Plain Pictures Of Plain Doctoring

MIT Press Series on the Humanistic and Social Dimensions of Medicine

Stanley Joel Reiser, General Editor

1 *Talking with Patients, Volume 1: The Theory of Doctor-Patient Communication*
Eric J. Cassell, 1985

2 *Talking with Patients, Volume 2: Clinical Technique*
Eric J. Cassell, 1985

3 *Plain Pictures of Plain Doctoring*
John D. Stoeckle and George Abbott White, 1985

The MIT Press
Cambridge, Massachusetts
London, England

Plain Pictures of Plain Doctoring

Vernacular Expression in New Deal Medicine and Photography

80 Photographs from the Farm Security Administration

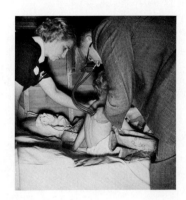

John D. Stoeckle, M.D., and George Abbott White

Reader's Note

All captions in this study are verbatim—with the exception of misleading spellings of proper nouns—from FSA mounted photographs in the Library of Congress. Other studies have either edited these captions for titles or retitled photographs.

A grant from the Margaret T. Morris Foundation has supported publication of this book.

Second printing, 1986

This book was set in Palatino by the MIT Press Computergraphics Department and printed and bound by Halliday Lithograph, Inc., in the United States of America

Library of Congress Cataloging in Publication Data

Stoeckle, John D.
 Plain pictures of plain doctoring.
 (MIT Press series on the humanistic and social dimensions of medicine; 3)
 Includes bibliographies and index.
 1. Family medicine—United States—History—20th century. 2. Medical care—United States—History—20th century. 3 Physician and patient—United States—History—20th century. 4. Depressions—1929—United States. I. White, George Abbott. II. Title. III. Series. [DNLM: 1. History of Medicine, 20th Cent.—United States—pictorial works. 2. Politics—history—United States—pictorial works. 3. Social Conditions—history—United States—pictorial works.
W1 MI938M v.3 / WZ 17 S864p]
R729.5.G4S76   1985   326.1'0973   85-123
ISBN 0-262-19236-5

This book is for Christopher Seiberling

No, I am not doing a seasonal sequence. It may be that the title of my next book will be The Auroras of Autumn, but this is some little distance ahead. . . . At the moment I am at work on a thing called An Ordinary Evening in New Haven . . . my interest is to try to get as close to the ordinary, the commonplace and the ugly as it is possible for a poet to get. It is not a question of grim reality but of plain reality.

—Wallace Stevens, *Letters of Wallace Stevens*, Number 691.

Contents

Series Foreword

What doctors and patients do in the intimacy and physical setting of the medical relationship, and how this relationship is affected by the social climate of the day, has been the subject of numerous essays and books in recent times. This work has been overwhelmingly verbal, pictorial evidence about such interactions limited by the canons of confidentiality that enclose medical relationships.

This book is unique and important from several perspectives. It provides rare visual insights into doctor-patient encounters and does so through the eyes of an extraordinary group of photographers, some of whom, like Walker Evans and Dorothy Lange, are numbered among the great American photographers of this century. It also examines the place of the political and social circumstances which placed these artists together in the mid-1930s under the auspices of the Farm Security Administration, one of many governmental creations of Franklin D. Roosevelt to fight the ravages of economic depression.

By understanding the subject, the artist, and the environment of the times in which they worked together, we are taken into the pictures to explore the interactions bounding their creation and the place of these pictures in the development of photography. We see the photographs as aesthetic objects, as social commentary about America in the mid-1930s, and as a view of how doctors and patients look when together. And since the physician-subjects of these pictures are generalists delivering a full spectrum of medical services to the rural patients who predominate in these scenes, the authors explore primary care medicine of the day as a medical and social movement.

This book is a fascinating account of interactions between the worlds of the artist, the doctor, and the politician. It brings us closer to recognizing the threads of continuity usually overlooked when these worlds and their people are examined apart from each other.

Stanley J. Reiser

Introduction

1
Siloam, Greene County, Ga. (vicinity). Nov.
1941.
Midwife going out on call.
JACK DELANO.

2
Kempton, W.Va. May 1939.
Company doctor leaving the home of a sick miner.
JOHN VACHON.

Some neglected photographs from the Depression years have become useful reminders of the roots of what we now call primary care medicine. They are also examples of an overlooked dimension in photography itself, the *vernacular*.[1] As much a function of the way in which they were made—and for whom and for what purposes—as for their content, these photographs may well provide us with a means of expanding how we see as well as expanding our documentation of the way in which medicine was practiced and people lived during a period of enormous transformation in American society.

In less than a decade, between 1935 and 1942, a handful of photographers with a New Deal agency, the Farm Security Administration (FSA), compiled more than a quarter million images of life in the United States. Surprisingly, given their vast accomplishment, these FSA photographers numbered only a dozen or so, with rarely more than half that number in the field at any one time. A few were well-trained professionals, but the majority were rank amateurs from the worlds of chemistry, Elizabethan poetry, and schoolteaching—looking for work. Giants emerged, such as Walker Evans and Dorothea Lange, Russell Lee and Arthur Rothstein and Gordon Parks. Yet whether their training was commercial or academic or on the job, during their time with the FSA they realized the height of whatever professional achievement they came to have.

The result has scarcely been approached in either scope or particularity. The FSA photographs capture small towns and sprawling cities, flood relief efforts and embittered strikers, lonely back roads, deserted farmhouses, stark cemeteries, black and white sharecroppers on the road, Chicanos in the fields, soiled miners, Southern policemen, country stores, women in cotton mills, family picnics, New Bedford fishing boats, and swirling, devastating dust storms. The viewer turns from them almost with a gasp, having seen a sweeping yet intimate inventory of working people's lives against the constant backdrop of a ravaged countryside.

A small fraction of the justly celebrated FSA photographs, two thousand or so unknown ones, record commonplace medical encounters: doctors and patients together. The doctor's office may be in a white frame Victorian or a teardrop trailer; the people waiting may be rural folk without shoes or town folk dressed for the occasion in neat but worn clothing; they may attend with a plump infant, a surly adolescent, a beaming family, or an aging adult. But these medical photographs are uncommon in two respects. They are linked to the most comprehensive and remarkable documentary photography effort ever attempted. And within the category of medical photography they are unique because doctors and patients are pictured together, not in the hospital operating room surrounded by surgical technology but for the first time in mundane scenes of everyday office medical practice, away from the hospital.

The FSA photographs originated in the Historical Section of the FSA's Information Division; they were taken under the direction of that section's extraordinary head, one Roy Emerson Stryker (himself responsible to FDR adviser Rexford Tugwell), who was both prop and prod to his tiny staff of photographers. As a kind of harbinger poverty program that attempted rural relief and rehabilitation, the FSA was constrained to justify its sometimes ad hoc, always controversial, activities before a skeptical Congress, and this, in turn, led to a seeming contradiction in the kinds of images with which the Historical Section sought to persuade Congress.

On the one hand, the FSA photographers identified previously ignored social evils which the administration of Franklin D. Roosevelt was at pains to correct. The conditions of the rural dispossessed and the unemployed in small towns required images that would, in short, condemn. But it was not enough simply to record the worn-out land or the horrendous living conditions under which one-third of a nation (or more) was ill-housed, ill-clad, and ill-nourished."[2] FSA cameras also had to focus on FSA programs that could work and, later in the 1930s after all that expenditure, were working. This second task required images that would celebrate.

FSA images which boldly condemned and glowingly celebrated have become the most well known; no study of the 1930s seems authentic without them, though by far the most numerous images the photographers actually generated were those showing neither the horror nor the heroism of the Depression but rather the apparent ordinariness of life as experienced by the bulk of the people. These photos usually co-opt the speech of their subjects: we call them vernacular photographs. The nature of this third kind of image, virtually unacknowledged and certainly unanalyzed until the present, was recognized by several FSA photographers at the time, notably Ben Shahn and John Vachon, as well as director Stryker. We will hear from them later. It is the burden of the essay that follows to construct a historic, medical, and aesthetic context for understanding these photographs and to conduct a new reading of a group of them. The book's first three sections address that context; the last two chapters address the text, the photographs, and their captions.

Why *medical* photographs? If our purpose were narrow, merely advancing another way of reading or emphasizing special social and political dimensions inherent in particular photographs, a selection of FSA images on games and sports or shots of churches and storefronts might suffice. Medicine cuts deeper. As physician and medical critic H. Jack Geiger observes,

We know—and our national debate reflects the knowledge—that there is more to medicine and medical care [than dollars and numbers]. The national health care system is part of the culture, a history, a political and economic order. It embodies our view of a basic social commitment to the care of the sick, the weak and the helpless. It speaks to issues of justice and equity and human rights. It expresses our belief in the power of science and our attitude towards physicians. It is the product of a century of political struggle.[3]

With the decline of mystery in the nineteenth century and the increase in uncertainty in the twentieth, we look to new places to cure our "ontological insecurity." Reason replaces God and, as Harvard sociologist Paul Starr asserts in *The Social Transformation of Medicine* (1983), "modern medicine is one of those extraordinary works of reason."[4] Starr subtitles his book *the rise of a sovereign profession and the making of a vast industry*. It is precisely this drama, authority transferred to new institutions of great size, life-and-death issues focused by new technologies, and charged questions of private morality and public policy that, in turn, force one not only to reexamine the distance medicine has travelled since the 1929 Crash but to wonder whether the personal cost has not sometimes exceeded the technological benefit.

Primary care medicine is predicated upon an initial, direct, and continuing relationship between doctor and patient. It was the work of the general practitioner; today, it is the work of the GP, family physician, pediatrician, and internist. Rather than a fantasied longing for a Golden Age of medicine that never existed, primary care—with its low-technology interventions, encouragement of collaborative care, promotion of prevention, and insistence upon mutuality and personal responsibility in fundamentally asymmetrical doctor-patient encounters—may accomplish a repossession of scale contemporary health care appears to be missing. This primary care is also, not surprisingly, congruent with the intent of the FSA program, which recorded itself in the 1930s and, moreover, funded a prepaid medical care plan in the doctor's office four decades before the sudden growth of health maintenance organizations (HMOs) and independent practice associations. The Kaiser Foundation Health Plan, first organized for Kaiser Industries employees in California in the early 1930s and opened to the public soon after WW II, is the best known of the early HMOs. FSA health care plans were preventative and directed toward low-income farm families as well as the down-and-out migrants who saw teams of doctors and nurses at FSA-supported health centers. No one has estimated the care provided in home visits by practitioners participating in FSA plans, but at their peak the plans enrolled over 600,000 individuals, while the health centers treated some 150,000 migratory workers and their families.[5]

Despite these numbers, few medical photographs were made. The reasons are many and they tell us more than the history of medical photography. For now, we may say that medicine's very mixed status in pre-New Deal American society—its marginal efficacy in treating injury and curing illness, and public ambivalence toward the figure of the doctor—account in part for the relative paucity of FSA medical images, matters traced in chapter 2. Who made such photographs, their purposes, as well as their procedures, technologies, and instructions, are additional, internal reasons, examined in chapter 3. Having named these, however, the fact remains that, as the FSA photographers turned their cameras from rural despair to rural success in the late 1930s, photographs of medical projects suddenly appeared, although in comparison with those documenting other areas of American life, the total was slight. Preparation for World War II both encouraged and reduced even further the rationale for medical photographs. Their moment came and went.

Yet answering why so few medical images (and why so few to begin with) introduces an important point of tangency between primary-care medicine and the FSA photographs. Students of American Studies are aware of a vernacular tradition.[6] In this examination, the vernacular is seen as linking both subject and vehicle, plain doctoring and plain pictures of plain doctoring, and the connection between the two is a radical one.

That is, these FSA medical photographs go to the root of matters by breaking with an earlier medical and photographic history, one informed by an ideology that isolated doctor from patient. Prior to the making of these images, the office visit had rarely been recorded. Since antiquity, of course, drawings depicted the doctor acting upon the patient, but absent was any sense of reciprocity in the relationship. From the nineteenth century on, commercial photography increased the sheer number of medical images and, in hospital after hospital, bed patients and their nurses were photographed time and again by administrators in order to demonstrate the accommodations of their wards. Additionally, medical staffs frequently enough recorded themselves—and those they trained—for posterity. In all of these, however, photographs of doctors and patients together were scarcely to be found; this view of the relationship remained pictorally off limits, perhaps because of prevailing societal notions regarding privacy.

Perhaps. But to the extent that the act of photographing something may be said to confer and convey value, the absence of such doctor-patient images may indicate that this kind of relationship was not valued.[7] By contrast, the great majority of FSA images do exhibit a valuing of similarly ordinary scenes. Thus, it is no accident that among them we have found these plain pictures of plain doctoring. And these pictures have a growing audience today, along with the oral histories of social movements and families and common individuals because society in general and the primary care movement in particular is attracted to their ordinariness. As black novelist Paule Marshall recently argued, "Common speech and the plain, workaday words that make it up are, after all, the stock in trade of some of the best fiction writers. . . . Perhaps the measure of a writer's talent is his skill in rendering everyday speech . . . as well as his ability to tap, to exploit, the beauty, poetry and wisdom it often contains."[8] Indeed, the focus—implicit and explicit—on the doctor-patient relationship within each of these photographs may impel the viewer to consider those elements in the medical-care delivery system of the 1930s that produced this kind of relationship. It may invite the viewer to consider afresh the New Deal. And it may ask us to reconsider the contributions, the distinctive embodiment of cultural differences, the vernacular can provide.

Acknowledgments

This book evolved as an overlapping series of projects. Initially, fifty-six of these photographs were selected and arranged as an exhibition—the extension of a project for a Harvard College General Education seminar, "Plain Doctoring in an Age of Technological Medicine." The seminar was given at Eliot House in the fall of 1977 (and again in 1979 and 1981), and Mark D. Smith, now a resident in primary care at the University of California Medical Center (San Francisco), prepared a paper using a dozen FSA photographs; we taught the seminar and from our own collection of FSA medical photographs expanded Dr. Smith's project.

The exhibition, "Primary Care in the 1930's. Working People Consulting the Doctor: 56 Photographs from the Farm Security Administration," was originally mounted at the Massachusetts General Hospital (Boston) from January to May 1979. It has since traveled to the Francis A. Countway Medical Library, Eliot House Library, Baylor College of Medicine, Brown University Medical School, Boston University Conference on Medical Sociology, Mayo Clinic, Barnard College/Columbia University, and Dartmouth Medical School.

Viewers of the exhibition and readers of the exhibition text encouraged us to deepen the argument of the text and to increase the number of FSA photographs. Preliminary versions of the book, then, were given as lectures at Baylor, Brown, St. Catherine's College (Oxford), Institute for United States Studies (University College, London), Department of American Studies, University of Hull, American Studies Program, Case Western Reserve University; printed versions appeared in the *Harvard Medical Alumni Bulletin* (April 1980) and *Studies in Visual Communication* (Winter 1983).

Many individuals and institutions gave considerable support and/or were generous hosts.

Michael Ross Grey, Thomas Andrew Dodds, Arthur Ciacchella, and Vickie Feldstein, students in the seminars and now medical students, did yeoman service helping crate, uncrate, mount, and arrange the exhibition at each of its locations. (Grey and Dodds generously shared their undergraduate research with us, and their contributions are cited in the Notes.) Ed Hogan (Aspect Composition) set the exhibition text, Charles Collins (formerly of Newtonville

Camera) consulted with us as to its mounting, and Stanley Joel Reiser (then of the Medical Humanities Program, Harvard Medical School) answered our questions regarding medical history and medical technology.

Alan Heimert, Master of Eliot House, deserves special mention. Without him the exhibition would not have existed because the seminar would not have existed. Professor Heimert helped us shape the course, guided it each time through the University bureaucracy, gave it meeting space, and paid for outside speakers. From his Master's Fund he also provided support (along with James Richter, Primary Care Fund, Massachusetts General Hospital) for mounting the exhibition and printing its poster.

For hosting the exhibition, we again thank C. R. (Robin) LeSuer, Librarian (Countway); Kevin Van Anglen and James Basker (Eliot House); Dean Ornish (Baylor); David S. Greer (Brown); Mark G. Field and Joel Kallish (Boston University); Barbara J. Callaway (Mayo Clinic); Nicholas Rango (Barnard/Columbia); Sherri Calkins (Mary Hitchcock Hospital/Dartmouth Medical School). Hosts for the talks included Duncan MacLeod (St. Catherine's); Peter Parrish and Howell Daniels (Institute for United States Studies); Maldwyn A. Jones (University College, London); Stephen Baskerville and P. A. M. Taylor (University of Hull); and Park Goist (Case Western Reserve).

Our research was speeded—indeed, made possible at several key junctures—by many libraries and their staff: at the Newton, Brookline, and Boston public libraries; at Harvard, including Eliot House, Widener, Lamont, Fogg, and Tozzer libraries; and, of course, at the Library of Congress. Leroy Bellamy, Reference Librarian, Department of Prints and Photographs, Library of Congress, was an invaluable colleague; few viewers of the FSA photographs can appreciate the assistance he has provided to students of this national treasure. Other librarians to be thanked specially are Mary Nelson and Dorothea Gaudet, Margaret Erskine Memorial Library, Newton South High School.

Our colleague John D. Goodson, Massachusetts General Hospital, representing a third generation of dedicated practitioners, made available to us valuable documents from his grandfather's practice.

Friends and colleagues in the Newton Public Schools (Massachusetts) provided a community of encouragement and stimulation. Particularly supportive were John M. Strand, Superintendent; Thomas P. O'Connor, Assistant Superintendent; Ernest Van B. Seasholes, Principal, Newton South High School; David Youngblood, Chair, English Department; and, certainly not least, Marshall A. Cohen and Douglas Worth.

Earlier versions of this essay were read and commented on, often at length, by F. Jack Hurley (Memphis State University), Davis Pratt (Fogg Art Museum), Grace Seiberling (University of Rochester), and Alan Trachtenberg (Yale University). Later versions received careful attention from David Bumke (*Harvard Medical Alumni Bulletin*), Tobia Worth (*Studies in Visual Communication*), Thomas Andrew Dodds (Dartmouth Medical College), James R. Green (College of Public and Community Service, University of Massachusetts, Boston), and Stu Cohen (Harvard School of Public Health). Howard S. Becker, Robert Coles, David Riesman, John R. Stilgoe, Harold W. Walsh, and Margaret Warner sent letters of encouragement and information. H. Ramsey Fowler (Memphis State University) gave the entire manuscript a last reading in an attempt to save the authors from their worst prose. Each reader had his or her disagreement— often considerable—with what we were saying; we list them not to imply blanket approval but to thank them for helping us say what we saw.

Work with the MIT Press was made easier through the generous efforts of our agent, Julian Bach, as was proofreading, thanks to Clyde Edwin Tressler, III.

Alice Stoeckle and Ann Withorn finally insisted we stop looking at the FSA medical photographs and start writing about them; good advice, though we wish we had taken it sooner.

From start to finish, however, one person gave unsparingly of his personal time (almost in the form of house calls) and his photographic experience (almost in the form of a tutorial in matters visual). For what we have learned about photographs from Christopher Seiberling, their appreciation and evaluation, we dedicate this imperfect work as but one means of redressing a debt. A considerable balance remains outstanding.

Finally, Walt Whitman once wrote that great poets require great audiences. Although it will become clear in the reading, we wish to state at the outset that we regard the FSA photographers and Roy Stryker as kinds of heroes and, no less, the people whose lives they touched. Some of these photographs of doctors and patients were made almost half a century ago, and many of those photographers and their subjects have gone. But for those who have not, or those who knew them, we would like to hear from them, and we encourage them to write us.

JDS
The Primary Care Program,
Massachusetts General Hospital
Division of Primary Care, Harvard Medical School

GAW
The Matthiessen Room
Eliot House, Harvard University

Plain Pictures of Plain Doctoring

1
Context of the Photographs: FDR, FERA, AAA, RA, FSA

3
Kempton, W.Va. May 1939.
Office of a company doctor.
JOHN VACHON.

4
Transylvania, La. June 1940.
The doctor's office on the U.S. Department of Agriculture, Farm Security Administration project.
MARION POST WOLCOTT.

5
Elkins (vicinity), W.Va. June 1939.
The Tygart valley subsistence homesteads, a proj-ect of the U.S. Resettlement Administration. Health center.
JOHN VACHON.

6
Oran, Mo. Feb. 1942.
Doctor receiving call in his office.
JOHN VACHON.

7
Peñasco, N.M. Jan. 1943.
*Clinic operated by the Taos County Cooperative
Health Association.*
JOHN COLLIER.

8
San Augustine, Tex. Apr. 1943.
Dr. Jones in his office.
JOHN VACHON.

9
Baltimore, Md. Apr. 1939.
Baltimore street.
ARTHUR ROTHSTEIN.

10
Chicago, Ill. Apr. 1941.
Doctor in his office in the south side.
RUSSELL LEE.

11
Shafter, Calif. Mar. 1940.
The Farm Security Administration camp for migratory workers. Patient leaving health clinic.
ARTHUR ROTHSTEIN.

12
Yakima, Wash. Sept. 1941.
FSA migratory labor camp for farm families. The clinic is a big drawing card.
RUSSELL LEE.

13
Faulkner County, Ark. May 1940.
A patient waiting at a doctor's office in the rear of a country store.
MARION POST WOLCOTT.

14
Scranton, Iowa. May 1940.
A doctor's office and a water tank.
JOHN VACHON.

15
Gee's Bend, Ala. May 1939.
Clay Coleman showing an interest in a food chart
while waiting in the health clinic.
MARION POST WOLCOTT.

16
Pittsburgh, Penna. May 1938.
Quack doctor's sign.
ARTHUR ROTHSTEIN.

17
Fairfield bench farms, an FSA scattered home-
stead development, Mont. May 1939.
*Doctor who is hired by the Farmers' Cooperative
Health Association.*
ARTHUR ROTHSTEIN.

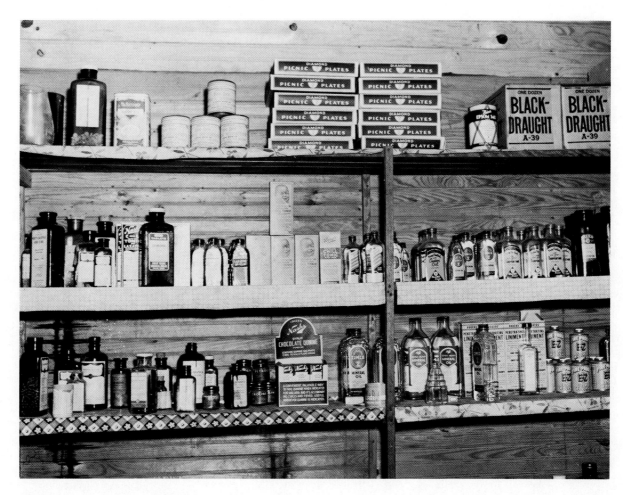

18
Faulkner County, Ark. May 1940.
A medicine and drug shelf in a country store
which has a doctor's office in the rear.
MARION POST WOLCOTT.

19
Merigold, Miss. Oct. 1938.
Negroes in front of a doctor's office.
MARION POST WOLCOTT.

20
San Augustine, Tex. Apr. 1943.
Dr. Rulfa in his office.
JOHN VACHON.

21
Circleville, Ohio. Summer 1938.
Doctor's office, on Main and Court streets.
BEN SHAHN.

The most comprehensive and remarkable series of documentary photographs ever attempted emerged in response to the Great Depression, thanks to President Roosevelt's "agrarian concern" and to the rapid success of conventional and experimental "alphabet soup" federal agencies we know today as the New Deal. Although serious argument continues as to the nature and content of FDR's concern, understanding the FSA photographs requires we at least outline that program's political and institutional context.[1]

In the first place, it was the *Great* Depression to those who experienced it just as it was the *Great* War to those who marched into battle or waited at home.[2] As gassed World War I victims were more than mere symbols to their children, so those who had been economically maimed impressed their experiences with a concreteness only a participant imparts. Half a century distant, however, witnesses of howling dust storms have all but retired from the scene, leaving the sufferings and dislocations to be qualified and reduced by time, unchallenged.

Until recently, that is.

Now, in the mid-1980s, urban infrastructure crumbles, steel mills shut in lockstep order, health-care benefits to the very young and the very old are reduced, and unemployment will never, we are told, be less than X or Y *millions.* Larger classes in public schools and fewer fire fighters, police officers, waitresses, salesclerks, orderlies, secretaries, telephone operators are to be the new norm, with the youngsters on porches, curbs, street corners, "hanging out." Network news anchors compete with one another to attach names to the numbers again. And, not unaware of echoes, the *New York Times* recently featured a midwestern farm supply dealer observing, "Fellow came by the other day and said, 'If I could just get back up to broke, I'd quit.' Thing is, he has to get back up to broke first."

The Crash and Its Aftermath

Then, as now, the numbers were very large; immense, really, because the United States contained far fewer people, because resources were fewer and much less available. The Great War across an ocean had called up a still-rural America from small towns and even smaller farms. A decade later, Americans who continued their inner migration to industrial centers had had their urbanizing pace rudely accelerated by the Great Depression.[3] Those still up in the hollows or on marginal Plains farms or working "shares" in the South were confronted with move or die, and perhaps die anyway. But it was the moving that made them realize how many they were, even if the country as a whole did not take much notice. As R. S. Mitchell, chief special agent, testified before a Senate subcommittee in 1935, "On the Missouri Pacific Railroad we have been trying to pay some attention to what we at one time called migratory labor; that is, the transient movement." When asked about his figures from 1928 to 1932, Mitchell replied: "We took official notice, in 1928, of 13,745 transients, trespassers that we found on our trains and property. In 1929 that figure was 13,675. In 1930 we took a record of 23,892. In 1931 that volume jumped to 186,028. . . ."[4]

Economic uncertainty was no stranger to Americans. There had been massive economic disruptions in 1873, 1893, 1907, and 1914, to name the more recent, and then the recession of 1920–21.[5] The unplanned and unregulated expansion of the 1920s had made many uneasy, but should anyone have thought to check even the most blatant danger—speculation—no adequate mechanism existed. Was the Great Crash felt all the greater precisely because the 1920s had been for a well-publicized few one smooth, unbroken ascent to privilege and economic insecurity for the rest made to appear a nightmare of the past? As late as 1928, Herbert Hoover, an orphaned Iowa farm boy become mining engineer, become millionaire, become president, declared, in his oft-cited Acceptance Address: "We in America today are nearer the final triumph over poverty than ever before in the history of the land. . . . We shall soon with the help of God be in sight of the day when poverty will be banished from this nation."[6]

Within a year, the stock market had plummeted, making a cruel mockery of Hoover's confident prophecy; within a month after the crash, stocks had lost over 40 percent of their face value, and it became terrifyingly clear that the speculative boom had been a noisy, glittery distraction from the ominous warnings that had assumed the substantial form of declining residential construction, trebling business inventories, and slackening industrial production, employment, and commodity prices.[7] Numerous reassurances by the President and prominent bankers aside, the Great Crash was an entirely accurate prognostication of things to come.

Economic announcements in the following three years went from disturbing to hideous. New capital issues, for example, a rough yardstick of investment, had totaled 10 billion dollars in 1929; in 1930 they slid to 7, dropped to 3 in 1931, and plunged to 1 in the year FDR was elected. Corporate profits fell from 8.4 billion in 1929 to 3.4 in 1932, and more than 100,000 businesses went under, along with 5,000 banks which were holding 26 billion in their 9 million savings accounts.[8] (William E. Leuchtenburg has noted that in the middle of 1932, steel operations were at "a sickening 12% of capacity,"[9] and John Kenneth Galbraith observed that the rich at the Crash were not only "indubitably rich"—5 percent of the population received at least 33 percent of all personal income—but they were neither investing nor purchasing, thus preventing the recirculation of at least a portion of the skewed monetary distribution.)[10] Industrial production itself fell more than 50 percent from 1929 to 1932, and unemployment mounted from 4 million in October 1930 to almost 11 million by the autumn of 1932. A few months later, by the time of FDR's inauguration, another 4 million would be looking for work.

Agricultural Disaster

On the farm matters were even worse. Historian Paul Conkin has determined that while overall farm prices in the 1920s seemed close to parity with the prosperous levels of 1909–1914, this was a misreading that led to a dangerous misperception since "all farmers did not share in the moderate prosperity." The total statistics included "millions of small, submarginal or inefficient farm units that contributed very little to industrial production."[11] Standing a current nostrum on its head, a falling tide dumps everyone in the muck, not just those in yachts; the Crash, therefore, led almost immediately to a severe drop in farm prices, 55 percent in the next three years, and that in turn meant plunging farm income, which went from 17 billion in 1919 to 2 billion in 1932. "Agriculture led all other industries into the Depression," Conkin concluded, "and suffered the most."[12]

Conkin's reference to agriculture as an "industry" is accurate and significant. Since a fifth of America's farmers harvested one-half of the nation's crops by the late 1920s,[13] it could be said that agribusiness was almost a reality and that a situation obtained in agriculture not unlike industry and commerce, namely, a concentration of wealth and power with comparable national organizations. Like the National Association of Manufacturers and the Chambers of Commerce, the large farmers and planters spoke to Washington directly about their losses. The problem was that no one, not the bankers, not the corporations, not the head of any major industry, and certainly not Herbert Hoover, had any solution other than the pre–New Deal remedies, namely, to cut federal spending, balance the federal budget, and wait until the economy "bottomed out."[14]

While those with large stakes in American society could caution nothing better than holding tight, there were other voices—threatening ones. By the spring of 1933 one out of every four American workers lacked a job, but in the countryside isolated unrest had already flared into organized violence. The intensity and scale of this threat are evidenced by Arthur Schlesinger's account in *The Crisis of the Old Order*:

Farmers stopped milk trucks along Iowa roads and poured milk into the ditches. Mobs halted mortgage sales, ran the men from the banks and insurance companies out of town, intimidated courts and judges, demanded a moratorium on debts. When a sales company in Nebraska invaded a farm and seized two trucks, the farmers in the Newman Grove district organized a posse, called it the "Red Army," and took the trucks back.[15]

This was no *lumpenproletariat*; rather, solid middle-class farmers no longer able to pay for seed, stock, equipment, or mortgages. They were also voters, although they were fast becoming disenchanted with electoral politics. A scant two months before Roosevelt took office, Edward A. O'Neal, an Alabama planter and head of the Farm Bureau Federation, bluntly warned a Senate committee that "unless something is done for the American farmer, we will have revolution in the countryside within less than twelve months."[16] About the same time, publisher William Randolph Hearst inquired as to the President-elect's agenda; he was told Mr. Roosevelt "considered farm relief the first priority; then unemployment relief and public works. . . ."[17]

Relief: RFC, FERA, AAA

Yet relief came first to the banks. "The commanding figure in the broadest range of relief activities," writes Albert U. Romasco in *The Politics of Recovery* (1983), was not President Roosevelt's close advisor, social activist and ex-social worker Harry Hopkins, but "in fact, Texas banker Jesse Jones, head of the Reconstruction Finance Corporation (RFC)."[18] By acting through the RFC as it did, the New Deal government intervened in the private sector as never before. Banks were closed, then opened on Washington's terms. They received massive loans and were invested in massively by Washington and, "by the end of 1937 when Congress had greatly enlarged the authority of the RFC by amending it some thirty times, more than 6,000 banks had received aid."[19] According to Romasco, the 10.5 billion spent by the beginning of World War II made the RFC "the world's largest, most powerful bank."[20]

Activist Hopkins received his half-billion for the Federal Emergency Relief Act (FERA) two months after the RFC was established and on the day of the passage of the momentous Agricultural Adjustment Act (AAA). While the RFC provided banks enormous relief, the government's stiff terms had resulted in nothing less than a fundamental restructuring of the financial system. The banks grumbled but acquiesced. The case with FERA and, to a greater extent, the AAA, was just the opposite; recipients held the upper hand; the federal government grumbled, and went along with only marginal intervention. As a result, neither the social welfare system nor agriculture was restructured, merely deflected from its original, ruinous course. Bills establishing FERA and the AAA had been drafted for quite different constituencies with quite different needs in mind, or so it seemed. Within a year the implications FERA and the AAA held would become clear and those implications would, shortly, bring about the creation of the Resettlement Administration (RA) in 1935, which, in turn, would be reorganized, separate from the U.S. Department of Agriculture, to become the Farm Security Administration (FSA) in 1937.

Current debates over social welfare policy would not have amused Hopkins (their dour attempts to define the "truly needy," for example, would have reminded him of Jonathan Swift at his most bitter), even as they recall for us the attacks upon FERA's expanding role.[21] At the depth of the Depression in early 1933, 15 million men and women were unemployed; no safety nets existed for them in the form of federal unemployment insurance or social security, and any savings likely had vanished with the local banks holding them. Beyond the pain these Americans and their families experienced, another, still darker world existed. Historians now estimate an additional 1 to 2 million men and women (and vagabond children) wandered the country during this period, un-accounted for by any statistic and only the dark tip of a still more desperate underclass.[22]

State and local government, and the private sector were the appropriate, the only agencies for relief, Hoover insisted.[23] That individuals could not be sup-ported by their own communities was neither a reflection on the communities nor the limits of those communities' resources but, as he saw it, a judgment on the individuals. Hopkins was forced to operate within the constraints of this philosophy of decentralized voluntarism, at least initially.[24] FERA was "only a middleman in the relief business," funneling its millions from the federal gov-ernment to the states and cities where "these in turn actually administered the distribution of funds by direct relief, that is, they made cash grants to those on the relief rolls."[25] In effect, the government was coming to the relief of local public-welfare agencies and private charity organizations which, administra-tively, was not unlike the AAA rescuing the larger farmers. What a contrast, however, each posed to the RFC, which rescued banks more than individuals, to be sure, but which set the terms of the rescue and then slowly—and funda-mentally—altered the rules of the entire financial game.

Neither Hopkins nor planners of similar mind, such as Henry Wallace and Rexford Tugwell in the Agriculture Department, would be slow to adopt the RFC's strategy; though fighting years of federal inaction and an ideology of So-cial Darwinism that blamed the victim, they would have far less success.[26] Al-most immediately, however, Hopkins persuaded FDR to create another agency, not for direct cash handouts ("dole") but for direct work relief (jobs),[27] and got the Civil Works Administration (CWA) for the winter of 1933–1934. Amid con-servative criticism of the CWA, Hopkins went back to Roosevelt in 1935 for a vastly expanded, permanent work-relief program, and thereby created the Works Progress Administration (WPA). This massive agency eventually spent no less than 10 billion dollars for relief and, like the RFC, was able to shape a new public policy that went far beyond simple relief to broad social welfare programs that included education, health care and the arts, and, significantly, agricultural relief and recovery programs that would overlap and then be in-corporated into the RA and, later, the FSA.[28]

"Talking agriculture, [Henry] Wallace could be exceedingly crisp, hard-hitting, and impressive," concedes his critic, Arthur M. Schlesinger, Jr. Moreover, "few Americans in 1933 were so steeped in the agricultural crisis, or had brooded over it so thoughtfully, or brought to it such acute and informed judgment [as he]."[29] Although Wallace's estimate of the crisis had a suspiciously pastoral tone to Schlesinger's ears ("the necessary balance between city and country" had been "upset," Wallace believed), three generations of Iowa cornfield farmers behind him gave Wallace an earth-bound awareness of the particular *economic* effects such an imbalance generated. Industry, faced with reduced demand, historically had protected itself by cutting output and maintaining price levels; farmers in a similar situation had had no choice but to literally produce what they had planted and watch their prices tumble at harvest time. "In agriculture," stated Wallace succinctly, "supply sets the price. In industry, price sets the supply."[30] The decline of foreign markets and the inflexibility of industrial prices (farm dollars bought less and less city goods) since World War I had accentuated the imbalance; the Depression turned this decline into a bobsled slide. As FDR's Secretary of Agriculture, Wallace intended to check the slide by increasing farm prices and reducing output; over the long haul, he intended to right the balance, and he had the President's support in using the AAA as the lever.

AAA Fails the Little Man

The AAA regulated farm production (over considerable conservative protest) by voluntary domestic allotment induced by benefit payments that were financed by a processing tax. Extensive other powers, however, lay with the Secretary, any one of which he could enforce or ignore. Schlesinger asserts that "probably never in American history had so much social and legal inventiveness gone into a single legislative measure."[31] An enumeration of only a few of the powers—to restrict or expand commodities through quotas and subsidies; to reduce production through government leasing of farmland (then to withdraw it from cultivation); to maintain prices through government purchase and storage, or foreign sale; to encourage innovative land-use policies through agreements with agricultural colleges and USDA agents; to provide direct relief to farmers through mortgage and equipment loans and grants—makes disagreement difficult, especially since within three years gross farm income increased 5 percent and cash receipts from marketing (including government payments) nearly doubled.[32]

All well and good for the large, already corporatized farmer, though the AAA avoided speaking to the knotty problem of how this increase was to be distributed other than in the existing pattern of American agriculture with its increasingly pyramidal structure of profit. But if there was political dynamite in altering the pattern, there was also political dynamite in encouraging it. The top 25 percent of the nation's farmers, the "four-hundred-acre-plus farmers," were represented in Washington by powerful lobbies; but the other 75 percent were, as suggested earlier, more than merely restless, and they were finding sympathizers within Washington and the New Deal too. Were there still *others*? In 1929, for example, almost 8 million people lived on farms yielding a *family* income of less than six hundred dollars a year. Looking closely, in reality almost half of the American farmers did not own the land they farmed; they worked it as tenants and sharecroppers whose numbers had been dramatically increasing since the turn of the century.[33] The cold numbers behind the bland statistics were that some 13 million people lived in tenant families, 3 million in sharecropper families, and another 3 million existed as wageworkers, day laborers, or part-time help on farms.[34]

Difficult in any region, nonownership, tenancy, and sharecropping took on a highly stratified, feudal quality in the South; and in a sense slavery without the name reasserted itself and settled more and more oppressively upon black and white alike.[35] As the Depression had forced big business to look to "the bottom line" around questions of employment and working conditions, so plantation owners and landlords, one eye on the banks and the other on the markets, economized in ever more stringent fashion with the one variable still under their control: manpower. Where landlords found it profitable through the AAA to reduce cotton acreage by a certain percentage, they did so in the "most economical way" by reducing "the number of tenants and sharecroppers by that amount."[36] In *The Forgotten Farmers: The Story of Sharecroppers and the New Deal* (1965), David Eugene Conrad comments bitterly on the consequences of the AAA's macroplanning:

Many hours and thousands of words were used in weighing the probable effects on farmers in general, consumers, producers, manufacturers, and even farmers in the Philippines and Puerto Rico, but little heed was given to the possible tragic results of the bill on the lower classes of farmers. Not a voice was heard to protest that drastic acreage reduction might mean the difference between a bare living and no living at all for marginal and sub-marginal farmers. No one warned that it would bring the eviction and displacement of thousands of tenant farmers and sharecroppers and the firing of many farmhands.

Conrad concludes:

But sharecroppers and hired hands had little representation in the high councils of the Department of Agriculture . . . or Congress. As it turned out, this was the blind side of the (AAA).[37]

More recent scholarship of the New Deal, including accounts by participants, reveals the farmers of the AAA as neither blind nor insensitive, unaware of these consequences. Ample evidence exists that Wallace knew, since the AAA paid benefits to the owners of the land, that middling and small farmers would gain little and tenants, sharecroppers, and farm laborers would be hurt. So did his right-hand planner and administrative assistant, later Under-Secretary of Agriculture Rexford Tugwell. (Though an economist at Columbia University who had been one of FDR's original brain-trusters, Tugwell grew up on a farm in western New York State and knew well what making crops involved.) Agricultural policy, like the New Deal, was very much in flux, still reactive to reactionary critique as *policy*, still conservative at heart and very political.

Rather than the clear articulation of powerful forces old and new, the Department of Agriculture was much more the focus of those forces in contention. Old-line farm leaders were joined by the major food processors and pushed in a direction best indicated by George Peek, the businessman who served as the AAA's first administrator. He said, "The sole aim and object of this act is to raise prices."[38] The editor of the Middle West's most influential farm journal, *Wallace's Farmer*, did not disagree with Peek, though now-Secretary Wallace was also drawn to the intellectual scope and technocratic expertise of a Tugwell, who had thought rationally and programmatically and who was "realistic about the realities of farm life.[39] No back-to-the-land Jeffersonian yearnings for Tugwell, who regarded family farms with something of the sophisticated distaste urban planners felt for the mom-and-pop store—archaic and inefficient, relics of the past—and who rapidly forced Peek's removal from the AAA for

policy reasons rather than purely personal ones. According to Bernard
Sternsher in *Rexford Tugwell and the New Deal* (1964), "Tugwell blamed a
faulty institutional structure for crises . . . asserted that business' expropriation
of governmental powers and its speculative, predatory practices were inevitable
in an uncoordinated economy."[40] Tugwell felt that crop restriction, while necessary, was only short term and that the long-term solution lay with proper
land utilization. Peek had wanted marketing, dumping the surplus abroad as in
the past, and this narrow view, worse, this narrow definition of Washington's
role in coordinating and regulating for the whole, had to go.[41]

Peek went, ironically appointed to an overseas post by FDR. But congruent
with the building of critical forces outside the department for greater conces-
sions to the larger farmers and less concern for the dispossessed, Wallace appointed Chester Davis, only a "more suave [and more effective] version of his
predecessor,"[42] who "believed his agency existed to bring higher prices to commercial farmers, not to reform the Southern social system."[43]

Even though Wallace demonstrated that he shared Davis's views of "political
realities" by firing the agency's legal counsel, Frank Davis, and his left-liberal
staff in February 1935 (for pushing a rereading of an AAA subclause that
passed cash benefits from landowner to tenant), Wallace showed himself sensitive to building critical forces inside the department. Those who argued for
greater intervention on behalf of the small farmer and the non-landholder
"slipping through the cracks of the AAA" were to be satisfied by the creation,
by Executive Order, of an agency that would finance the removal of low-
income farmers and sharecroppers onto subsistence homesteads on good land.
This new agency only partially satisfied because, although conceived by Tugwell and Hopkins, the Resettlement Administration actually was not a "pure"
agency; the RA necessarily inherited the rural relief and rehabilitation programs of the old FERA and the uncompleted communities of the Division of
Subsistence Homesteads in the Department of the Interior.

Resettlement Administration

The RA was severely compromised from the beginning by the usual problem
of limited funds in the face of great needs, by the difficulties involved in ab-

sorbing FERA's programs and staff, and by confrontations with the new agency's critics, who included right and left wings, inside and outside the New Deal. Tugwell took the view that subsistence and small farmers were doomed, and that suburbs were where they should go; he wanted to resettle urban slum-dwellers in autonomous garden cities and sub-marginal farmers in new, productive farm villages. Actually much of the RA he inherited was not to Tugwell's taste: he disapproved of the homestead approach, believed the self-contained community to be an anachronism, and wanted most to press for the wholesale retirement of exhausted land (which was a considerable amount and growing)[44] and the wholesale retirement and retraining of exhausted farmers . . . in or near cities.[45]

Unfortunately, the largest share of his funds had to be used to continue rural relief, and even the RA's slightest *reform* programs, whether rational land use or personal renewal, rapidly stirred hornets' nests. Resettling people into model communities smacked of "waste" and "socialism" (Senator McKellar of Tennessee criticized the installation of electricity and use of stone in building as "luxuries"), tenant purchase of farmland was more of the same (since the RA subsidized the purchases through low interest), and establishing cooperatives—for farming, marketing, and equipment buying—was "collectivism" and "sovietism" in the popular as well as Congressional mind.[46] Sharing FDR's alienation from the business community and openly contemptuous of the Agriculture Department's conventional Extension Service and the old boy links to the Grange and the Farm Bureau Federation, Tugwell used the RA to set up a duplicate, parallel farm organization with its own agents and support system of social scientists who would attack the causes and not merely the symptoms of the problem[47] and who were, according to Conkin, "dedicated only to the exploited and underprivileged." The RA had its internal differences but exhibited a greater uniformity of purpose than other federal agencies of the time, refusing to patronize its clients and making conscious efforts not to compromise racial equality in the delivery of its many services. It constructed migratory camps for the "rootless" Arkies and Okies (the "good" camps in John Steinbeck's *The Grapes of Wrath*) and challenged the conventional medical system by setting up group medical plans and forming cooperative associations of practitioners for those holding its loans. "It was not only one of the most honest but probably the most class-conscious of New Deal agencies," acknowledges Conkin. "Soon it antagonized practically every vested interest, a good mark of its relative effectiveness."[48]

Effectiveness for the oppressed and dispossessed had its price. Under constant congressional attack and with practical restrictions upon its prerogatives increasing, the RA had to move under the wing of the USDA in December 1936 and, after months of legislative infighting, became the FSA in September 1937, not by direct congressional action and approval but by executive order again.[49] Tugwell had resigned at the time of the transfer—his name more a red-flag hindrance than a help—and the now even larger agency became the charge of a Southern liberal critic of the AAA, the clergyman, educator, and expert on race relations, William ("Dr. Will") Alexander.[50]

Any social change invites criticism as well as support, engenders hostility as well as reassurance. Attempts to alleviate poverty, much less strike at its roots, threatened many established interests and offered an opportunity for opportunists. Disappointed claimants for patronage joined bureaucratic competitors, disapproving Republicans on the Outs linked arms with Southern Democrats on the In whose "way of life" was at risk, personal foes of the President and public foes of the New Deal found it convenient to attack through a favored associate and his agency, and the entire expected range of strictly ideological opposition from bigoted nativists to "reds-under-beds" reactionaries found in Tugwell and the RA a controversial target they seemed to have waited for all their lives.[51] Courts heard honest as well as dishonest petitioners (the explicitly top-down style of the New Deal was not always as "liberal" in practice as in conception), and experts were suspect for sound as well as irrational reasons. The American press needed a good story every day, and any federal agency that grew from a dozen to 16,000 employees within a year had its share of good stories.

An enormous transformation of American society was in progress, in part the result of a process of industrialization that had begun more than a century earlier, in part the result of specific federal interventions by New Deal agencies that reached down to local levels and altered everyday life every day. When it could be understood, like other transformations, the New Deal was criticized and opposed.

Always the planner, however, Tugwell had anticipated the critics his RA would earn and, well before the agency had assumed national visibility, he had launched "an ambitious public information program," designed in Baldwin's words, "to propagate the faith of the new agency and its prophet."[52] Baldwin's image may be overdrawn but is apt in that the RA was an arm of federal policy and was also, as Tugwell understood, part of a movement for institutional and social change. The RA and, even more, the FSA would gather under an establishment roof many left-wing reformers and radicals; when the mud flew, a vocal mass of supporters would be required to defend the FSA's mission. To inform these yet-to-be-organized supporters, five sections were formed under an Information Division—including a press and editorial section, a special publications section, a radio section, and a documentary film section. Mass circulation photographic magazines called *Life* and *Look* were about to be invented and, with shrewd foresight, the RA's fifth section was to be "a photograph section in which photography was employed for the purposes of historical record, immediacy and news value, and works of art."[53] While all sections were tasked with reaching sophisticated as well as mass audiences, the photograph section was especially encouraged from the outset to reach the widest possible audience with the FSA's message.

Stryker and Tugwell

Roy Emerson Stryker, the photograph section's director, seemed destined for this special New Deal role. The son of a modest Colorado farmer who was a native radical with an enthusiasm for books and learning, Stryker gained first-hand instruction in agriculture by observing the poor farm-and-ranch conditions around his community under the lash of his father's populist jeremiads. A reader of the still-Progressive *New Republic* and *Nation* magazines and influenced by the ideas of social gospelist Walter Rauschenbusch through a minister friend, Stryker had always intended to go East for his education but was forced to do so almost as much by the disastrous falling prices of 1920–1921 as by the notion that rural problems had their sources in the city and that solutions would come from city not country roots. After a stint working full time at a Manhattan settlement house which was a project of the Union Theological

School, Stryker finally began to study economics at Columbia University. His instructor was a fast-rising academic by the name of Tugwell. Others must have wondered what that cool, urbane intellectual saw in the unpolished, informally prepared westerner; Tugwell "always avoided personal contacts" but, from their first meeting, was impressed by this older student who appeared so eager and so committed.

It is just possible that Tugwell, recalling his western New York State youth, appreciated doing economics with someone who actually knew how hard rural life could be and what the economics of failing equipment and delayed plantings and poor harvests and uncertain markets actually meant. Whatever the case, there was a strong relationship between the two, and Tugwell became Stryker's mentor at the university. As a provocative young economist with a reputation for being a stimulating teacher, Tugwell was keen on "descriptive economics"; he believed students studying economics should make visual contact with the economic institutions they were studying by taking trips around New York City.

One version of Stryker's tutorial for his FSA directorship has Stryker, as graduate assistant to Tugwell, instructing himself by ferrying undergraduates the length and breadth of Manhattan. Another version, by a farm insurance company publicist who describes himself as Stryker's "last and most receptive student" in the 1950s, has fledgling instructor Stryker confronting

a gaggle of students . . . as dismal as the science he was supposed to teach [by] almost in desperation, bringing in pictures to the class—mostly illustrations from the newspapers and magazines of the day. He would tack them to the walls and point. "You want to know about economics?" he would ask. "Economics is not money. Economics is people. *This* is economics." And then he would take them to Wall Street and Park Avenue; through night courts, banks, produce markets, jails, garment factories, and slaughterhouses. He moved them excitedly, back and forth, among the text, his pictures, and the streets, until finally they were able to draw their own conclusions between economic theory and the real world.[54]

In addition to the trips Stryker organized during his first year as a graduate student and as Tugwell's assistant in 1924, Stryker was also invited to help Tugwell with his book, *American Economic Life*, which was to carry illustrations. F. Jack Hurley describes Stryker's attempt to gather appropriate illustrations for Tugwell's book as the beginning of Stryker's self-education in the *use* of photographs. In *Portrait of a Decade: Roy Stryker and the Development of Documentary Photography in the Thirties* (1972), Hurley writes that populist Stryker's extensive survey of the general media and even specialized publications did not provide suitable images. "The magazines of the day," writes Hurley, ". . . used photographs to present an idealized view of life as it ought to be, rather than life as it was." Moreover, Stryker felt "the top magazine photographers were extremely skilled technicians and often sensitive artists, but they tended to see the photograph as an end in itself, a thing of beauty with no message beyond its own perfection."[55]

Stryker was not against the beauty of aesthetic formalism, but he had a firm political orientation ("I was basically a radical. I was basically from a socialist home," he remembered), and from this stemmed a more social and utilitarian, though aesthetically complex, concept of beauty. His survey served as a rich apprenticeship in that, beyond the study of the immediate and the commercial, it had Stryker assessing photographers as aesthetically diverse as Edward Steichen and Edward Weston, as historically distant and important as Mathew Brady and Jacob Riis.

Eventually Stryker discovered Lewis Hine's powerful documentary work and even contacted Hine who, with characteristic enthusiasm and generosity, would "come to Columbia with great armloads of pictures drawn from his vast experience in the areas of child labor, poverty, and industrial photography."[56] Hine's achievement went into eclipse in the 1930s and was not recognized until three decades later. Critics like Judith Mara Gutman and Alan Trachtenberg repossessed Hine in the activist 1960s and 1970s by demonstrating what others had acknowledged in years past (the relevance of Hine's documentary efforts to current concerns for political equality and social justice) and by demonstrating for the first time a direct relationship between Hine's technical mastery of situation and medium, and the wide range of images he was therefore able to capture—a relationship Hine's detractors either denied or minimized. Gutman relates an interview with "photographer *extraordinaire*" Paul Strand, who studied with Hine in 1908 and for whom the word 'courage' recaptured, for Strand, "some of the flavor of Hine." Strand reminded Gutman that "when nobody else dared, Hine photographed conflict. Photographing child labor, especially in the South," he underscored, "was akin to entering an armed camp."[57] And, examining Hine's nationwide investigations for the National Child Labor Committee, Trachtenberg suggests how that kind of social and political risk-taking could result in an expanded or a new aesthetic.

Hine was a model for Stryker, if unacknowledged as one until now, in two respects. To gain images, whether as illustrations or as visions, the photographer had to get out of his or her studio, get into the field, and go to the people. The America of the first third of the twentieth century that lay beyond the cities' edge could be penetrated, as John R. Stilgoe has detailed for us in *Metropolitan Corridor* (1983), by rail.[58] From station to site, however, the roads were dirt and the vehicle was Ford. Neither was predictable, and crisscrossing ten or twenty thousand miles of that America under conditions of extreme heat, cold, dust, and rain demanded perseverance and physical endurance. Once there, factory police and hulking foremen demanded other qualities:

To gain entry into mines and mills, Hine was forced to assume many guises . . . a marvellous actor . . . his repertory ranged from fire inspector, postcard vendor, and Bible salesman to broken-down schoolteacher selling insurance. Sometimes he was an industrial photographer making a record of factory equipment [but] hidden in his pocket was a little notebook in which he wrote vital statistics [of the children] such as age, working conditions, years of service, and schooling.[59]

Through imagination and guile, Hine disclosed the politically and socially unseen. This, Trachtenberg argues, had aesthetic implications. Although Hine was critical of the photographer-as-artist and the photograph-as-art (the Photo-Successionists of the turn of the century whom Hine saw as too detached and whose fine-print work he judged as too precious and idealized), his photographs can be seen in retrospect as a substantive challenge to both role and product. Hine's artist was a communicator and a witness; Hine's photograph was an active embodiment of his Progressive beliefs in that, through it, the brutalizing effects of industrialism were, not unlike what lay beyond the shadows of a Stieglitz print, hidden information waiting to be brought into consciousness, into public view. The system, according to the Progressivism of his era, required rehabilitation not demolition, reform not revolution; the purpose of Hine's art, therefore, was not to shock or condemn so much as to provide a necessary completeness, "to persuade the viewer that the full picture, the complete scene, includes contradictory evidence."[60] The artist who could search out such information provided one model, the manner of presentation was another.

Hine accomplished the latter, technically, in three ways: by expanding the range of the dominant aesthetic in terms of subject (sympathetically including the working class, the labor process, and the work itself), by more fully developing the scene (posing individuals in groups, in context, with their implements, or at their work stations), and by presenting completed images innovatively. Rather than neatly hung in well-lit, spacious galleries, as the Photo-Successionists' photographs were, Hine's photographs went onto posters and flyers, into newspapers and social welfare journals. And there the hitherto unseen was not presented as a single, individual moment, but as a montage, a series, as time exposures grouped for a comprehensive effect.

Hine's photographs were not for books or newspapers alone, he had been commissioned by legislative committees and private contractors (like those who built the Empire State Building) to produce specific images. As a result, when Stryker or Tugwell required the photographic correlative of an abstract concept for their economics text, Hine could easily present the type, a contrasting image, indeed, virtually any image they named, either from his personal files or from where only Hine, in his wisdom and experience, knew to look.

According to Hurley, up until that point "the experience of hunting pictures to illustrate abstract ideas had been the most exciting thing [Stryker] had ever done."[61] For several years, until 1935, Stryker would continue to use photographs in his economics teaching at Columbia with greater variety and growing sophistication; Tugwell, who was head of the department during this time, helped institutionalize Stryker's repeated visits to his preselected sites. Tugwell was well aware that, after tours of factories, banks, slums, slaughterhouses, and the like, Stryker's discussions afterward would be complemented by the use of appropriate photographs.

Small wonder, then, when Tugwell left Columbia for Washington, Stryker would not be far behind. In the summer of 1934, when Tugwell was still assistant secretary of Agriculture, he found Stryker a job within the Information Division of the Agricultural Adjustment Administration. Stryker's reputation as a specialist in the use of illustrations had him working under Milton Eisenhower and, as the summer progressed and Stryker became more and more aware of the value of the picture file maintained by the Department of Agriculture's extension service, he passed on his interest and his ideas to Tugwell.

The project that emerged from these conversations was to be a picture book on agriculture. Tugwell saw it as "a source book for the historian or economist." But before it could come to completion, Tugwell had been named director of the newly formed Resettlement Administration. Under its Information Division, historical section, someone who knew how to use photographs, as records and as propaganda, was needed. Stryker was Tugwell's obvious and immediate choice. The small number of medical photographs Stryker's section would make, relative to the vast documentary corpus that was to take shape, was probably the last thing on Stryker's mind when he settled into Washington that hot muggy summer of 1935.

2
Primary Care in the 1930s

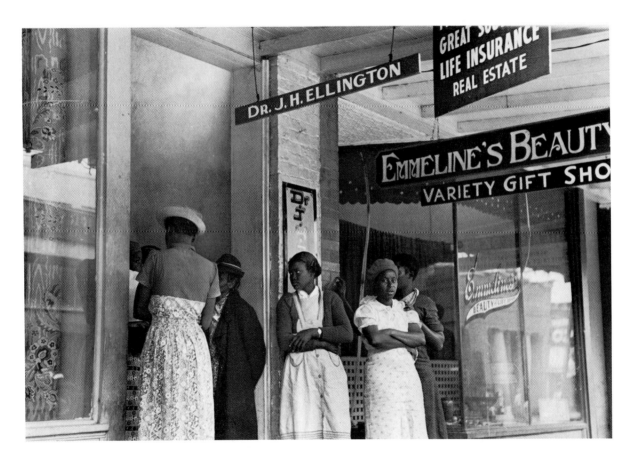

22
San Augustine, Tex. Apr. 1939.
Line of women waiting to see the doctor on Satur-
day morning.
RUSSELL LEE.

23
West Aliquippa, Penna. Jan. 1941.
House.
JOHN VACHON.

24
Greene County, Ga. June 1941.
A young boy in bed with measles in the home of a
Farm Security Administration borrower.
JACK DELANO.

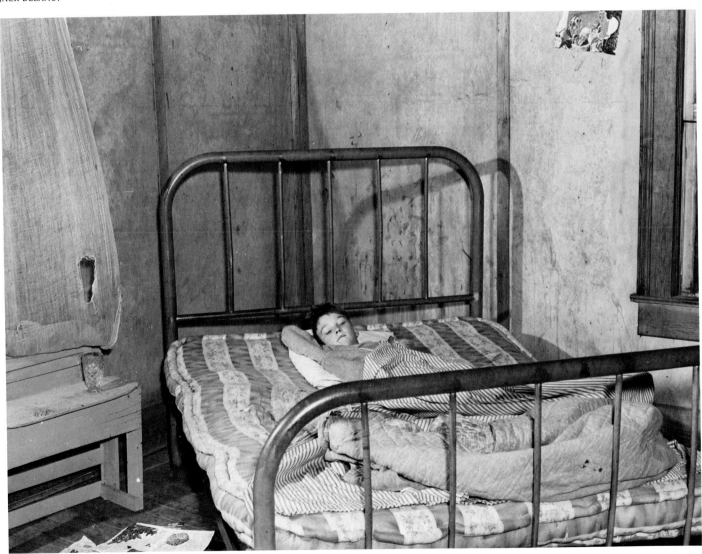

25
Belle Glade, Fla. June 1940.
The waiting room at the health clinic on typhoid
inoculation day at the Osceola migratory labor
camp, a Farm Security Administration project.
MARION POST WOLCOTT.

26
Woodville, Calif. Mar. 1941.
Agricultural workers waiting in the clinic at the
Farm Security Administration farm workers'
community.
RUSSELL LEE.

27
Oran, Mo. Feb. 1942.
Farmer waiting to see the doctor.
JOHN VACHON.

28
Penasco, N.M. Jan. 1943.
The waiting room of a clinic operated by the Taos County Cooperative Health Association.
JOHN COLLIER.

29
Irwinville Farms, a U.S. Resettlement Administration project, near Irwinville, Ga. May 1938.
Women and children waiting to see the doctor who visits the project once a week.
JOHN VACHON.

30
Oran, Mo. Feb. 1942.
Doctor's office and waiting room.
JOHN VACHON.

31
Questa, N.M. Jan. 1943.
The waiting room of the clinic operated by the
Taos County Cooperative Health Association.
JOHN COLLIER.

32
Chicago, Ill. Apr. 1942.
Provident Hospital. In the waiting room of the clinic.
JACK DELANO.

33
Eleven Mile Corner, Ariz. Feb. 1942.
Cairns General Hospital, Farm Security Administration farm workers' community. The waiting room at the clinic.
RUSSELL LEE.

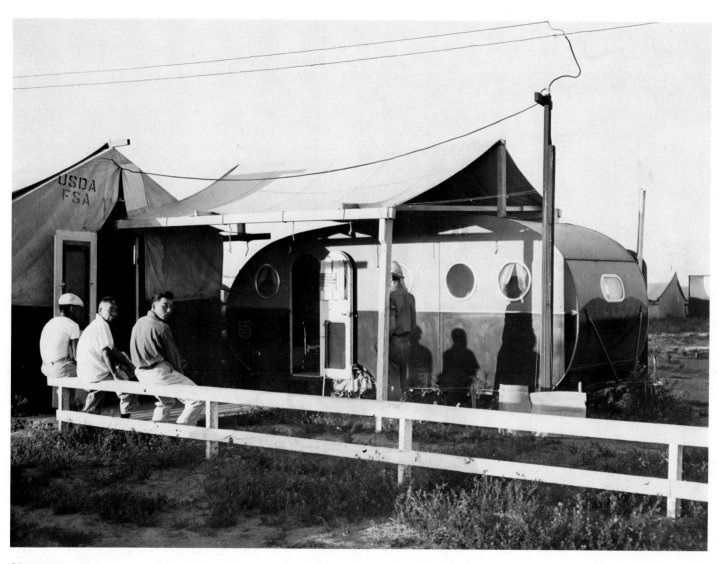

34
Nyssa, Ore. July 1942.
FSA mobile camp. Japanese-Americans patronize
the camp clinic.
RUSSELL LEE.

The first volume of a projected three-volume biography of former President Lyndon Baines Johnson, by Robert A. Caro, contains a set piece on farm life in the Austin, Texas, area—Hill Country—during the late 1920s, which is as unsettling and unforgettable as his subject.

With electricity, Caro observes, a farmer worked from dawn to dusk. Without it—the condition of many until widespread rural electrification in the late 1930s—a farmer arose at three-thirty or four in the morning to milk the cows (by hand which took several hours for twenty cows) and worked late into the evening at tasks electricity could have done for him during the day: pumping water (which otherwise had to be carried bucket by bucket into the house or out to the stock), lugging ice (to cool milk or food), pitchforking hay into a barn loft, grinding feed for the stock. Without electric motors, cottonseed was unloaded, wood was sawed, and clothing was washed—all by hand. The lack of electricity or the inability to pay for it where it did exist meant radical limitations in a farmer's life and excessive expenditures of time and energy for him and his wife. On the simplest level for her, it meant that vegetables or fruit had to be canned the day they came ripe.

So, added to a rural wife's summer burdens—cooking, cleaning, washing, ironing, dumping the ash box, childbearing and tending—she kept constant attendance on the fire and the stove, and canned. There was no respite.

Because in that fierce Hill Country heat [wrote Caro], fruit and vegetables spoiled very quickly. And once the canning process was begun, it could not stop. "If you peeled six dozen peaches, and then, later that day, you felt sick, "you couldn't stop, says Gay Harris. "Because you can't can something if it's rotten. The job has to be done, no matter what." Sick or not, in the Hill Country, when it was time to can, a woman canned, standing hour after hour, trapped between a blazing sun and a blazing wood fire. "We had no choice, you see," Mrs. Harris says.[1]

Others had even less choice, however; they had no peaches to can.

But peaches or no, the cost of this sheer unending labor was high. It exhausted men and women, and it wore them out like machines turned on but never turned off. This, then, conditioned health. This was the context of medical practice.

By the 1930s major reforms in American medicine were already in place, though not fully developed or implemented. With Abraham Flexner's report of 1910 and the ensuing reforms, medical education had come under the aegis of the university, eliminating the proprietary schools and many poorly educated and untrained doctors.[2] Flexner may have given little weight to the *art* of medicine, but his report did much to make certain that medicine would henceforth be solidly based on *science*; the doctor was to be a scientist (more a metaphor, since it was technologies not science doctors used), and every clinical situation was to be treated as a scientific research project which in teaching institutions might make patients believe that they were being experimented on.[3] Hospitals and medical schools had also launched systematic research in basic and clinical science, which was promising new cures for disease and a scientific rationale for practice.

Medical Care

Medical care was another matter entirely. With the new increase in knowledge and technique it had become specialized, but that gain did little or nothing to change the extensive poverty or ill health of the 1920s. The public and the profession were well aware that society was not appropriately organized to support those essential functions of *primary* medical care—initial access without delay, integration of specialized services, and continuity throughout the life cycle—and least of all for the poor and dispossessed.

In the following decade, the 1930s, medical care was reexamined, most often accepted as immutable, though sometimes purposely changed to bring better care to the poor and nonpoor alike. Still, as Robert and Helen Merrell Lynd remind us in their classic study *Middletown* (1929), precisely how much authoritative medical advice filtered down from the newly scientific medical schools to the hinterland and precisely how much those new medical doctors were able to actually use was doubtful. "One must recall," they observed, "how close is the pioneer background of Middletown with its cures of 'nanny tea' and bleeding."[4] Besides avoiding the doctor by home cures, even Middletown's solid citizens made their way to "crones" in outlying villages, while "a downtown barber regularly takes patients into a back room for magical treatment for everything from headache to cancer."[5]

The medical scene was entirely different from our 1980s. For one thing, the reigning popular concept was a more narrow *medical* care, not our more inclusive *health* care. People expected less, got less, and complained less about what little they got. Now, Americans are more and more accustomed to conveniently "seeing the doctor" for a wide range of needs. This was not always the case. In the 1930s, for example, the number of visits was 2.6 per person per year, with only half the population making those visits in any one year. This is in contrast with, say, 1982 when 4.5 visits per person per year were made, with 80 percent of the nation's population attending the doctor.[6] It is true that there were fewer doctors to see in those years, even as there were more diseases and illnesses that were untreatable. The burden of illness was so often "just lived with," handled by home remedies or "fixed up" with patent medicines. To us, the realistic alternative would be to go to the doctor no matter what; but then the doctor was also frequently unavailable and, when available, viewed as the absolute last resort in coping with what, after all, was understood as the inevitable. The tone was stoical, with a streak of puritanism that encouraged people to believe that what could not be purchased was likely not deserved. The net effect was silence or muted complaint on the part of the patient.

Yet, gradually, this unvoiced, unattended residue of national ill health was revealed. Public-health medical officers and a new generation of scholars in urban and rural sociology went into the field. They conducted surveys in the cities and small towns, in farm counties and industrial regions of the country. For the first time households were counted, as were individuals with untreated disorders, handicaps, and disabilities. Such actuarial accounts were complemented by reports on the costs of health care and the use of medical services, since the distribution of and access to care were important social issues of the day. Poverty, evident everywhere, seemed clearly to affect health, if not care, so that substantiated evidence about both would surely bring the necessary remedial action.

These accounts depicted a collective, quantitative picture of health, illness, and treatment. The touchstone, by the Committee on the Costs of Medical Care (CCMC), was published in twenty-seven volumes in 1932, and although the product of a very mixed group in terms of political persuasions and technical orientations, its members had united to express deep concern regarding the adequacy of medical care and the general health of the American people.[7] Comparing the underserved to the served and paying particular attention to the rural population, the CCMC went so far as to call for fewer specialists and more generalists to meet the crisis they depicted, and they stressed that questions of access and cost were barriers to a lasting solution. The CCMC report and other period studies left little doubt as to the seriousness of general conditions, but the picture of the *individual's* experience with illness and the doctor's work in practice was blurred and much harder to find.

The inside of the doctor-patient encounter was a very private matter then, off limits, certainly, to the intrusive, intensive kind of scholarship practiced today. Glimpses could be caught, if one knew enough to look in ordinary places: popular novels, magazines and movies; newspaper human interest stories, poems and advice columns; gossip, rumors and family anecdotes. We have been able to reconstruct that relationship at this distance by drawing upon those sources in the manner of social history and by supplementing and correcting accounts through the use of individual physicians' or clinics' records of that time. Medical schools and hospitals, medical publications, and the correspondence of individuals also have their ordinary—if overlooked—value in such exercises. Added to oral histories, from doctors as well as patients, all these have provided us with what we believe to be valid pieces in the medical care puzzle.

Home Remedies

In coping with illness, self-treatment tactics were as, if not more common, than medical visits. On the subject of home remedies the Lynds' keen eyes picked the titles of numerous popular medical advice books; middle- more than working-class sources, they judged. One such example was,

Dr Chase's
Third, Last and Complete
Receipt Book
and Household Physician
or
Practical Knowledge for the People
From
The Life Long observation of the Author,
Embracing the Choicest, Most Valuable and
Entirely New Receipts in Every Department of
Medicine, Mechanics, and Household Economy . . .

Several substantial quotes from this text were provided by the Lynds so that a reader might fairly judge Doctor Chase's counsel (1,200 families bought the last two editions, or so the advertising went), one of the "choicest" quotes being,

It is claimed by many scientific men that it is best to always lie with the head to the north, on account of the fact—a supposed fact, at least—that there is an electric current passing through the system when one is lying down, whether awake or asleep, and that its influence is best with the head to the north. Invalids, at least, had better do it, if the situation of their room will allow it.[8]

From new academic centers like the University of North Carolina came the new tradition in sociology and a new kind of researcher: curious but sensitive, diligent but tactful, principled but nonjudgmental. These early field workers questioned people about what they thought and did, without elaborate protocols or instruments; they listened attentively. Uncensored by intellectual preconception or ideological bias, the enormous (and odd) variety of home remedies emerged. Charles S. Johnson's 1934 study, *Shadows of the Plantation*, showed that "Whooping cough is treated by tying a leather string around the child's neck. A necklace of cork and mole's feet is used to make teething easy. 'White Wonder Salve' softens up old injuries; 'Thread Salve' cures 'yellow trash.' "[9] Johnson took the unusual clinical step, for an academic then, of attempting to report verbatim, without tidying up the informant's language, without shoehorning their sense of their experiences into standard English. Thus,

A woman said: "Papa died with pneumonia. He wouldn't use nothin but rubbin medicine, and wouldn't call no doctor." Another woman, with enormous sores of long standing on her arm and breast, was trying to nurse her baby.

"Dese boils hurt so bad," she complained, "Dey's sore from de kernel. I been so sick I could hardly stand up," She put sulphur and vaseline on these sores.[10]

Authenticity achieved, Johnson went on to draw his own conclusion: "There was, however, a sense of the possibility of contagion. She talked of weaning the baby 'so de boils won't turn on it.' " And "still another woman kept a string around the children's necks to keep off disease. Pomegranate hull tea and brook-straw root tea are used for 'back weakness.' Peach-tree leaves and elephant tongue are good for fever."[11] The lay skepticism of doctors' remedies may be gleaned from the following:

The woman who gave this formula said "Doctor ain't no good when it comes to fevers." Boiled firewood and lard make an excellent salve for burns. Sheep-nanny, tea, kerosene, and sugar may be used for whooping cough, or red onions alone. If swollen feet are sweated first in pine top and mullen, then in cedar water, they will give no more trouble. Pepper and salt will cure spasms.[12]

Johnson was also alert to the lay rationales behind the remedies for sickness, the structural "pictures" a patient had in his or her mind:

Complaints are generalized into merely "feelin' kinda poorly" or "I ain't no good," and generalized complaints call for the generalized measures of patent medicines, or home herb remedies. "Black Draught," "666," salts, and castor oil make up a large part of the treatment of disease. Other standard remedies are 'White Wonder Salve," calomel, and quinine.[13]

Patent Medicines

More sophisticated than home cures were patent medicines. Their effectiveness was reinforced not only by patients' specific ignorance of how their bodies functioned but by testimonials and the easy availability of substances dispensed by "professionals" who might know more. Arthur F. Raper's important study, *Preface to Peasantry* (1936), underscores this and suggests something more.

While medical service is provided by the planters for the workers on a few of the larger plantations, and doctors and druggists do a considerable amount of charity and near-charity work [Raper observes], the mass of poorest people of both races rely largely upon the midwives and the tonics and heart, liver, and kidney remedies sold from the shelves of the general store.[14]

Did the ill turn to patent medicine as a result of misinformation or lack of information, or was this more a matter of how much medical service was unavailable and how little access to it most Americans had? Raper lends weight to the latter by his use of the words "a few" and "largest" [plantations], suggesting that medical services were unavailable elsewhere. At the same time we know from the official professional response to the CCMC that this unavailability and inaccessibility of medical service was largely unacknowledged. Moreover, solutions other than solo practice, such as group or institutional modes, were loudly denounced as "socialist dogma," even if organized privately, by fee-for-service medicine. "There is the question of Americanism versus Sovietism for the American people," was the AMA's widely publicized position.[15]

What resulted from the absence of alternatives, in either the delivery of medical services or in the kind and cost of services delivered, was implied, sardonically, if understated, by Raper:

When a family goes a whole year without the services of the physician, as did nearly one-half of them [in Greene and Macon, the two Georgia counties under survey], it means much unnecessary suffering and death. With the paucity of physicians on the one hand and the low incomes on the other, the mass of farm tenants have no choice but midwives and patent medicines. The services of midwives are cheap, usually five dollars or less; patent medicines can often be bought on credit.[16]

Further, although there were eight physicians in Greene County (one was "a Negro, respected by both races and with a large practice, not all Negro") and in Macon County, the thirty-two midwives in Greene and the twenty-six in Macon (all black), delivered half the babies, and

the same families who employ midwives rely almost wholly on patent medicines in case of sickness. [Moreover] the Black Belt storekeeper sells medicines he knows little or nothing about, for sick people whose conditions he is wholly unable either to diagnose or prescribe for.[17]

Exactly what such data on "alternative health practices" or self-help in those days meant, to what extent patent medicines and home cures were the symptom and to what extent the cause, was uncertain. What was certain was that neither quack medicines nor quack cures were peculiar to rural America but common, as the Lynds discovered, in small-town America too:

Akin to these time-honored [personal and folk] methods of treatment but far more potent in shaping Middletown's habits today are the numerous and constant newspaper advertisements of "patent medicines." A locally made "Winter Pep Cough Syrup" is publicly recommended by the president of a highly respected Middletown life insurance company, by the judge of the circuit and juvenile courts, the judge of the city court, and the chief of police. In the leading Middletown paper one morning in January, 1925, there were sixty-eight display advertisements of one inch or larger, exclusive of amusement, agriculture, financial, and classified advertisements; thirty-seven of the sixty-eight concerned various salves, soaps, and remedies.[18]

To make more doctors available, whether for the untreated or self-treated illnesses, the CCMC had opposed both voluntary and compulsory health insurance, yet their report thoroughly documented the unregulated and uncoordinated maldistribution of resources characteristic of the 1930s. The Lynds lost no time in noting the same contradiction several years later in *Middletown in Transition* (1937):

In such a world, in which sickness and money are so closely related and the institutional world encourages self-help, it is not surprising that patent medicines flourish today [1932] as in 1925. Middletown papers still carry doctor's advertisements of the "No knife, No pain, No drugs, No danger, and No high rates" sort and patent-medicine advertisements promising: Stomach ulcers, gas pains, indigestion victims, why suffer? For quick relief get a free sample of *Ugda,* a doctor's prescription at (the largest drugstore in the city).[19]

The Medical Visit

No matter what the barrier to professional help, eventually the doctor would be visited or called and then waited for. "Waiting for the doctor," a prevalent theme in the FSA medical photographs, is an anxious time; one's thoughts and feelings are least under control and often at their most private. Contemporary poets have powerfully registered sickness and this experience of waiting. L. E. Sissman's collections, *Hello, Darkness* (1979), *Scattered Returns* (1969), and *Dying: An Introduction* (1968), poignantly detail how this feels inside or in the shadow of the modern hospital. Robert Penn Warren, a distinguished older poet with roots in rural Kentucky, reaches back to the 1920s and 1930s with arresting memories of "just waiting."

It was October. It was the Depression, Money
Was tight, Hoover was not a bad
Man, and my mother
Died—and God
Kept on, and keeps on
Trying to tie things together, but

It doesn't always work . . .
Propped in a chair, lying down she
Could not breathe, dying
Erect, breath
Slow from the hole of the mouth . . .

"Tale of Time"

The Federal Writer's Project (FWP) captured the experience too; these writers were early oral historians who wrote down the intimate "as told by the people":

After that [said one woman], things didn't go on so good. Another baby came on and we had our hands full takin' care of the two children and lookin' after the farm work. When the second baby was four years old, he started gettin' pale and thin. We put him to bed one day because he looked so sick we thought he was goin' to die. We didn't call a doctor for a long while. You see, we didn't have any money then, and we'd heard that the doctor up in the town wouldn't come unless you had the money.[20]

and

The only other two children we lost was the twins. They died five days after they was born. I don't believe we would have lost them if we could have got to a doctor. I could see that they was weakly as soon as they was born. We didn't know what to do for them. We just used the home remedies for sick babies. Guess we done something wrong. They was the only doctor in that end of Madison County then, and the snow in the mountains was awful deep when the twins come. I sent for the doctor. He didn't git my word until three days later. Seems he was away from home with the sick and by the time he was found three days had passed. It took him two days more to git to us. . . .[21]

From the doctor's perspective, feelings could be confused, mixed, and anxious too. Dr. Lewis Thomas, in *The Youngest Science: Notes of a Medicine-Watcher* (1983), turns autobiographical and relates a disturbing talk with his physician-father, Lewis Thomas, Sr.: "The general drift of his conversation was intended to make clear to me, early on, the aspect of medicine that troubled him most through his professional life; there were so many people needing help, and so little he could do for any of them."[22] In the tradition of celebrated Yorkshireman James Herriot's *All Creatures Great and Small* (1972) and the earlier salty reflections of the Kansas *Horse and Buggy Doctor*, Arthur E. Hertzler (which became a best-seller in 1938), however, these doctors had learned something. They did their duty; at least they *attended.* "It was necessary for him to be available, and to make all these calls [Dr. Lewis Thomas, Sr., stressed], but I was not to have the idea that he could do anything much to change the course of their illness."[23] Rain or shine, first by bicycle, then by mule (Hertzler practiced in Kansas rather than Thomas's Flushing, New York), horse and buggy, and later automobile, these stoic physicians made their home visits. Why did they go and go more often than today, when only 1 percent of the doctor-patient encounters take place in the home as opposed to 40 percent then?[24] "The patients lived in the country and it was necessary for the doctor to drive out into the country to visit them," Dr. Hertzler would answer. Further, "There was very little office practice because patients were treated with simple remedies at home unless or until the state of the disease seemed to be threatening or the pain became too great to bear."[25]

Such practice naturally divided itself into two parts: first, transportation to the bedside; second, what the doctor did after he arrived. The transportation part had its humorous ("Though the mule occasionally backfires," Dr. Hertzler observed, "he does not run out of gas—no dead batteries, no flat tires. But one must learn to respect his individuality") as well as its terrifying aspects ("After we had missed a few cattle lying in the road by a narrow margin, I admonished my driver to slow down. His reply was, 'Doc, the gas won't shut off and I can't get at the brakes!' ").[26] Humor and terror held true for the bedside, and often side by side.

But when doctors did make those home visits, the encounters meant more than prescribing for the kids with "the croup," diarrhea, and earache. Dr. Thomas, Sr., notwithstanding, there were many things a doctor could do, and we would seriously misrepresent the medical practice of this time if we allowed his reflections to stand as the last word. Given so many others with untreatable medical needs, such doctors might view their own technical acts of such little consequence to mean they provided marginal assistance. Their commonplace misperception ignores the vital helping function of "doctoring," regardless of technique. Doctors provided patients with explanations of their illness, hence control, meaning, and so relief.

Delivering babies who did not always come into this world as "naturally" as some contemporary writers would have us believe, is one area of practice where a doctor's experience and a doctor's intervention could make a difference. Then, removing those annoying and infected tonsils, treating for painful sexual diseases (and reassuring equally anxious patients about sexual dysfunction), setting broken bones, draining abcesses, and sewing up those frequent industrial accidents and farm wounds (the "kitchen surgery" so vividly detailed by Doctor Hertzler) were other areas—even while making people comfortable by insisting with a doctor's authority on something as basic as bed rest in the years before the pneumonias could be treated with the new sulfa drugs of the late 1930s, and with penicillin and other "miracle drugs" a few short years later. The failing hearts and the heart attacks of aging grandparents could at least be diagnosed, appropriate care prescribed, and doctors could show more than their professional respect by attending to the dying old folks whose deaths had not yet been institutionalized at hospitals or nursing homes where they would be treated by strangers.

In the middle of America, a look at the fifty-three years of Dr. William Hammack Goodson's records, beginning just before the turn of the century and extending into the 1950s, reiterates the everyday elements of this plain doctoring so obviously necessary to average citizens but so easily lost on researchers unattuned to the rhythms of such common lives. As a general practitioner around Liberty, Missouri, Doctor Goodson's manner of following the lives of his patients seems, not unlike the poetry of another doctor, William Carlos Williams, almost as worthy of our attention as the lives themselves. On individual 3-by-5 sheets their lives accrue, move suddenly in fits and starts, then explode with illness or accident; his patients are routinely overwhelmed, cured; their lives are resolved one moment, concluded another: sheet after sheet, neatly typed names, dates, symptoms, and treatments. A sampling of these and the accompanying notes, diagrams, sketches, maps, stapled letters and test results, dunning notes and personal communications, the frequent asides—scribbled in Doctor Goodson's own hand—bring the experience of medical care then very close:

Mrs VP	9/22/33	Dislocation of right elbow in a fall to the floor while dancing. Reduced under Ethyl Chloride, and put in a sling. X-RAY made and showed no break of any of the bones of the arm. Service: 15:00 Rec'd On Act 1.00
Mr BW	8/10/35	Find that BW had been losing strength for some weeks, ever since the calls last spring. Nothing special hurts but he looks bad. R/more food, milk, etc.
	8/12/35	Visit. Said that he had had a sinking spell. His hands are cold, and he is conscious but very weak.
	8/13/35	Visit 5 A.M. P died a short time before. Posted [the autopsy like the operation was often done at home] and find stomach all right, and nothing apparent to cause death unless an anaemia of some sort or just starvation, or general arteriosclerosis.
		[*Note in Dr. Goodson's hand*] Loaned 5.00 to help bury him. Sara and Ellie said they would pay
Miss JG	3/24/35	Was called out about 10 A.M. and went out and remained about four hours when she had had no trouble much. Vag ex showed the cervix dilated for one finger. Baby was definitely premature and small. Advised to keep it for a short time and see if it might not live. The father of the child is not known. Mother works at a sporting house in Kansas City. Remained till about 4 P.M. then gave hypo morphine and came home. Back about 7 P.M. and baby was born almost at once. Placenta delivered normally and baby girl all right. Dressed and put in a box to keep extra warm and feed.
	3/25/35	Visit. Mother and baby all right. R/ mother's milk with a dropper for the baby.

	3/26/35	Baby is being kept very warm by the stove.
	3/27/35	Visit. Doing all right. Mother and baby. Service: 35.00 [*Note in his hand:*] Mrs TF says she will pay in installments. . .
Mrs CJK	4/6/37	Visit. P. having trouble with nervousness and some pain in the side of abdomen especially the right side and some on left. Thinks she has some trouble with kidneys for there was slight amount of blood for her when she went to stool. Urine by cathet showed nothing the matter there. Thought it might be something like a stone in bladder or kidney. R/ bromide solution and Bismuth acc colitic probab.
	4/10/37	Visit. Had to have more relief from the pain and this time had some blood with the urine she thought. I could find little. Urine showed a little pus but no blood.
	4/15/37	Visit. It is probably true that the blood which was thought to have come from the bladder, came from the vagina. Had some talk with her about pain on intercourse, and she says it wrecks her for several days. I hurt her a good deal in vag ex, but found nothing and she was not a wreck either. Advised to be a good sport about it, and take it without so much trouble. Asked for office exam to see.
	4/18/37	Off vag shows no erosion but a disturbance of the mucous membrane like a senile vaginitis. Touched with Agno 3.
	4/21/37	Off touched vagina with 10% Agno 3 solution. Find that she does not eat as she should. R/ milk daily. 1000 cc whole milk. $30.00
Mrs OCB	7/18/38	Visit. Has just been brought to this neighborhood. Has been sick for three weeks with something which she cannot get over. Was first thought to be flu. Now shows definite rose spots and the dicrotic pulse, the anxious facies, and the dry tongue. Evidently has had no water, and does not care. R/ water 8oz ASA lq2h
	7/19/38	Visit. T 103 Abdomen tight R/ soda 4gmqtid
	7/21/38	Visit. P. in about the same condition though she is more distended and there appeared fine water blisters apparently non inflammatory very thick over the lower abdomen. These little blisters look as if

they were droplets of sweat which only lacked wiping off. A cloth rubbed over them however ruptures them and leaves a mark very much like a healed pock mark after a fresh smallpox, that is with a very faint red base, and a very slight depression. There had been no local applications used before this and the character of the fluid was not like that of a pus sac. Fluid was clear. I thought at first that it was perspiration pure and simple, but there was this very thin membrane over the area.

7/22/38   Visit. 2 P.M. P. in about the same condition though possibly a little worse. She does not take fluid well though did take it out of a spoon. Abdomen is more distended and there has been a haemorrhage from the bowel. About a pint of fresh blood. AREA of the ERUPTION noted yesterday is the same.

7/22/38   Cont. though now shows over an area from the pubes to just about the costal margin. Larger spots where they had not been ruptured the day before and the pocklike marks have disappeared and new blisters appear. P. has started to flow from the vagina and menstruated about two weeks ago. Hot stupes advised and cent the water. Heart appears very weak and has taken digitalis from some doctor at Platte City.

7/22/38   Visit. 10 P.M. Mrs B died just as they called me to come. I went on out, and found abdomen greatly distended.[27]

Attached to these slips ran a parallel account of Mrs. B.'s husband, "who has been feeling sick for some time but has had to look after his wife who was sick first." Dr. Goodson noted that, even though Mr. OCB "was vaccinated against typhoid fever five years ago," he "now has symptoms which resemble those of his wife." Dr. Goodson reports a temperature variation of between 103 and 104 degrees for three days; Mr. OCB was given 125 and 200 million typhoid baccilli hypes, and his temperature fell back to normal; however, an attending nurse "was also sick from the vaccine and the fact that she is not strong, she had fainted." Several days later, Dr. Goodson visits and notes: "Find that he is doing well. Though still troubled some because he is off mentally." Apparently some time after, Dr. Goodson received the following note from the patient's sister:

I will write you a few lines to let you know we have not forgotten you all though it rather looks like it. Willie is getting long fine and has just worked about two weeks now it is the first work he has had to do he wonted me to write and tell you he will send you a little money in a week or two as soon as they get the job settled he will do the best he can he has to pay some on the funeral expence to well I will close as ever your friend. . . .[28]

In his five decades and more of plain doctoring, Dr. Goodson treated tens of thousands of workmen, laborers (black and white), housewives, drivers, craftsmen, and small businessmen. His 3-by-5 slips give us a feel for his transportation difficulties, because in pen and ink are sketches of alternative routes around muck, bridge washouts, fallen trees, and too-steep grades for the vehicle he is driving; he had, after all, to make return trips. While the home site of care may appear, in retrospect, a continuous advantage for patient and doctor alike (comfortable, support and supervision easily available), this was not always the case. Homes differed in their organization and in what they could offer. Resources were slight in the South and as Dr. B. K. Harris relates,

Not only have I prescribed for patients, but in some cases I've had to nurse and see about food for them. In labor cases, sometimes, with nobody in the house but the husband and me, I've had to bathe and dress the baby. I was called to a pneumonia patient where everybody in the house was sick and the little thirteen-months-old baby was crawling all over the mother's bed, with nobody but the sick mother to do anything for him, and no money to hire anybody. The mother needed food more than medicine; so I had some chicken soup made for her. I took the soup on my next visit, but it was too late; she died.[29]

As Dr. Goodson would at times drive out and bring his patients home for nursing, so Dr. Harris crossed the convenience (and color) line to care:

A colored man very ill with flu sent for me. Living alone, he had nobody to look after him. I left him with some medicine, but warned him what he needed most was plenty of cold water to drink and a warm room. There was no wood cut; so I went to the wood-pile and cut the nigger enough wood to last through the night, brought him a bucket of cold water, and told him how to take the pills I left.[30]

Despite the trials and gratifications of home visits and the high volume (15–20 house calls to 6–8 office visits per day),[31] the Depression years saw more and more of the doctor's encounters shift to the office, as patients had transportation, while increasingly important backup hospital medical work was just beginning to grow. This latter shift was promoted by the provision of hospital insurance to workers in exchange for wages.

Financing by the workplace would soon prove crucial to the nature and structure of health care, making diagnosis and treatment in the hospital a modern patient-doctor convenience, if not a clinical necessity. By the early 1940s, most home medical practice had moved into the doctor's office and the hospital, and an era of care and a particular context for the doctor-patient relationship had come to an end.[32] Medicine would radically change, not least for technical and institutional reasons which had been building for decades; World War II only accelerated one aspect of this process, as the Depression accelerated another.

Looking back, medical life in the 1930s was certainly a time-consuming, demanding job, less technical than today but not without its own technology. The applied science of the home visit was, in addition to what we have seen, the doctor's bag, while in the most up-to-date offices of those days were added the EKG for chest pains and palpitations, an X-ray machine that made films of bones and chests, and the microscope for blood cell counts, urine tests, and sputum smears. Of Doctor Goodson's black bag, which was carried throughout Clay County in those years of house calls, his son, Dr. William H. Goodson, Jr., has written:

> In his car, my father carried two bags, one for routine use, another for obstetrical use. In the first was his stethoscope, otoscope, sphygmomanometer, and a little leather case conaining several small scalpels, a pair of tweezers, scissors, and a tenaculum along with rolls of two-inch bulk sterilized cotton. There were bottles of ST34, tincture of Merthiolate, 1% silver nitrate, phenol and tincture of cocaine. For injections, the bag contained a luer syringe, 3–4 needles, and tubes of 1/4 grain morphine, atropine and nitroglycerine hopotables. Other medications included capsules of seconal or nembutal and pink, green, brown, black and white tablets—all aspirin. A few catheters and pairs of rubber gloves were also included.[33]

This black bag (then a potent, universal symbol of family medical practice) became insufficient for medical diagnosis even though the doctor had the information from the patient's history and from the physical exam conducted in the bed or on the kitchen table. The focus in the office now was on the *individual* patient (apart from the seeming distractions of family, friends, neighbors, and milieu), and much more of the individual could be seen and examined with testing equipment; moreover, the office was more efficient, capable of handling many more patients than could be seen in a day of all those house calls. An office offered the opportunity of putting things in one place (that great pile on top of the doctor's desk, as our FSA photographs show); it also offered "beneficial distancing" through the secretary, nurse, or simply being on the doctor's "turf." "The chief convenience of the house visit," according to Doctor Hertzler, "was that the patient was definitely anchored and one could at once gain a reasonable proximity by simply clawing off the comforter or feather bed."[34] But to him, "the one great advantage of office practice" was that "if the young doctor does not know what is wrong with the patient he can adopt the lawyer's tactics and stall. He can give the patient something to take and ask him to return, and in the interval, read up on the various possibilities."[35]

The Doctor's Pay, the Patient's Cost

If the technical aspects in the 1930s make the doctor's job seem easy, the varied accounts cited should dispel such a notion. Plain doctoring remained a hard, 24-hour-a-day job with no free weekends.[36] Part of the reason for this was economics, pure and simple. (Doctor Hertzler remarked, apropos "reading up," that "the doctor must read fast, for it is not his habit to charge a retaining fee and there is a possibility that in the meantime the patient may stray off to another doctor.")[37] Competition for patients (at least the paying ones), whether in the office, home, or hospital, was keen. The saying went, "A doctor's worst enemy is another doctor." In *Poor Man's Doctor* (1945), Lewis R. Tryon would write, "I don't think the average layman realizes the amount of professional jealousy which exists among doctors, especially in small towns, where there is a definite limit to the total number of available patients." More recent accounts of the period have reported doctors fist fighting in hospital parking lots over "patient stealing."[38]

The Lynds took a somewhat less sympathetic view. "With the increase of medical skills," they wrote, "have inevitably come vested interests. Says one of the city's leading medical experts, 'Our Medical Association refuses to recognize the right of an outside medical man to come here and earn money raised in this county.' "[39] Bottom-line economics encouraged other compromises, some large, some small. According to the Lynds, certain diseases went unreported by doctors—venereal disease, for example—"rather than lose the case" and "competition is so keen [they observed] that even the best doctors in many cases supplement their incomes by putting up their own prescriptions."[40] It was not unheard of, even in Boston, for a patient to make calls to three doctors, paying only the one who arrived first! In that decade fee splitting was also a professional issue, as specialists, in order to get referrals, sometimes exchanged rewards with general practitioners: Two dollars might be returned with the report of an X-ray examination. Although certain national studies reported that doctors did fairly well during the Depression, relative to the rest of the population, the word from the Middle West was that these were "years of the locust." Thomas Neville Bonner noted that in Kansas "reception rooms were unfilled, appointment books more or less blank, and telephones more silent than any time in years. Checker and cribbage boards were dusted off and put back into action." More seriously,

Not a few doctors were themselves forced onto the relief rolls. It was . . . "the most serious time this generation of doctors has known." Most threatening of all was the desertion of long-time patients for other doctors in the embarrassment of not being able to pay old bills, let alone pay for new services.[41]

From Atlantic City, New Jersey, emigré physician Benjamin J. Gordon wrote of similar circumstances.

Days passed without my seeing a patient, and those who came to consult me did anything but inspire me with hope. On the third day after I had opened my office, an elderly woman, well-dressed and bedecked with precious stones, walked into my reception room. When I came out to greet her, I found her looking around my little waiting room with an air of superiority. The size of my room and its furnishings did not appear to measure up to her expectations.[42]

At the public clinics that filled those blank private appointment hours, medical work was paid at the rate of $3.00 per hour by welfare departments. The municipal and voluntary hospital clinics were where doctors might donate their time, exchanging this duty for the privilege of hospitalizing their paying patients or for the chance to pick up a paying patient to bring to their own office; neither alternative was satisfactory to the profession, though circumstances forced them to tolerate it—and to tolerate the FSA medical programs. Visits to the private practitioner were cheap by today's standards, sometimes as low as half a dollar to a dollar and a half in the country, and between three and five dollars in the city—often with the extra charge of half a dollar per mile for the doctor to drive his Chevy out to the home, an extra that, like laboratory tests today, netted the doctor more income than the visit itself. In rural regions, such mileage could add up. "Rural calls are expensive and time-consuming to make," Charles S. Johnson wrote, "whether the physician takes into account the ability of patients to pay or not."[43] While the fee for an office consultation could vary from $2.50 to $3.00, "fees for rural calls appear to vary according to distance and accessibility, sometimes amounting to $12.00."[44]

In Minnesota health costs differed; doctors charged only "fifty cents a mile on country calls, "but when your cash income was only $1,000 a year, "you just can't afford to get sick" either, said the Handevidt family. Twice in the past twelve years, however, "serious illness for Mrs. Handevidt has set them back financially." Hospitalization insurance was not available in their region, so, like many working people they tried to look after themselves, and trusted to a combination of background, environment, diet, and common sense to keep their annual medical expenses "down close to $50.00."[45] The Walter W. Kriebel family in Seattle, Washington, attempted a similar strategy but, according to a *Ladies' Home Journal* survey,

their luck has been terrible. Every time they get one three-figured charge for an operation paid off, trouble strikes again in a different part of their anatomies. On one such occasion a ruptured appendix almost carried Jack off at the age of ten. Walt has always managed so far to arrange short-term installments for doctors and hospitals, $5 a month here, $2.50 a month there. But the cumulative effect has been crippling. . . .[46]

Home deliveries were but $25 and, when done by midwives, cheaper still at $5. Despite what appear to be inexpensive charges, few working people could easily pay for such visits from what little out-of-pocket cash they had. Money was that tight, and the spread between middle and working class much less. The median income was $1,500 for patients and $3,000 for doctors. (Lewis Thomas's best friend in the Harvard Medical School class of 1937 put out the yearbook and at the same time sent a questionnaire to Harvard graduates of the previous classes of 1927, 1917, and 1907. Responses were instructive. "The average income for the ten-year graduates was $3,500," Thomas wrote, rising to $7,500 for the twenty-year men. "One man, a urologist, reported an income of $50,000, but he was an anomaly; all the rest made, by the standards of 1937, respectable but very modest sums of money."[47] If professional incomes everywhere were low, those of ordinary rural folk were drastically low, especially in the South: $270 per year in South Carolina, for example, which also had the lowest ratio of doctors in the country—1:1,431 as compared to 1:621 in New York.[48] Disease, as noted earlier, followed the falling curve of income like a vulture. Arthur Raper wrote:

It is generally known that about half the South's people are unable to pay for medical care, that there are over 1,500,000 cases of malaria in seven Southern states, that hookworm and pellagra are most common in areas where tenancy is highest, income lowest, and educational rating poorest.[49]

Mining regions did no better; from the miners' $27- or $30-a-month wage came "deducts," as the miners called them, the $2 paid to the company doctor. Overloading an already conflicted relationship, complaints were many, such that outsiders could easily pinpoint the crux of the problem: "The miners have no power to hire and fire these doctors and the doctors being quite independent of their clients and paid by the coal companies, do as they like and as they find convenient about coming when they are called."[50]

If under such circumstances there was no cash nexus to the encounter of doctor and patient, as the Depresssion worsened the doctor either was postponed or avoided; and when he finally visited, he was "paid in kind." Dr. B. K. Harris tartly recalled "what Doc Johnson said to me one day, he said, 'I've eaten just about all the fried chicken and black-eyed peas I can stand!' And I know it to be a fact, a lot of his pay was in just that, you know." The flexible collection and management of fees—as seen with Dr. Goodson's patients—changed still further. "It used to be the rule not to charge widows any doctor's fees," Dr. Harris reported, but

since the various relief agencies there is less charity, less private charity, and this had had its bearing among doctors, too. A great deal of charity is still being done by rural doctors, has to be done, but they are accepting pay that is offered by their patients even though it is in produce rather than coin. I have been paid for 'medical services rendered' in molasses, hogs, chickens, eggs, corn, potatoes, ham, beans, all kinds of vegetables. The biggest item I ever accepted in payment for medical service was 200 plow beams. I still have some of those plow beams.[51]

This was no different than the Middle West, where, according to Dr. Joseph A. Jerger,

we frequently were much amused by serious intentions to pay us for Tommy's tonsils, papa's gall bladder or Mary's cholera morbus, with hand-painted china, ships in bottles, live suckling pigs, homemade ties, and many other articles. One morning I found a young mule I had admired, hitched to a post behind the house, labelled, " 'John,' and look out for her, she kicks like hell!"[52]

After attending at six deliveries without being paid, a Southern country doctor attended at the seventh, and "after it was all over and she was comfortable [the mother] looked up at me and said, with the utmost sincerity: 'Doctor Cain, I've never been able to pay you nothin' for delivin' my other six children, so I'll give you this one.' "[53] More traditionally, "A husband, feeling very grateful after his wife had borne him a nice son, said to me on one occasion: 'Doc, I've got nothin' to pay you with, but I'll name my boy for you.' Years after that I saw the man in Anton one day."[54]

Not all the exchanges were so friendly, nor was the charge for service so often scaled, reduced, or dismissed. Charles S. Johnson wrote that, according to his research, certain "doctors insist upon some security for the debt before calling. Ownership of a cow, or mule, or other property will suffice, and these are taken in if the bills are not paid within a reasonable time." A patient bitterly complained to Johnson:

They just gets all our money when we is sick. A poor nigger has a hard time. You phones them and they say, "is you got the money?" If you ain't, you need not 'spect them. You gotta have that money right on the table or you just lies here and dies.[55]

If nowadays such testimony, anecdotes, and statistics do not move us, if we take the matter of payment for granted, this is only because 60 percent of the population has some coverage of office care through Medicaid, Medicare, or private insurance, whereas in the past insurance coverage was nil. As a result, then, the charitable urban hospital outpatient departments (OPDs) were jammed with nonpaying patients, while rural doctors ran OPDs from their own small offices by not charging, discounting bills, or not collecting at all, a situation that continued until after World War II. Doctors' collection rates during the Depression were, not surprisingly, 40 percent or less, which explained the average decline in physician net income of 17 percent or more, especially in those rural dust-bowl states of Kansas, Texas, and Oklahoma, where the decline was 50 percent.[56] A general practitioner from Kentucky during those years, Dr. William Wright, revealingly summarized the negative aspects of the situation when he said:

The doctor did the best he could. He seldom went out of town. Sometimes you got paid, sometimes you didn't get paid. Sometimes you'd get a brokered deal. They bring in food or they work for you. That kind of thing. There wasn't a whole lot of money and there wasn't a whole lot of care.[57]

With the kinds of illness and disease, social and economic conditions, site of care, payment, scope of illness, and technology of practice all different during the Depression, was the doctor-patient relationship also different?

Very likely so, if these elements are judged to be part of that relationship.

We have so few direct observations of these encounters, though more pieces can be added by the doctors (at least the writing ones) whose memoirs and personal letters convey a devotion to their patients quite surpassing the prudent limits of restrained science, the current desires for academic status, institutional power, and straight cash accumulation. These were the plain doctors, exemplified by the gangling, Lincolnesque, and tireless Hertzler of *Horse and Buggy Doctor*; the wry but hopeful sort who strove always to "go to the patient" no matter how difficult the journey or how little a doctor like Hertzler might offer technically when he arrived.

The relationship and examples of both the patient and doctor's perspectives can be seen in American fiction if we search it carefully, especially in authors and works formerly overlooked. The novels, stories, and poetry of William Carlos Williams are an obvious and rich resource. He captures with "Ashcan" realism, the weariness and frustration of the average physician trudging up one tenement stair after another; he renders with lyric impressionism moments of extreme joy and extreme sorrow; and, always congruent with the vernacular, he renders the plain speech of the participants: their vulgar rebukes and crude recriminations, their anguished incomprehension and cold acceptance, their understated gratitude and humbling attempts at recompense.

Southern Gothic humor in the extreme can be found in Faulkner's treatment of a "grieving" family's bumbling journey with their mother's coffin in *As I Lay*

Dying; and the intensity and duration of anxiety a life-threatening illness generates literally brings Sinclair Lewis's *Babbitt* to a standstill. Several of Hemingway's Nick Adams stories revolve around the youthful protagonist's initiation into manhood via doctor-patient conflicts involving race and class. Nick's doctor-father in "Indian Camp," for example, is elated with his medical prowess, having successfully completed a caesarian with nothing but a jackknife and fly-fishing leader. He has "saved" both suffering mother and unborn child, though his objectification of the squaw is dramatized by the fact that he has lost her "brave" (the ignored father-to-be has slit his throat from ear to ear in the upper bunk during the operation), and the burden of Dr. Adams' insensitivity falls upon Nick for whom the interventions of a doctor will never again be—if they ever were—an unqualified good. A story of the period by Don Marquis, "Country Doctor," gives us the practitioner's point of view where, we are told,

nobody ever heard him say anything about loving these people [his patients], nor did they talk about loving him. Nor did anybody hear the word "service," so popular since, from his lips. . . . But [significantly] there was a pretty good understanding between the doctor and his people. . . . They took him as naturally as they did the sunlight and rain and changes of seasons, and, some of them, thoughtlessly.[58]

A well-made British novel of the day, Helen Ashton's *Doctor Serocold: A Page from His Day-Book* (1930), discloses the back-and-forth nature of the relationship with psychological deftness. For example, one of the characters muses that "he knew all our circumstances, just as he knew the life story of every other person in the little town. It was the fruit and burden of his forty years there that he learned a thousand troubles besides his own."[59] And, out of his hearing, the speaker concludes as though speaking to her doctor directly:

Of course we couldn't do without you. . . . Think, you've been here as long as most of us can remember! You know everything about us. We don't have to explain our bodies or our minds to you. . . . We just come to you whenever there's anything wrong; we know that you will help us if you can, and that if there's no help, at any rate, you'll understand.[60]

The evidence weighs heavily on the doctor in these accounts; it seems their lives contain a good deal of what in the current idiom is termed "grief and aggravation." Yet should doctoring during the 1930s seem bleak compared to our present affluent practices (for some), the patient's lot was even bleaker. With one worker in four without a job, family medical costs ran from $15 to $30 a year, and more than half of 8,500 white families with incomes under $1,200, for example, received *no* medical care in twelve consecutive months during the period 1928–1931.[61] Medical expenses, like income, were unequally distributed. Poor rural families, for example, spent a far greater percentage of their yearly income for far fewer medical services than the wealthiest.[62] The poor health that was so often a part of joblessness and economic failure was not the only acute complaint that brought the doctor to the house or the patient to the office. These complaints also included the angst of coping with personal failure ("because he is off mentally," as Doctor Goodson noted) and the grief from "being ill" when so much else had to be done "no matter how the housewife might feel that day," as Robert Caro observed.

This psychological burden from ill health was also compounded and lessened, in a way, by the commonplace occurrence of chronic disease and handicaps— as public health surveys of the period demonstrated when enumerating the prevalence of dental caries, impaired vision and hearing, malnutrition, hypertension, arthritis, varicose veins, and gastrointestinal disorders. In one study these and other disorders, together, made for no less than 4.9 defects per person.[63]

The benchmark CCMC report in 1932 only made public what, in fact, had been private knowledge for years: Medical care for the bulk of the American people prior to the Depression was wholly inadequate and getting no better. Each year after 1929, for example, medical statistics followed and then exceeded the downward curve of economic indicators. And this, despite the aforementioned medical school reforms and the significant advances in medical technology and medical research. Plain doctoring existed, but it was not reaching plain people. Then, as now, questions of access and financing posed major obstacles to improvement, as did matters internal to the medical profession: the rural-urban distribution of doctors, over-specialization, two- and three-tiered quality of care, inter-professional rivalry, and, inescapably, a conflicted ideology among practitioners (and the public) who saw medicine as a right on the one hand and a commodity like any other on the other.

The FSA Medical Care Plans

As the New Deal provided direct relief, it was inevitable that various agencies would involve themselves in medical care. To the extent that the New Deal went further and attempted rehabilitation and fundamental change, it was inevitable that certain forms of medical care and kinds of practitioners would emerge who would challenge the status quo. FERA, recall, provided direct aid, and its socially responsible, progressive director, Hopkins, surely had a hand in framing the famous "Category 7" under FERA's Rules and Regulations, which stated: "Federal Funds granted to the State may be used to pay for medical attention and medical supplies for families on relief."[64] Although, as Michael Ross Grey acknowledges in "Primary Care in the Great Depression: The Medical Program of the Farm Security Administration (1980)," "no organizational reform, in terms of financing or delivery of care, was involved in the FERA medical aid program,"[65] there is no mistaking, nor does Grey fail to develop, the fact the government camel had put its nose into the medical care tent for more than its traditional provision of services to Indians, seamen, veterans, and members of the armed services.

When the inner councils of the New Deal planners decided as early as in 1934 that relief without reform was a dead-end policy, it was only a matter of time before the technical "advice" proferred ailing farmers, tenants, sharecroppers, and farm laborers would include more than merely information about diet and the use of professional services. It was obvious that a reform of services would be required for any lasting rehabilitation. Direct medical relief initially took the form of direct, federal payments to medical practitioners, paralleling FERA's direct payments to state welfare agencies; it would go further by becoming a federally organized, but locally directed program in three stages. First the clients would be encouraged to form medical cooperatives, and they or their government field supervisor would approach local medical societies and individual physicians, soliciting their participation. Later the government would take it upon itself to provide medical services through government-contracted services in a particular area. Finally, the reform phase would come about through government-organized but locally directed cooperatives, generally reformed because they were now based on group prepayment and internally reformed because they were organized on our prevailing model of prepaid group practice, the HMO, for primary care.

Discussions about medical care had begun with the FERA planners, but it was within the RA that the first eight medical cooperatives were begun, though as experiments. As could be expected, these were roundly denounced for their "sovietism," but the RA refused to be swayed from their policy; they did not believe that collective action by small and marginal farmers was un-American or that such action would be unsuccessful. The RA argued that large farmers had established cooperatives of their own by lobbying through large national organizations and that the success of their action, in the form of the AAA, could hardly be denied. Policy makers within the successor FSA found a way to answer later critics by turning the weakest link in the FSA program, loan default (a constant source of the conservative criticism, that RA, later FSA, clients couldn't be rehabilitated),[66] into a justification for RA/FSA-sponsored medical care. In numerous surveys of its client population, Grey writes, "the RA found that ill-health was a large contributory factor in loan defaults . . . ill-health was thus an obstacle to successful rehabilitation." And in the fall of 1937, when the RA was reorganized under Dr. Will Alexander, it was argued even more forcefully, according to Grey, that "a family in good health was a better credit risk than a family in bad health. So far as the government was concerned the program [health cooperatives] was simply a matter of good business."[67]

Yet organized medicine remained hostile; indeed, when the CCMC proposals appeared some years earlier, the American Medical Association editorialized in its national journal in support of the disagreeing minority, describing the majority's mild proposals for *some* movement toward group practice and *some* form of national health insurance as an "incitement to revolution." The AMA had asserted, in the face of all the public and private research to the contrary, that "present indicators are that these counties are receiving all the medical care that they demand and considerably more than they can pay for." Moreover, "no evidence has been found to show that the people who live in these counties have complained of any lack of services."[68]

The hookworm population must have rejoiced at the AMA's myopic self-assurance and, needless to say, the RA/FSA's "good business" arguments did little to allay the AMA's fear that "socialized medicine" was about to stalk the land under the federal government's banner.

A commentary from Kansas indicates that the FSA program was one option, among others, which attempted to deal in a programmatic way with the medical care needs of the unemployed and those with a low income. Other options were the old county medical roster, and the use of salaried county welfare physicians, and a third was prepayment by the county to individual providers.

Under [FERA] the county medical society in a number of instances was made officially responsible for the medical care of relief patients. The society was reimbursed by local authorities at the rate of one dollar per month for the care of each family on relief.

The technical arrangements and physicians' responses were predictable: "These funds were divided among participating physicians. Most doctors approved of this program because it maintained the doctor-patient relationship and kept the care of the sick in the hands of the local profession." "Control" and "local" are the operative concepts. "By 1939," the account continued,

a number of variations of this plan . . . were in operation. In fifty-five counties of Kansas a county physician or physicians were paid salaries by local authorities. In forty other counties a number of participating doctors were paid fees for their services according to a schedule usually set in agreement with the county medical society. Finally, eleven counties still relied directly upon the county medical society to furnish medical services to relief patients, for which the county paid a lump sum into the society's treasury at stated intervals.

How much need was actually being addressed by these plans is difficult to estimate, but "a mammoth problem" was what the situation was called in Kansas because in 1938 alone 20,000 were "on the relief rolls in [one county] Shawnee . . . with only one physician to look after their health." Responding to the size of the problem, that county medical society in 1942, for example, "took a bold step forward in assuming medical and hospital care of these indigent persons in return for payment of three dollars per month from each of the families concerned." More than 90 percent of eligible families paid this fee the first month, attesting to the popularity of the concept. "This was the first time in Kansas and almost in the United States," the report fairly crowed, "that a county sought to guarantee such complete medical and hospital care, including drugs and all necessary tests, to its unemployed."

The concept of a prepayment plan rapidly drew other supporters in that state because, in western Kansas, "another emergency health insurance plan was started . . . and included more than one thousand Farm Security Administration clients." Even though the commentary described the FSA plan as a response to an "emergency," suggesting, perhaps, that medical organization would change once the country went back to "normal," the figures spoke for themselves in terms of acceptance: "With all fifty-five physicians in the nineteen-county area taking part, the participating farmers were assured emergency medical and hospital care for themselves and their families for thirty dollars per year."[69]

None of these plans, with the exception of the FSA program, were long-range solutions. All may have been a response to an emergency, but only the FSA's was intended to go beyond, to act as a model for continuous prevention and maintenance in the future. The thrust of Grey's thesis is to demonstrate that this FSA model failed nationally not because the decline in client numbers in the early 1940s reflected an inadequate model and an inefficient and ineffective program, as has been argued, but because of the grudging participation of local medical societies and local physicians from the beginning, whose participation was withdrawn the moment the economy picked up, the moment they could leave the FSA and return to older models of narrow medical care rather than broader, more inclusive health care, and to more lucrative private fee-for-service practices. That said, it must also be qualified, for it was hardly professional *dominance* that caused the demise. As the postwar economy expanded, political support for the FSA program waned—as it did for the plan urged by no less than President Truman, in the late 1940's, national health insurance.

General statistics that cover the years of the Great Depression, roughly 1929 to 1940, tell us that the aggregate national health-care expenditures as measured against the gross national product rose one-half of a percentage point during that time, hardly a huge amount, but that there was a significant shift of almost seven percentage points from private to public funding of these expenditures. In actual dollars it means that, out of $3,863 million spent for health care in 1940, some $782 million as opposed to $477 million in 1929 was being spent by the government. Four out of every five dollars were still being spent privately ($3,081 million in 1940 as opposed to $3,112 million in 1929) but the trend, a function of the New Deal and the FSA in particular, accelerated and increased until the present when approximately one out of every two dollars spent for health care is a public dollar.[70]

Despite criticism from the left and the right, the significance of this shift for actual medical practice is a story that remains to be told. Grey went to the original FSA sources and interviewed FSA participants, including physicians and administrators. He came to understand a little of the day-to-day activity of FSA doctors; he could give his readers some of the quality of the doctor-patient relationship by quoting from pamphlets and flyers administrators addressed to clients/patients ("Remember, the physician is only human, after all, and that he enjoys an occasional pat on the back. A good physician deserves more of that than he receives") and to local directors ("The families should be encouraged to express appreciation to the physicians for services rendered").[71]

Grey also looked closely at one location, the state of North Carolina, in order to provide evidence that the FSA health care model was flexible, that it could and did adapt successfully to local conditions and local needs. But here, as elswhere in his study, Grey's aim was less descriptive than political. He was at pains to answer the program's critics, and he wanted to draw parallels from this New Deal success to our present condition.

We learn about the FSA's experiment in primary care medicine during the Depression more from Grey's research than from many recent and seemingly more inclusive and extensive studies. These studies tell us how the bulk of government dollars, a vast amount, has gone to finance medical schools and medical training, hospital construction and hospital operation, and, of course, medical research. Valuable information, though our principal source of knowledge for the medical practice of the 1930s, will, along with Grey, remain the several thousand FSA medical photographs of its operation. Until, one hopes, scholars delve into the FSA files again in order to explain to us the full nature of medical care that reached 120,000 families in more than 1,000 rural counties in every part of the United States and two-thirds of that number in the American South.[72]

3
Medical Photographs and the Doctor-Patient Relationship

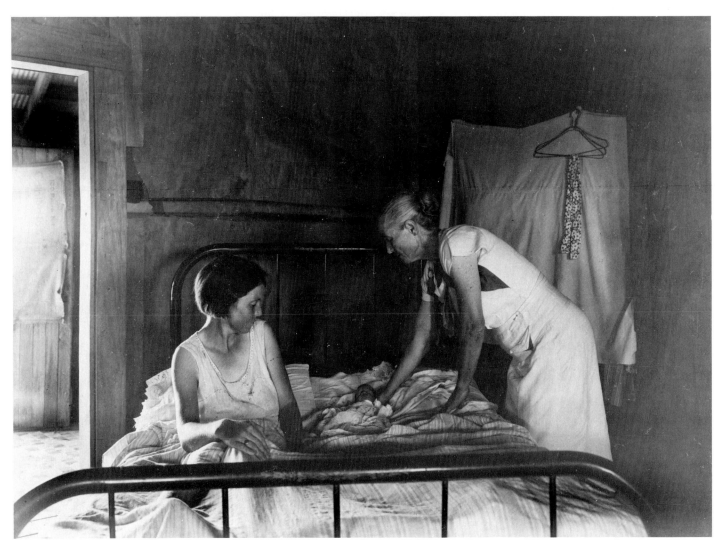

35
Cleveland (vicinity), Miss., in the Delta area.
June 1937.
*Grandmother, mother, and newborn baby of a
sharecropper.*
DOROTHEA LANGE.

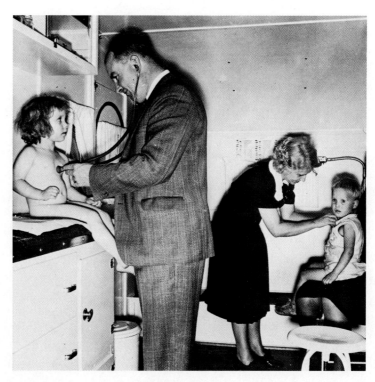

36
Merrill, Klamath County, Ore. Oct. 1939.
Farm Security Administration mobile camp for mi-
gratory farm labor. Doctor examining children in
the trailer clinic.
DOROTHEA LANGE.

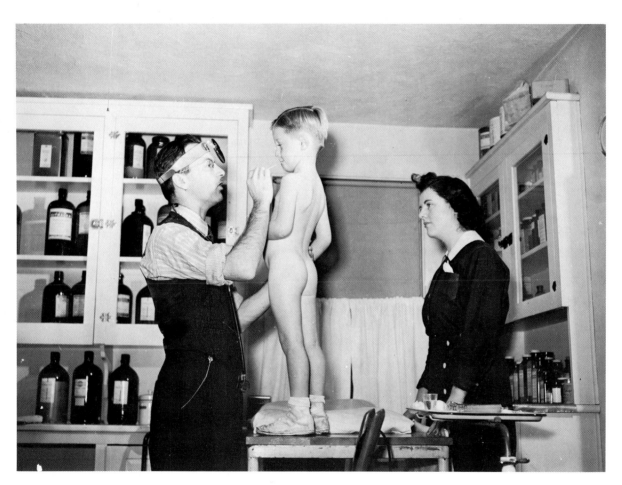

37
Dailey, W.Va. Dec. 1941. Tygart valley homesteads, and Farm Security Administration project, 11 miles southwest of Elkins, W.Va.
*Dr. Tabor examining Randolph Darkey before in-
oculating him against measles, in the community
health center.*
ARTHUR ROTHSTEIN.

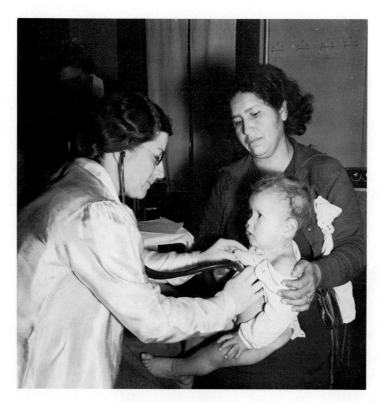

38
Calipatria, Imperial County, Calif. Feb. 1939.
*The Farm Security Administration emergency
camp for workers in the pea harvest. Visiting pub-
lic health doctor conducting a well-baby clinic in
a local school building adjacent to the pea harvest.
Many migratory mothers bring their children.*
DOROTHEA LANGE.

39
Bridgeton, N.J. June 1942.
Farm Security Administration agricultural workers'
camp. The camp clinic.
JOHN COLLIER.

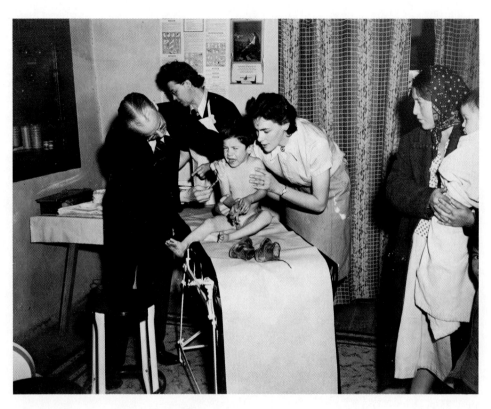

40
Penasco, N.M. Jan. 1943.
*Preventive medicine is an important part of the
program of the clinic operated by the Taos County
Cooperative Health Association.*
JOHN COLLIER.

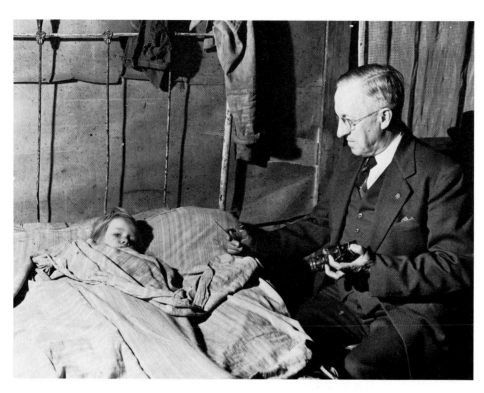

41
Scott County, Mo. Feb. 1942.
Doctor at bedside of sick child.
JOHN VACHON.

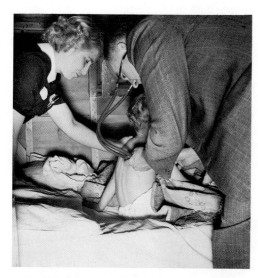

42
Merrill, Klamath County, Ore. Oct. 1939.
Farm Security Administration mobile camp for migratory farm labor. The doctor examining a boy from Texas.
DOROTHEA LANGE.

43
Southington, Conn. May 1942.
At the health center, the people of Southington may receive medical advice and a certain amount of medical care (such as physical checkups, which this girl is receiving) without cost.
FENNO JACOBS.

44
St. Charles County, Mo. Nov. 1939.
*A physician cooperating with an FSA medical
health plan, visiting the home of a rehabilitation
client.*
ARTHUR ROTHSTEIN.

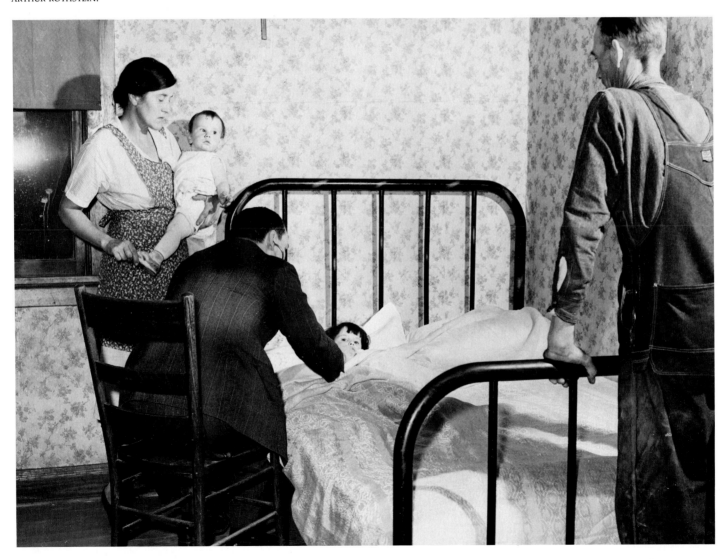

45
Bridgeton, N.J. June 1942.
*Farm Security Administration agricultural workers'
camp. The camp doctor has a large practice in
Bridgeton but also gives his time to the migrant
camp, where he works to curb venereal disease,
malnutrition, and general run-down conditions of
health.*
JOHN COLLIER.

46
Chaffee, Mo. Feb. 1942.
*Little girl who was bitten by a dog receiving
antihydrophobia vaccine.*
JOHN VACHON.

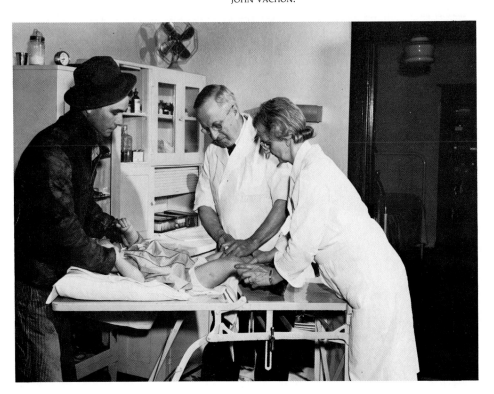

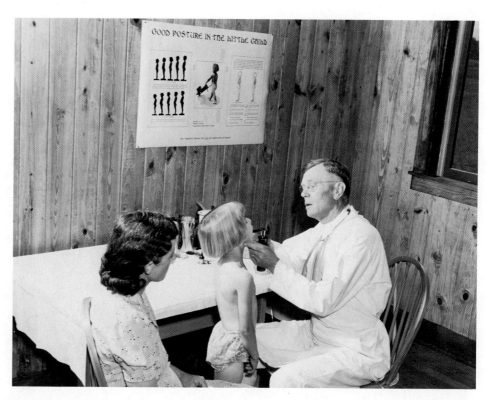

47
Transylvania, La. June 1940.
*A U.S. Department of Agriculture, Farm Security
Administration project. Mrs. M. E. Chappell with
her daughter, Sybil Lee, being examined by Dr.
F. A. Williams, Director of East Carroll Parish
health unit, in the project school clinic.*
MARION POST WOLCOTT.

48
Caswell County, N.C. Oct. 1940.
Dr. S. A. Malloy examining Louis Graves and his family on their front porch.
MARION POST WOLCOTT.

49
Greendale, Wis. Sept. 1939 [?].
A community planned by the suburban division of the U.S. Resettlement Administration. Boy being examined by the doctor. This is the Greendale branch of the Milwaukee Group Health Association.
JOHN VACHON.

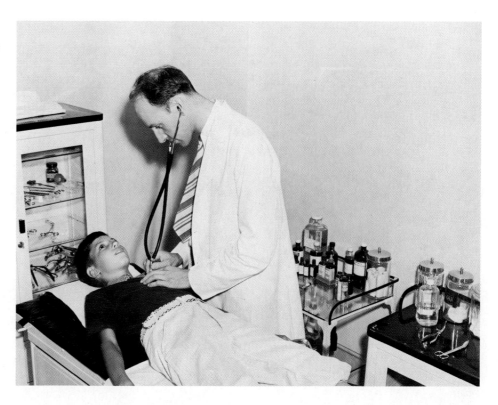

50
Coffee County, Ala. Apr. 1939.
A doctor and a nurse (Miss Teal) examining and advising about treatment for a child at the health room of the Goodman Consolidated School.
MARION POST WOLCOTT.

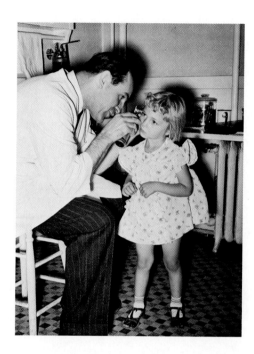

51
Box Elder, Utah. Aug. 1940.
Medical cooperative of the FSA.
RUSSELL LEE.

52
Blanch, N.C. Oct. 1940.
Dr. S. A. Malloy examining Mrs. William H. Willis and her family. Mr. Willis is a Farm Security Administration borrower.
MARION POST WOLCOTT.

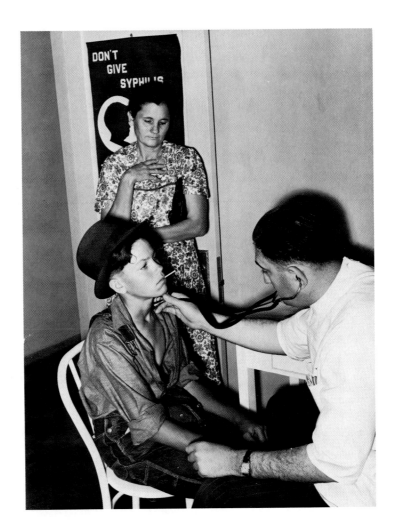

53
Maricopa County, Ariz. May 1940.
*The Aqua Fria Farm Security Administration camp
for migratory workers. Doctor at the clinic exam-
ining the son of an agricultural worker.*
RUSSELL LEE.

54
Bridgeton, N.J. July 1942.
Farm Security Administration agricultural workers'
camp. The clinic.
JOHN COLLIER.

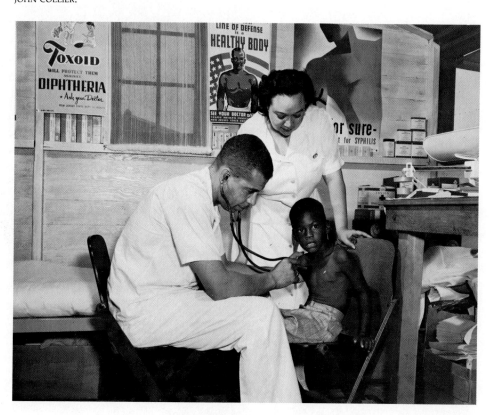

55
Scott County, Mo. Feb. 1942.
Country doctor examining child in farmhouse.
JOHN VACHON.

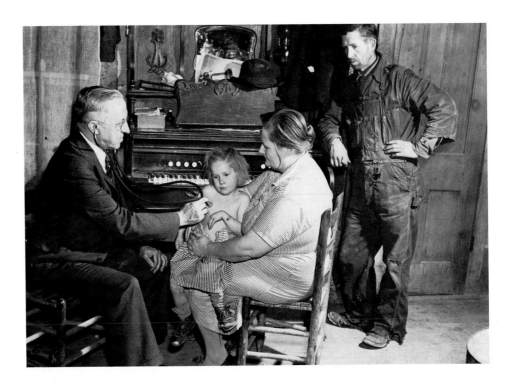

56
Blanch, N.C. Oct. 1940.
Dr. S. A. Malloy examining Mr. William H. Willis's son Bobby in their home. Mr. Willis is a Farm Security Administration borrower.
MARION POST WOLCOTT.

57
Bridgeton, N.J. June 1942.
Farm Security Administration agricultural workers'
camp. Patients at the camp clinic receiving injec-
tions for the treatment of venereal disease.
JOHN COLLIER.

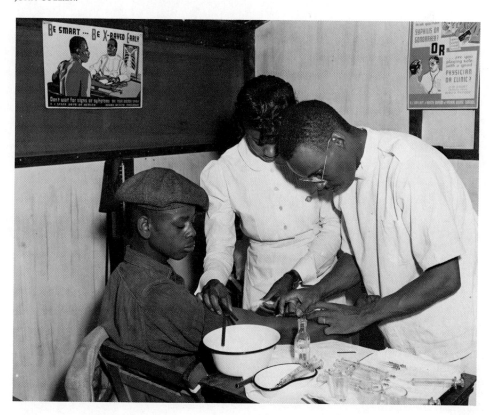

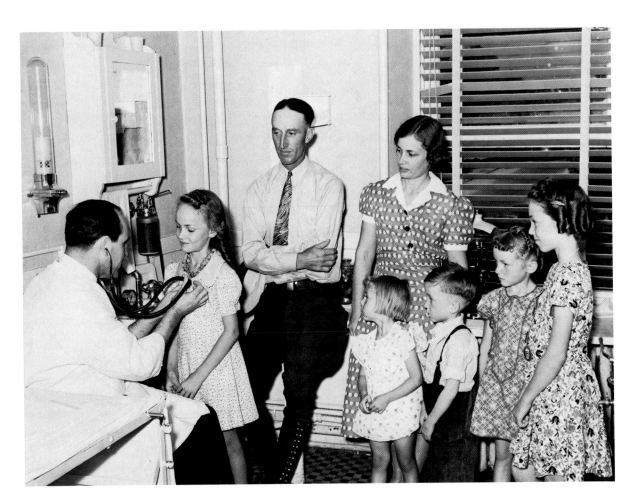

58
Box Elder, Utah. Aug. 1940.
*Doctor with a family who are members of the FSA
medical cooperative.*
RUSSELL LEE.

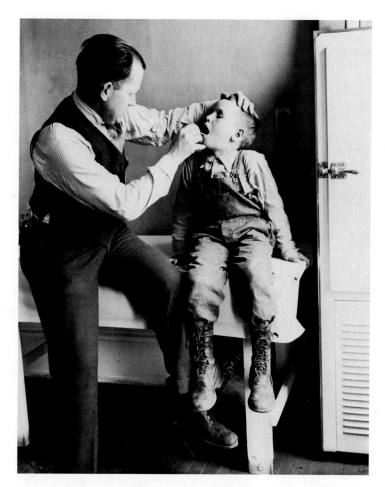

59
Reedsville, W.Va. Apr. 1935.
The Arthurdale subsistence homestead project of
the U.S. Resettlement Administration. Doctor ex-
amining a boy's throat.
ARTHUR ROTHSTEIN.

60

Penasco, N.M. Jan. 1943.
Dr. Onstine, of the clinic operated by the Taos County Cooperative Health Association, and Majorie Muller (right), resident Red Cross nurse.
JOHN COLLIER.

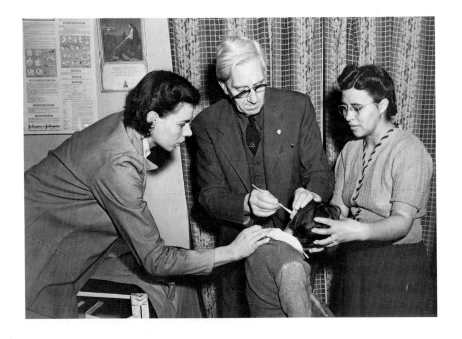

61

Dailey, W.Va. Dec. 1941.
Tygart valley homesteads, and Farm Security Administration project, 11 miles southwest of Elkins, W.Va. Dr. Tabor writing instructions for medicine for Roscoe Loupin.
ARTHUR ROTHSTEIN.

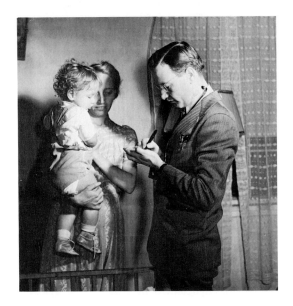

62
San Augustine, Tex. April 1943.
Dr. Schreiber of San Augustine giving typhoid in-
oculation at rural school.
JOHN VACHON.

No less than the ubiquitous snapshot or the discreet formal portrait, medical photographs are part of a tradition, and their form and content are dictated by convention. They oscillate uneasily. They are not exactly snapshots (despite their accidental and often stereotypical content) nor are they formal portraits (despite their formal commission and photographer-subject compliance). Their most common though most deeply conflicting characteristic lies in a relationship; all three kinds of photographs suggest both more and less of a relationship than the image actually presents. The meaning of medical photographs, therefore, is best approached through an appreciation of shared conventions and technical differences and an understanding of the structure and process of the doctor-patient relationship that medical photographs imply and also withhold, deny, and leave ambiguous. The multiple dimensions of this doctor-patient relationship are illuminated by the psychological work of Sigmund Freud, Harry Stack Sullivan, and Jay Haley, and it is to such work that plain doctoring turns as well.

You Push the Button, We Do the Rest

With his own upper-middle class Pennsylvania Quaker family as a source, John A. Kouwenhoven's useful essay, "Living in a Snapshot World," is framed, as it were, by a quotation from the Museum of Modern Art's noted photography curator, John Szarkowski:

Painting was difficult, expensive, and precious, and it recorded what was known to be important. Photography was easy, cheap, and ubiquitous, . . . and it recorded anything. And once made objective and permanent, immortalized in a picture, these trivial things took on an importance. By the end of the century even the poorest man knew what his ancestors had looked like.[1]

Skirting the issue of why even in "our mobile, throwaway society," people hang on to photographs, Kouwenhoven analyzes his family snapshots following Szarkowski's lead, noting that, unlike the early and more expensive daguerreotypes, his family's could be photographed quickly with a minimum of deliberate posing on the part of the subjects and a minimum of deliberate selectivity on the part of the photographer.[2] He tends to see their relative inexpensiveness, when contrasted with the luxurious and elegant settings of the daguerreotype studio, as a major factor in their popularization. (Photography historian Dan Schiller supports this conclusion; Schiller writes that, by 1850, "Americans spent between eight and twelve million dollars a year on photographs" and estimates that, by the 1870s, 50 million photographs were being made each year!)[3] An album assembled between 1885 and 1915 by his aunts is Kouwenhoven's focus; the book has large pages (10 3/4 by 13 1/2 inches), each of which holds fifteen or so pictures. There are individuals and groups, not all self-consciously posed, he sees; some distant relative is "caught," as the advertisements promised only a camera could; similarly, medical photographers would catch smallpox spots they weren't looking for or hidden bullets in newly set limbs.

The differences between snapshots and painted pictures that Szarkowski suggested are probed by Kouwenhoven on the level of conventions. Except for accidental snapshots, from what he knows of his family (valuable information in decoding anything visual), the then-young lady who took the first pictures in the album "saw the world about her with eyes accustomed to seeing what the pictures by well-known painters and illustrators [of the time] had taught her to see." The major clue for Kouwenhoven lies with the interior shots ("some are quite lovely," he admits) that, technically, not only required careful time exposures, tripod placement (to utilize gas or window light), and hung white sheets, but also something like a visual inventory of conventions because "they could not have been composed or lighted by someone who had never seen paintings or engraved reproductions of paintings by . . . Sargent, or . . . Eakins."[4]

It occurs to Kouwenhoven that paintings allow for an enormous selection of reality; more than photographs, they are heavily *edited* by an artist who combines perceptions acquired over time and who can concentrate, select, omit, or alter those perceptions. Snapshots remind him that the selection is decided beforehand, the photographer "at most determines the instant at which the unedited details will be recorded." When he says, however, that the photographer "cannot select some details and ignore others visible at that instant," he forgets the considerable powers of the darkroom. True, it is a *via negativa*; the darkroom can only say No. That, however, may make a large difference to what has been said Yes to already. And when he argues that photography "cannot incorporate details that were visible at other moments no matter how significant the photographer might consider them to be," he neglects the motor-drive camera and its micro-second appetite, although it must be conceded that such a camera still cannot go backward in time.

Yet even the hint of a darkroom has us crossing a threshold, from the amateur who has been given "permission" to be intrusive by familial agreement or a generalized freedom with natural objects like mountains, canyons, rivers or public objects like cathedrals, monuments, and public buildings ("AIR, This Is Your Country, Dont Let The Big Men Take It Away FROM YOU" says the garage sign in Dorothea Lange's Depression photograph), to the professional who has not been given permission so much as entered into an agreement or brokered a contract about what the image is to contain.

Representation of Self

Erving Goffman's exhaustive study, "Gender Advertisements," which first appeared in *Studies in Visual Anthropology*, opens with the statement that a portrait is a "decorative representation of self that serves to present one's social identity."[5] The purchaser of this commodity intends to record "who" he or she is for either an explicit audience in the present (shareholders in a corporation report, the press corps in Washington, colleagues at the hospital), or an implicit one in the future.

As wills and trusts attempt to control future behavior through gifts with conditions attached, so does the formal portrait photograph attempt to direct posterity by means of an official image of the individual. Distribution of such portraits is strictly limited and is part of the contract, though to whom the limits apply is a function of the relative prominence of both client and photographer. While the expense involved in formal portraits would have us believe that their audiences are primarily commercial, the biographers of portrait photographers suggest a sizable domestic consumption, especially with the extended families of the rising middle class in the late nineteenth and early twentieth centuries. As Dorothea Lange observed while reflecting upon her early work, formal portraits may also commemorate a special occasion in people's lives;

like the large church wedding, as opposed to a small civil ceremony, the complexity of such an event and the addition and/or subtraction of objects, add significant depth to an otherwise familiar ritual.[6]

Late nineteenth-century portraits were staged, the military parade ground not too distant. Faces were frozen into socially acceptable norms of dignity; the wet-plate procedure prior to the 1880s required a certain amount of bracing in order to keep still, but customers also wanted to be uniformly and properly presented to the outside world. (With the dry plate came greater flexibility in holding the pose. Conventions die hard though, and the stiff pose continued for several decades more, even until today, even as snapshots mimic it in satire.) Goffman explains that canvas backdrops had sylvan or Hellenic scenes, allusions to the classical heritage that, through privileged access to Greek and Latin, only the very well-off actually possessed; and neither strict posing nor "touching-up" and "tinting" were considered unnatural. Like any other *thing*, one was buying what one wanted.

Moreover, in order to receive one's social "due," one had to style himself or herself "so that others present can immediately know the social (and sometimes the personal) identity of he/she who is to be dealt with."[7] The portraitist was being paid to idealize the subject, with everything "important" in place; the unexpected was for snapshots, for informal summer outings like Kouwenhoven's family, in Rockport, Massachusetts, though in the 1920s and 1930s conventions again changed. Customers wanted "warmth," so a second camera was added, along with more photographer-client time for "warm-up."

Hairstyle, clothing, and decorations such as jewelry, medals, and Phi Beta Kappa keys were the more obvious clues the formal portrait was to organize and present. (Their analogues in the medical photograph should be obvious, though here again medical photographers couldn't control everything, as we shall see with the FSA.) Not for nothing did youngsters at the turn of the century make themselves "presentable" before adults by "correct" carriage and bowing or curtseying; adults presented themselves to one another, indicating social deference or social rank, through the "salute" of raising or tipping hats or the extension of the hand to be kissed—and also through the scrutiny of the "calling card," which had been handed to a servant or placed in a small wicker basket in the entryway. Decorous typography and elegant engraving thereby presented individuals, though they maintained plenty of social distance by their form and by the manner of their presentation. With the formal portrait, one also got one's due, not only from the placement of the camera's lens relative to the client—in frontal fashion ("open," "frank," "direct") or at some elevation and angle ("higher-to-lower" and "the good side")—but from the client's position relative to the camera's lens. Goffman's study catalogues the manifold gestures and postures of men and women with respect to social valuation. "Women, more than men," he observes, "are shown using their fingers in commercial advertising; men usually appear larger and taller than women."[8] And one can easily see the ways in which power, status, and desired values are enhanced in the older portraits simply by an individual's placement.

Accidents within snapshots—not simply technical mishaps like blurred images—receive little attention. An awkward gesture, a stranger in the frame, or an unwanted object is not, in the course of things, a matter for much concern; it is not something to be reflexively edited out. One takes a snap and moves on. The stereotypical occasions for snapshots (family picnics, weddings, friends, travel, military service, pets, first children) are situational and do not encourage the costly taking of duplicates. (No one sits around long for a snapshot, after all.) Quite the contrary is the case with the formal portrait, where the identity of self is clear to the client or is made clear by the photographer's contractual provision of an array of proofs and/or a return sitting, should it be necessary. A recent study of social and business portraits revealed a division between men and women on how best one might pose for a contemporary presentation before an employer or family. There was no division on the categories of posing—the cant, bow, and smile—when multiple alternatives were made available in the form of proofs.[9]

Compliance is "understood" with snapshots, since it is also understood—or was—where the boundaries of family and others are drawn; and, in any event, rarely would anyone outside the family circle show interest. Portraits involve a more explicit exchange, and more explicit rules bind each party. Discreet ads in *The New Yorker* cue prospective clients nowadays; they are to telephone for appointments, suggesting how high-status clients should regard high-status image makers. But a prominent portrait photographer told one of the authors that, during the Depression, it was not uncommon for a firm to give free sittings to professionals in order to encourage business; and, during the 1920s, when it was becoming more acceptable to be presented in a photograph than in a painting, Dorothea Lange recalls making "house calls" to her "San Francisco merchant princes."[10] As conventions have altered radically for both snapshots and formal portraits, so has compliance for medical photographs, fluctuating between the understood, the informal trust that came with the doctor-patient relationship, and the legally contractual. Perhaps this shift to the latter was in reaction to adversarial times, but perhaps it was also in reaction to the demonstrated decline in satisfaction with the doctor-patient relationship as expressed in numerous surveys of patients.

That is, although medical photographs are normally taken by relative strangers—usually an attendant or aide, rather than a physician or the patient's physician—like the formal portrait, the medical structure of limited access implies a hierarchy of trust, just as the cash nexus implies a hierarchy of responsibility in the case of the formal or professional portraitist. Hidden parts of the human body should not be exposed to just anyone, we believe, not without authorization, in much the same way that social access to the prominent, they believe, must be carefully screened and regulated. And implicit in the giving of permission is that it is an act of trust: a prime element in the doctor-patient relationship. Consent, then, passed from the individual photographed through the responsible doctor(s) to a technician. All this was to be thoroughly explained to the patient well beforehand, as well as the rationale and the uses to which such images would be put. Or such was the protocol.

Wounds, Idiots, New Buildings

The historical justification for medical photography was and remains illustration and instruction. Mid-nineteenth-century medical photographs showed to other physicians examples of skin diseases, spinal curvature, physical deformities, and signs of disease (clubbed nails, exophthalmos, goiters) that could be learned from body inspection as well as from Siamese twins, idiots, missing body members, operating arenas, cadavers during postmortems, and organ specimens removed at the post mortems.[11] As much a matter of sharing information with their colleagues, doctors used images of the body and its condition over time in order to instruct students. The number of before-and-after photographs, particularly surgical, bulked large enough during the Civil War to be published immediately afterward by the Surgeon General; he selected and apportioned them into six thick volumes, as proof of the effectiveness of mid-nineteenth-century treatment, one assumes. More affective disorders, on the whole, were brought before the camera, later in the century; Jean Martin Charcot, at the famous Hospice de la Salpetrière, actually instituted a photographic service in 1878. A decade later, his photographic director, Albert Londe, was innovating away, turning to chronography (the taking of photographs at rapid and regular intervals) in order to describe the natural history of nervous disease.[12]

By the century's end, the medical press had begun to use photographs in greater numbers. Practical advice in the medical journals for the picture-taking doctor also increased about this time, as did attempts to look more closely, in microscopic ways. Few physicians and far fewer medical facilities were photographed before 1900 than after, although procedures such as the physical examination were the subject of numerous textbooks, notably those by Dr. Richard C. Cabot of the Massachusetts General Hospital, from 1900 to the 1930s.

The avalanche of images in medical advertising—for the promotion of building funds and special medical equipment, public relations for the doctor and image making for the hospital, and those massive campaigns for drugs, old and new—did not begin to overwhelm the public and the profession until the 1960s. In the 1970s and 1980s, fictionalized television doctors such as "Ben Casey," "Marcus Welby," and "Trapper John" projected their image to tens of millions of viewers and they received dozens of letters a week asking for, of course, medical advice. Currently, photographs of body lesions appear in throwaway medical journals in multicolored separations that would draw envy from the publishers of the elegant Sierra Club books.

Doubts concerning the validity of medical photographs and their effect upon the doctor-patient relationship portrayed arose early. This photography seemed as mysterious as the doctors themselves in mid-nineteenth-century America. The novelist Hawthorne uses their mysteriousness interchangeably—to plumb, analyze, and unsettle conventional society—in works with a questionable doctor (*The Blithedale Romance*) and a disquieting daguerreotypist (*The House of the Seven Gables*).[13] What the artist had intuited and given imaginative form to had become palpable reality by the century's end; both figures were objects of widespread public adulation and scorn.[14]

Doctors, however, held opinions that differed from the public at large. Enthused by the new empiricism and the new emphasis on medicine as a science, many regarded photographs highly, believing they possessed "literal truth" or "detailed exactitude." The concept of "realism" had entered American culture after the Civil War and was increasingly influential well past the turn of the century. A period of great industrial and economic expansion, with "pride in precision and detail," followed, observe Daniel M. Fox and James Terry in "Photography and the American Physician, 1880–1920," and this pride "was reinforced," they say, by these and "other events of the period."[15] A minority remained unconvinced. Life was more complex than what fitted into a photograph's frame; the mechanical aspects of photography, rather than reassuring these doctors, only raised the same doubts as those two slightly sinister characters in Hawthorne's novels did. Indeed, the claim that the photograph was "frozen reality" raised "grave problems for the medical profession because pictures were easily accessible to the laity." Fox and Terry quote a Dr. William Keiller, who wrote to the editor of *The New York Medical Journal* in 1894, "deploring the 'craze for photographs' which 'expose the person quite unnecessarily and therefore indecently.'"

Sex was on Dr. Keiller's mind, naturally. He worried mainly about photographs of "'nude women in innumerable modifications of the dorsal, dorsolateral, and Trendenberg positions,'"[16] but he had a point. What other doctor was worrying about the "exposure" all those nineteenth-century "imbeciles" and "idiots" were receiving, the publicity accorded to the subjects of countless open-ended phrenological investigations? What kind of relationship could Dr. Charcot have had with his patients, determined as he was to establish a "scientific basis" for mental illness? We must infer, from descriptions of his assistant, Londe's photographic "style" as Londe amassed photographic "data":

Usually a new patient was photographed full-length, nude, against a plain grey background in a glazed studio in which the lighting was controlled by curtains and white screen reflectors. According to the condition, a front, back, three-quarters, or profile view, standing or sitting, was taken. Any particular parts of the body that were affected, were photographed separately.

Rather than wait, Londe was not above provoking behavior for purposes of "instruction," as when

On one occasion, half a dozen women, subject to hysteria, were brought to the studio on the pretext of having their portrait taken. At the sudden beating of a loud gong, all six fell into a state of catalepsy, in which it was easy to photograph their characteristic expressions.[17]

Freud had described his mentor, Charcot, as a commanding teacher and a pioneering researcher; however, the man who wrote the classic self-critical account of a failed doctor-patient relationship, "Dora," made no mention of this questionable aspect of the older man's work.

Concerned physicians did take steps to guard the privacy of the doctor-patient relationship, though it was qualified. Bodies were draped to conceal identities; eyes in photographs were crossed out with bold, black lines; heads were cut off before photographs were printed or distributed; and "private parts" were often enough covered with triangles. But the "sacred trust" of the Hippocratic oath was, like all absolute vows, not absolutely impervious to the intrusions of class privilege and changes in social convention. We know from photographs taken during the same period, of private offices and public clinics, that two systems were operative. Home offices for well-off patients resembled, to some extent, the homes of the well-off, as did their hospital quarters: there were plants, comfortable furniture, pleasant drapes and lighting, even fireplaces and their own toilets as at the Phillips House, Massachusetts General Hospital, which was opened in 1917. Not so pleasant were the examining spaces for the poor, especially during the period when waves of immigrants were examined, en masse, in New York and San Francisco. Unlikely to be laid out in a resident's handbook, it was nevertheless "acceptable," a convention of the times, to photographically portray the lower class, the criminal element, and those with "social diseases." In charity wards, aside from the expected bureaucratic insensitivity and impersonality, the cash nexus was understood in yet another manner: use my body in exchange for free treatment. Although modified by photographers who, like James Agee and Walker Evans were acutely aware of their own intrusions and the possible violation of privacy inherent in them (discussed later), this situation can be seen in the FSA medical photographs where patients look uncomfortable and annoyed. But their distress is a far cry from the present, when patients from all classes feel free to express their unwillingness to serve as subjects for teaching or as "guinea pigs," and *informed consent* and *release waivers* must be brokered prior to the camera's, now the video camera's, introduction into the doctor-patient relationship, that is regularly seen and heard for purposes of teaching and research.

A considerable literature has been generated discrediting an entire range of late nineteenth-century "sciences" whose purpose was to advance one group over another on the basis of "inherited" characteristics.[18] These appeals were based on a biological determinism that rode, crudely, to be sure, on the work of Darwin. The fact that medical photographs were used as "scientific proof" in these frauds should give us pause. How creditable are medical photographs, then? Photography critic Stu Cohen has addressed this question, arguing that there needs always be a distinction "between treating specific photographs as 'documents' and the idea of a 'documentary tradition' in photography." Concerning credibility, he says:

Individual photographs are often treated as documents insofar as they present the viewer with 'information.' A photograph, in this sense, is similar to a land deed, a social security card or any other document. A photograph can present a viewer with deliberately falsified "information" just as a land-title can. Despite the fact that all photographs can be defined as documents, not all photographs are documentary.

Additionally, and especially relevant to the FSA medical photographs, "documentary photography implies a certain relationship between the photographer and his expected audience. More than any other kinds of photographs, documentary images are purposefully manipulative in intent. . . ." So, particularly with these kinds of photographs, says Cohen, the entire range of interpretative effort must be attempted, from the structural and iconographic, through the biographic, historic, economic, and psychological. This strategy not only delimits their inherent tendency to fraudulence but shifts the burden of meaning from the producer (the photographer, who, like the artist, often knows far more than he or she can easily acknowledge) to the consumer (the audience, who, like audiences in classical drama, has a role to play in the meaning of the production as much as the actors and the author do).

And, as if in response to Dr. Keiller's admonition about the inappropriate distribution of images, Cohen observes: "Those forces which have conditioned the production and part of the distribution of documentary photographs have never been able to restrict their use and extended distribution to groups of consumers other than those originally intended." Lewis Hine's poignant images of child-labor exploitation have been used in liberal reform efforts, but, Cohen argues, they have also been used to stir radicals to direct action. A documentary photograph can sustain more than one analysis of its meaning, within a range. "No photograph," states Cohen, "no matter how eloquent, is in and of itself an analysis of the situation it portrays. At best, a documentary image is a piece of evidence, nothing more (the question of such images as works of art is not under discussion here)."[19]

Mick Gidley's compressed but incisive pamphlet, *American Photography* (1983), raises the crucial question of generalization, which arises less from the nature of photographs as documents than from the documentary uses to which photographs are put. Examining an American Heritage collection, *American Album* (1968), Gidley is quick to affirm the value of what a viewer can learn. "It is possible to follow the varieties of taste and necessity in dress, hairstyles, beards and mustaches through the years, regions and occupations. . . . There are photographs presenting a range of jobs in great detail. . . . And there are people's amusements. . . ." The viewer can also see the people in all their variety, their dwellings, and the land itself, the sweep of "forest, prairie, desert, mountain, river, lake and tilled field." But for all these visions that constitute "a land, a nation, an era," Gidley rightly wonders that, "although the title *American Album* is appropriate, it probably seems more so than it is." Just how representative is the compilation? Moving to another collection, *The American Image* (1979), we are told it contains some two hundred photographs from the National Archives. But there are *five million* photographs in these archives. Explicit principles of selection, of inclusion and exclusion, Gidley stresses, are all too often absent in such projects, where "lavishly designed and bound, they can all too easily present the point of view—often a nostalgic one—held by the present-day compilers towards past eras."[20]

Fox and Terry similarly caution. Following the lead of French communications theorist Roland Barthes, they highlight the complex and elongated selection procedures involved in creating any image, since photographs are, in reality, "collections of images consciously or unconsciously selected by some combination of subject, photographer and collector."[21] Again, following Barthes, they also point out the importance of "correlative texts," the old-fashioned written data, and the problems inherent in establishing meaning without them. Although medical photographs from the late nineteenth and early twentieth centuries "are plentiful and have common characteristics," these images, unfortunately, lack "a clearly documented contemporary explanation." According to Fox and Terry, "if anyone wrote down why a [medical] photograph was taken, why it was composed as it was and why it was worth preserving, the written records have not yet been found." This may be overstating the situation, but in support of their position, they note that "Harvey Cushing, the only physician we have discovered who cared deeply enough about both writing and photography to record the medical life of his times in both words and pictures, provided no written explanation for the photographs he preserved."[22] Much must be inferred though, increasingly, inferences have more solidity through the careful reconstruction of context by new methods in social history and new modes of conceptualization, such as Barthes'.[23]

The old methods were not entirely inadequate, however, not if one knew how to apply them. In the case of the Mathew Brady photographs of Civil War wounds, medical care, hospital maltreatment, and the surgeons themselves, we have been unable to find any commentary by Brady or his associates.[24] On the other hand we do have a contemporary account, Walt Whitman's *Specimen Days*. True, observations filtered through the consciousness of a great poet produce different sorts of truth than a clinical trial, but the truth of the imagination—with Crane's *Red Badge of Courage* as an example—can often bring us closer to an event than all the testimonials of those who were at its presumed center. A recent edition of Whitman's book parallels original and seldom-published photographs with the 1882 text:

O heavens, what scene is this?—is this indeed *humanity*—these butchers' shambles? There are several of them. There they lie, in the largest, in an open space in the woods, from 200 to 300 poor fellows—the groans and the screams—the odor of blood, mixed with the fresh scent of the night, the grass, the trees—that slaughterhouse! . . . One man is shot by a shell, both in the arm and leg—both are amputated—there lie the rejected members. Some have their legs blown off—some bullets through the breast—some indescribably horrid wounds in the face or head, all mutilated, sickening, torn, gouged out—some in the abdomen—some mere boys—many rebels, badly hurt—they take their regular turns with the rest, just the same as any—the surgeons use them just the same.[25]

When Whitman writes the account of field hospitals, we can look to a photograph on the adjoining page, "Ambulance Train at City Point Hospital," with five large, horse-drawn vans with white canvas tops, a single man before each van, near the horse. The men's faces are blank, the trees leafless behind the vans. Are the vans empty? Because they have deposited *those* wounded? Of the men who wielded the knives Whitman says:

I must bear my most emphatic testimony to the zeal, manliness, and professional spirit and capacity generally prevailing among the surgeons, many of them young men,. . . . I will not say much about the exceptions, for they are few (but I have met some of those few, and very incompetent and airish they were).[26]

The three medical men pictured are not young, with the possible exception of Lieutenant Colonel Peter Pineo, who is identified as a "Medical Examiner." How one infers competence seems to be the question. Each is dressed differently (one with cape over part of his shoulder, one with arms folded across his chest, a third with hat on); all stand erect. Two have beards (maturity?), one a moustache; one looks at the camera, two stare into the distance. Their hands, so important for surgeons, are either hidden from the camera or out of focus. Next text.

The released prisoners of war are now coming up from the Southern prisons. The sight is worse than any sight of the battlefields, or any collection of wounded, even the bloodiest. There was (as a sample) one large boatload, of several hundreds . . . and out of the whole number only three individuals were able to walk from the boat. The rest were carried ashore. . . . Can those be *men*—those little livid brown, ash-streaked, monkey-looking dwarfs?[27]

There are two photographs, under the heading "Soldiers Returned from Richmond Prison." One shows a clearly emaciated man with his thin arm around another (attendant?), the second man is holding the first's head up with his hand under the first man's chin. The contrast between the men in general appearance and bulk, is striking, made even more so by the fact that the first man is naked and the second is neatly attired. The second photograph shows two men (doctors?) examining a third man who has his back to the camera and is naked from the waist up; a fourth man (doctor?) looks on, staring into the camera. The bones of the man being examined are evident. More could be said about the relationships these photographs suggest, a series of transactions between text and image, sides not only by the sparse captions (which, as in the case of the FSA photographs in general and Dorothea Lange's in particular, can have a life all their own), but by conditions surrounding Whitman's words which, he tells us, were taken in part from notebooks and journals and in part from his own newspaper accounts published at the time of the events.[28]

Snapshots without captions are a frequent source of frustration in families who, at a certain point in time, wish to establish relationships with the past, an identity with those ancestors John Szarkowski mentioned. This is seldom a problem with the formal portrait, as others soon enough become custodians of memory for the prominent, from the clerk at the studio who logs the name (and perhaps a good deal of other information, for which the photograph becomes the explanatory link), to the accountant who writes off the cost of this commodity as a business expense, to the manager of the office responsible for all the objects in his or her space. Whitman's text therefore adds to the information base of the caption, even as it validates the photograph; and, as Kouwenhoven reminds us, the photograph and text are therefore trapped within the situation of *transmission* that affects all snapshots, portraits, and medical photographs—no matter what their time of origin. For when Brady's assistants were taking those grim pictures of dead soldiers on the battlefields of America's Civil War,

it was a quarter of an hour before they even saw the unarguable realities recorded on their glass plates, several weeks before the public saw even secondhand, and therefore suspect, engraved translations of them, and several years before the photographs themselves were seen by more than a handful of people.[29]

Dr. Freud, Who Else Is in the Room?

Freud suggested that it is difficult to be objective about our own death. An individual's response to his or her own illness seldom is rational; nor can the doctor, unless he or she is aware of these "sentiments" (Dr. L. J. Henderson's word), be of much help. Speaking to the medical staff at the Massachusetts General Hospital in 1935, Henderson (without acknowledgment) translated Freud's insights regarding the therapeutic encounter into advice about how physicians could manage the doctor-patient relationship to the patient's ultimate benefit.

These photographic scenes of practice—of doctor and patient—address no particular theory of the relationship. Yet theories of what that relationship is like illuminate the pictures in different ways—take Freud, Sullivan, and Haley.

Prior to the twentieth century, medical literature on practice had an almost Platonic quality to it. Patients were regarded as passive entities, idealized Diseases; the doctor acted upon them and, with the weight of solid logic behind the doctor, the patients responded. Freud's investigations revealed quite a different picture. Rather than a simple matter of authoritarian directives and deferential compliance, the relationship between doctor and patient was competitive, even fundamentally conflicted, and far from simple. Medical truth, unless correctly applied, would not make a patient free, in the sense that patients would not give additional or accurate information about their condition, openly express misgivings about the course of their treatment, or consult with the doctor again as to alternatives. The patient with mixed feelings—about illness, treatment, and the very person of the physicians—of which the patient was generally unaware, "resisted" seemingly appropriate interventions and reasonable advice. In "Physician and Patient as a Social System," Dr. Henderson cast Freud's central concepts of *transference* and *countertransference* in other terms and set them within what today we might call a form of gestalt theory.[30]

"A physician and a patient make up a social system," wrote Henderson, and "in any social system the sentiments [the affective life] and the interactions of the sentiments are likely to be the most important phenomena."[31] Quoting one of Lord Chesterfield's letters on the choice of words and the manner in which they should be spoken, Henderson stressed that, because of their condition, patients were rarely "in a favorable state of mind to appreciate the precise significance of a logical statement."[32]

Should the doctor, then, cultivate illogic? Hardly. The physician, determined to be useful, "should see to it that the patient's sentiments do not act upon his sentiments and, above all, do not thereby modify his behavior, and he should endeavor to act upon the patient's sentiments according to a well-considered plan."[33] Because the sentiments are "resistant to change" and the patient usually unconscious of them, the physician's tactic should be to "utilize some part of the sentiments that the patient has in order to modify his subjective attitude." Although it has a quaint ring, Henderson was on firm ground when he urged upon doctors Freud's oft-cited dictum that "the first aim of treatment consists in attaching [the patient] to the treatment and to the person of the physician." In order to ensure this, Henderson, like Freud, believed the necessary requirement to be time, and time was gained by paying serious attention to the patient, mainly by *listening*. Henderson suggested that the doctor pay attention to what patients wanted to tell, what they did not want to tell, and what they could not tell.[34]

If Freud's approach responded to the turmoil and confusion *within*—unconscious conflict—psychiatrist Harry Stack Sullivan directed attention to conflicts in the space *between* individuals. What, in the fundamental nature of communication, created barriers and encouraged misunderstandings? In a series of lectures that became *The Psychiatric Interview* (1954), Sullivan explored anxiety's central role in distorting and confusing, taking the doctor-patient relationship as his *inter*-personal paradigm.[35]

More than many, Sullivan emphasized the importance of a patient's social situation; he observed that anxiety was provoked as much by economic threats that were conscious as by past emotional threats that had been internalized. An individual's natural state was defensive, and his or her principal defensive weapon was language. Paradoxically, this language actually increased anxiety because, in the course of its use, the resultant communication distanced indiscriminately: it put off helpful people while it threatened others.

The "noise" of this communication also distanced the individual from him or herself. Sullivan broke this paradox by developing Freud's observation that *what* patients said was always a function of *who* they were and *how* they said it. The latter could be a tone of voice or facial gesture, a patient's position in a chair or the way he or she holds a pencil. He called this modifying mode *prototaxic* communication. As for what patients said, the same words coming from a child or from an adult, from a woman in a white coat or a man in dirty overalls (as in the FSA medical photographs), were interpreted in quite different ways. A communication in this modality was *parataxic*. Closest to true communication was the *syntaxic* mode and, for Sullivan, one achieved this by a back-and-forth process of mutual definition and redefinition which he termed *consensual validation*.

Illness was no absolute for Freud but more a spectrum of efficient functioning from high to low, and the doctor was also a patient. As such (echoed by Henderson) doctoring required considerable insight into the doctor's own behavior. In order to achieve this, Freud insisted that a psychoanalyst first submit to analysis and become a patient; over-intellectualizing, thereafter, would be more difficult, he thought, and the doctor would, he hoped, become more sensitive to the subjective—though no less painful—dimension of the patient's suffering. Similarly, Sullivan argued that the doctor continuously monitor his or her own involvement with the patient, not with the intent of further (professional) distancing but to gather more data for the patient's benefit. This was *participant-observation*, and he stressed that "there are no psychiatric data that can be observed from a detached position by a person in no way involved . . . psychiatric data arise from participation in the situation that is observed."[36] Within the psychoanalytic encounter, the patients would move toward greater efficiency by insight into *intra* personal communications, conversations within the self; implementing Sullivan's *intra*-personal theory, the patients' anxieties would be reduced through increasingly clear communications between themselves and others—which they would not only understand better but control better.

Jay Haley's work takes for granted the dynamic ground of Freud and Sullivan, focusing instead on communication as purely abstract behavior: a series of patterns within a total field. Haley would agree that no relationship is without conflict. He is more interested, however, in locating the behavioral *products* of conflicts than their *sources*. Symptoms, therefore, are "tactics," albeit unconsciously deployed, in an "interactional game." The name of the game is power, one individual over or under the other, and "a basic rule of communications theory demonstrates . . . that it is impossible for a person to avoid defining, or taking control of, his relationship with another."[37]

Communication, according to Haley, contains not only messages and reports but, simultaneously, influences and commands. Without reference to the unconscious or to anxiety, Haley wishes to unpack the total manipulative intent behind the surface of statements in this game of power. For example,

"I feel badly today," [states Haley] is not merely a description of the internal state of the speaker. It also expresses something like "Do something about this," or "Think of me as a person who feels badly." Every message from one person to another tends to define the kind of interchange which is to take place between them.

In Haley's analysis, something *does* come of nothing, *King Lear* notwithstanding, because even "if one tries not to influence the other person by remaining silent, his silences become an influencing factor in the interchange."[38]

The various titles of Haley's essays—"The Art of Schizophrenia" and "The Power Tactics of Jesus Christ" are two—may suggest a breezy contribution to the doctor-patient relationship. Analyzing communication as communication reminds one, on second thought, of the strictly iconographic approach to reading images and, as such, has considerable descriptive power.

Because it analyzes behavior within an interactional field, as well as language within a culturally referential field, Haley's work has proved helpful to doctors and therapists whose relationships are broader than their essentially white, middle-class training norms, and whose patients may distrust the actions within those relationships as much as the words spoken while they take place. Its explanatory usefulness is limited, however, by the very abstractness which is its strength; and its underlying assumptions are functionalist in a way that, if applied in isolation, would leave out much of the world the FSA patients brought with them into the consulting room. Like Talcott Parsons' seminal formulation of the "sick role," Haley's game-theory approach (which analyzes the game in the room only within a clearly circumscribed system) tends to be complementary, static, and exclusionary of everything beyond the system under analysis. In effect, the doctor or therapist is the expert, affectively neutral and limited by what the patient brings as his or her "complaint."

Even with extensive brokering, Sullivan never assumed that consensual validation would make a consensus of the conflicting social and economic forces that comprised the patient's world and, although Freud was optimistic about the ability of the psychoanalyzed individual to withstand the pressures and intrusions of the state, he never believed that such individuals—apart from political movements, organizations, or parties—could change the state. The world that made the FSA necessary and brought the FSA patient into the picture's frame had its difficult, even overwhelming, qualities, and any approach, like Haley's, that could sort and clarify the patient's communications was valuable—though not, of course, if in the process it simplified the patients and their problems out of existence.

The general practitioners and their patients in the FSA medical photographs were hardly grounded in these theories of relationships, nor were they self-reflective enough to explain to others what they were about, even if they had the time, which they did not. Yet self-awareness can come through action as well as discourse, and these photographs do capture action. In doing so they "speak" to these dynamics again and again, even though we lack many of the other validating materials of the present: the authenticating tapes of conversation and actual movement in the consulting room. Audio tapes of that discourse (and then only of psychiatrist and patient) came in the 1940s, while modern videotaping of the medical encounter began in the 1960s.[39]

In some pictures, the doctor acts directly enough on the patient as he/she accepts the physical examination and the intimate proximity this requires. In others, the postures of doctor and patient reflect definition and redefinition in the course of communication. We see, especially, the doctor listening and, therefore, learning, as Henderson suggests; the doctor coming to understand something of the patient's perspective on his or her illness. In still others, the settings change, often radically, from the "turf" of the doctor's office to the "middle space" of the outdoors or porch, to the patient's "turf" of his or her bedroom. We see the patient alone, and with escorts and guardians, circumstances that are bound to impress themselves, as Sullivan suggests, on the doctor-as-participant. Finally, even though the photographs are without words—leaving aside the confirmatory, supplemental, or purely additive nature of the accompanying captions—the combination of gestures and postures, the changing distances between doctor and patient, the alterations of place and the elements that compose these places—the clear "complaints" of the patient and the clear "advice" of the doctor do demonstrate those behavioral tactics of the game between doctor and patient. We will see them all and more, and we will hear the many voices with which the photographs can be made to speak.

4
Ideology and the Vernacular

63
Penasco, N.M. Jan. 1943.
Doctor Onstine making an examination in the
clinic operated by the Taos County Cooperative
Health Association.
JOHN COLLIER.

64
Crystal City, Tex. March 1939.
Mexican with an advanced case of tuberculosis.
He was in a bed at home with other members of
the family sleeping and living in the same room.
RUSSELL LEE.

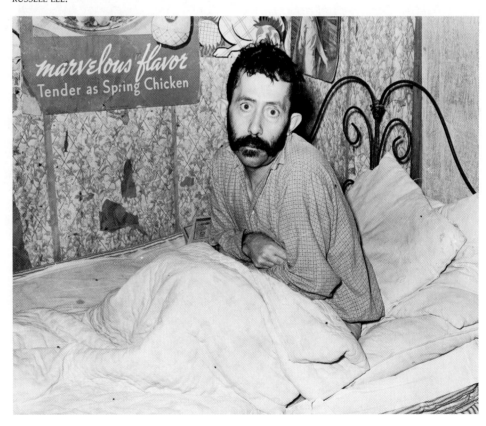

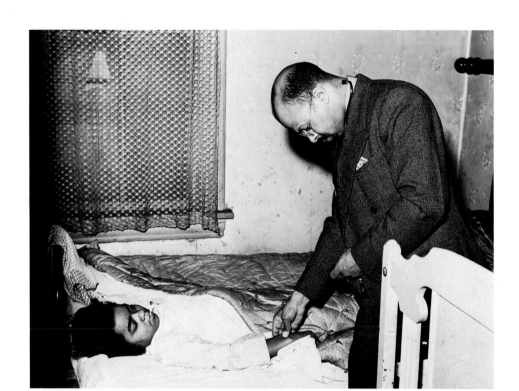

65
Chicago, Ill. Apr. 1941.
Doctor examining a patient in her home. The patient is on relief.
RUSSELL LEE.

66
Corpus Christi, Tex. Jan. 1942.
*Privately supported tuberculosis clinic supervised
by a retired doctor. Majority of patients are Latin-
American. Doctor recording medical history of pa-
tient. Map shows number of cases in area.*
ARTHUR ROTHSTEIN.

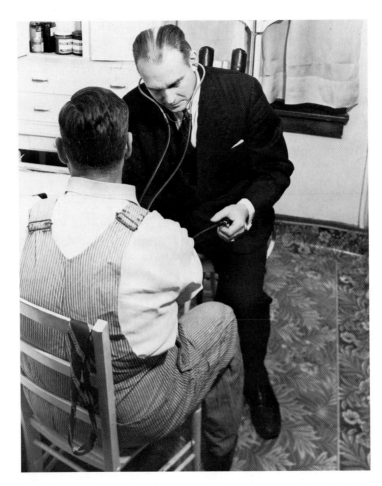

67
Washington, D.C. Jan. 1942.
Self-help client getting medical examination before
he applies for work.
JOHN COLLIER.

68
Kempton, W.Va. May 1939.
Company doctor in a coal town examining a patient. Miners pay $2 a month for medical care.
JOHN VACHON.

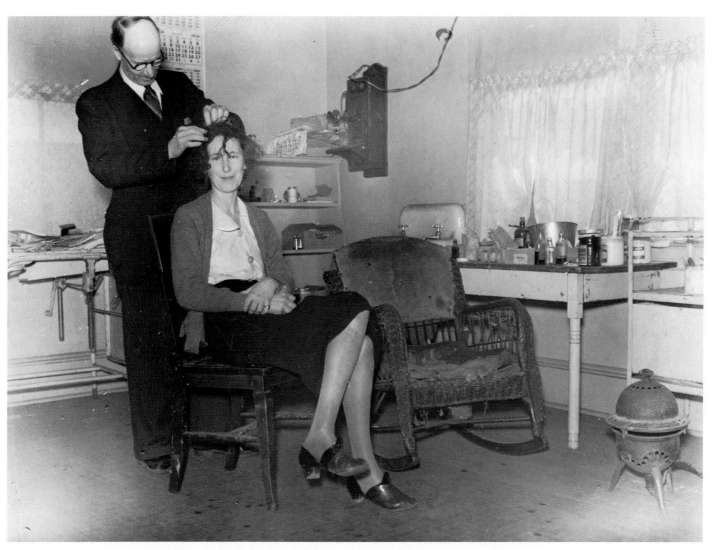

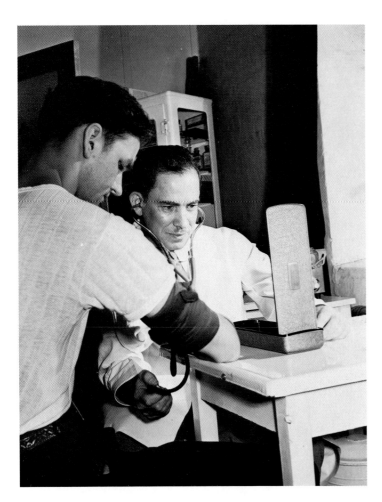

69
Brooklyn, N.Y. Aug. 1942.
State physician checking the blood pressure of a
factory worker.
ARTHUR ROTHSTEIN.

70
Questa, N.M. Jan. 1943.
Examination in the clinic operated by the Taos
County Cooperative Health Association.
JOHN COLLIER.

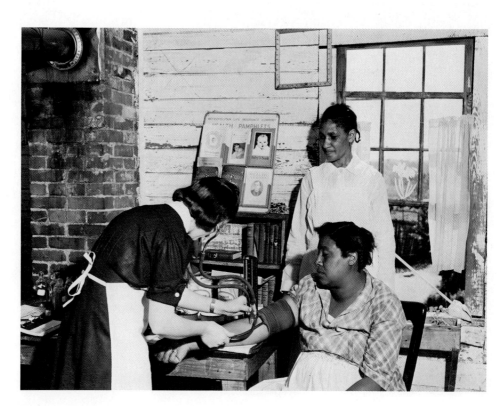

71
Woodville, Ga. June 1941.
At a cooperative prenatal clinic.
JACK DELANO.

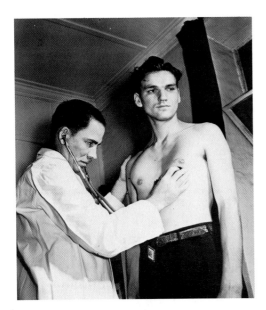

72
Brooklyn, N.Y. Aug. 1942.
State industrial hygiene physician examining the heart of a factory worker.
ARTHUR ROTHSTEIN.

73
Wilder, Idaho. May 1941.
Mobile unit of the Farm Security Administration camp for migratory workers. Examination in the trailer clinic.
RUSSELL LEE.

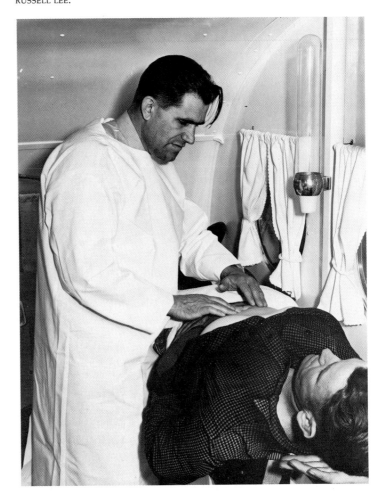

74
New York, N.Y. Jan. 1943.
Italian surgeon bandaging a patient's arm.
MARJORY COLLINS.

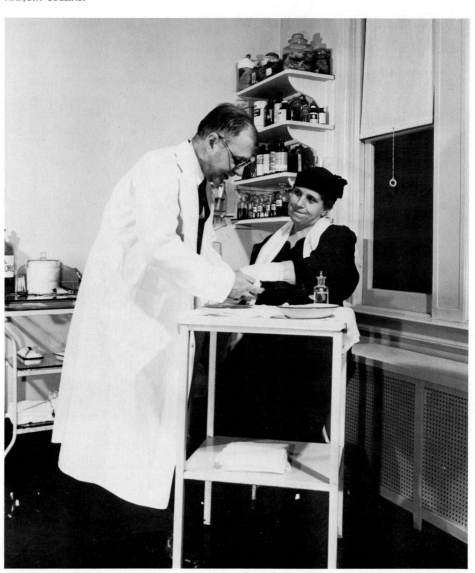

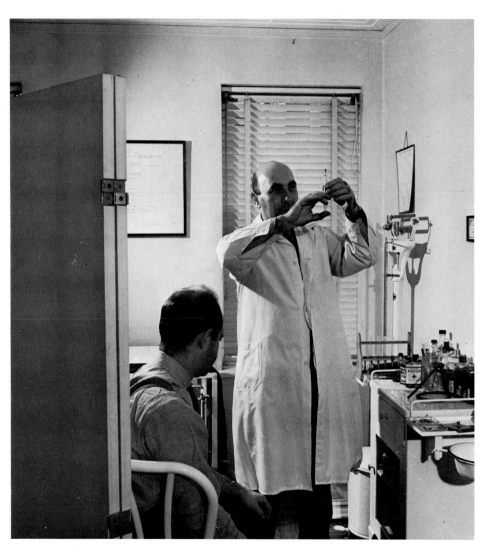

75
New York, N.Y. Oct. 1942.
Dr. Winn, a Czech-American, has his office in his
apartment at 425 East 72 St.
MAJORY COLLINS.

76
Colp, Ill. Jan. 1939.
Dr. Springs giving prescription to patient.
ARTHUR ROTHSTEIN.

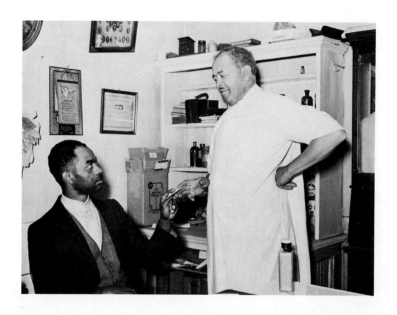

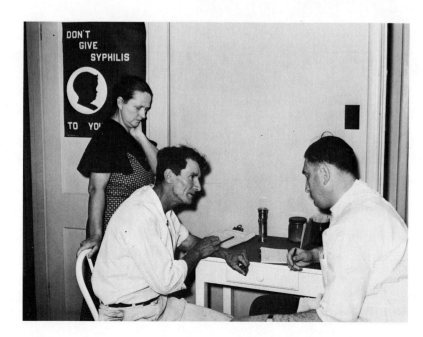

77
Maricopa County, Ariz. May 1940.
The Aqua Fria FSA camp for migratory workers.
Doctor at clinic taking case history of agricultural
worker.
RUSSELL LEE.

78
Crystal City, Tex. Mar. 1939.
*After much persuasion by a local physician, this
small shed was constructed to house a tuberculosis
patient. This was the first time in this section that
a tuberculosis patient was isolated from his family.*
RUSSELL LEE.

Examining the vernacular in the FSA photographs could begin with any of the collections in which FSA photographs have appeared. A good example would be the year 1978, when a spate of FSA books was published: *Walker Evans: First and Last Photographs; Russell Lee, Photographer; Dorothea Lange. A Photographer's Life;* and *The Depression Years, As Photographed by Arthur Rothstein.*[1] These gave us a much larger inventory of FSA photographs and, with Dorothea Lange and Russell Lee, the best inventory to date of biographical material about two of the FSA photographers themselves. Yet it could be argued that quantity is no virtue. Indeed, in the case of the FSA photographs, increasing the sheer number of them only compounded the problem.

And what *is* the problem? That, once again, two very similar kinds of FSA photographs were roused from their Library of Congress file drawers. For what purpose? To reinforce, in their standard condemnatory/celebratory, testimonial manner, the image of the period and its people they had already imprinted upon us the first (or was it the fifth?) time around.[2] Absent then, as now, was a thoroughgoing examination of what FSA photographic work during those eight mid- and post-Depression years was all about, what those nearly one-quarter of a million images may be said to have meant, if anything at all.

That examination will require more than this essay, though the making of three assertions might perhaps begin it.

First, what have become the "classic" FSA photographs of the 1930s, rather than containing in themselves—by way of raw information or more processed allusions and implications—anything like a comprehensive definition of that time and its people, as we have been taught to believe by seeing them again and again, are complex articulations of a dominant ideology that actually discouraged a comprehensive, structural definition.[3] What needs explanation, however, is the way in which these oft-reproduced photographs both consciously and unconsciously fulfilled two modes of visual representation suggested earlier, that were ideologically acceptable. We would call them superficial *condemnation* and superficial *celebration.*

Second, the process by which the classic photographs were made and then came to achieve their wide acceptance in itself constitutes an important element of the ideology. Both aesthetic and political dimensions of this process require close examination in order to force an awareness of the large number—the bulk—of FSA photographs that were made in other ways and did not achieve classic status.

Third, it is just these *vernacular* pictures, organized around plain, seemingly mundane themes such as games and sports or primary-care medicine, that may well provide us with a far more inclusive, fully adequate visual experience of the period, precisely because they break with the dominant ideology instead of reinforcing it. FSA photographer John Collier implied as much when he said,

The pictures that we find to be the most important are going to be the ones that people think of as dull. It is the pedestrian shape of the file that holds the great cultural vision. The dramatic pictures will never finally be the thing that will tell us what was going on.[4]

Yet, until now, for reasons Collier did not or could not name, only the "dramatic" photographs were read in careful, thoughtful ways. Understanding the reasons for misreadings—then placing these doctor-patient pictures, for example, within a different ideological framework, thereby reading them in new as well as old ways—may convince us that the FSA photographers knew far more than they, or we, ever suspected.

Who Pays the Piper, Etc.

In a 1937 budget memo, the director of photography in the Roosevelt Resettlement Administration (RA), Roy Emerson Stryker, wrote the following straightforward justification for his monumental documentary project: "The sole purpose behind [the photographer's work] . . . has been the simple and unspectacular attempt to give information."[5] Some four decades later, speaking in a packed Boston University auditorium where the audience had just viewed the slides of his corpus and asked what he believed his FSA photographs were for, Russell Lee replied, without a moment's hesitation, "The country was in terrible shape. The people in Washington just didn't know what it looked like. . . ." And, responding to a similar line of inquiry, artist Ben Shahn, who had made photographs for the RA/FSA from 1935 to 1938, observed:

We tried to present the ordinary in an extraordinary manner. But that's a paradox, because the only thing extraordinary about it was that it was so ordinary.

Nobody had ever done it before, deliberately. Now, it's just called documentary, which I suppose is all right. . . . We just took pictures that cried out to be taken.[6]

Shahn is close to key insights about the process and about the nature of vernacular pictures—their dumb or inarticulate ordinariness; but at this moment we must raise another question, whether in fact the pictures did the crying out. That is, tucked into all three candid statements is the assumption that certain conditions of American life were not known to middle-class photographers and their (essentially) middle-class audience, to departments and agencies of the federal bureaucracy, to the centers of power, to "Washington." Moreover, there is an even greater assumption about what would happen: that the conditions would suddenly, through the powerfully enabling medium of photography, become conscious to the American public, and that mysteriously this rise in mass consciousness would translate into political action that would, in turn, result in appropriate social remedies.[7]

But let us assume that the national situation was entirely other.[8] Let us assume that America's economic and social inequities wrought, in the 1930s in particular, terrible physical and psychological injury throughout the land that was well known—if not in specific detail, certainly as public statistics—and pervaded public consciousness by any index one wished to judge it by: newspapers, novels, radio shows, newsreels, and the like. Suppose that one quite variegated group at the highest levels of national power continued to find themselves agreed upon the proposition that it was possible to justify the existence of those inequities, whereas another group, similar in many respects, nevertheless agreed upon the necessity of denouncing the results of those inequities. In effect, the first group would be blind to what the second group would see.

The New Dealers, of course, were the ones who saw. Characteristic of that evangelical strain in the American political tradition and tapping into the "enthusiastic" moralism so much a part of America's civil religion, they gained federal power by eloquently announcing a vision, and they defended their power by legitimizing a new way of seeing—no small thanks to agencies like the FSA, whose photographers they employed and whose pictures they rapidly and widely distributed.[9] The institutional function of those FSA photographers was thus always clear, if at times in apparent contradiction with public policy. And this contradiction was the case—apart from a few cattle skulls in the Dakotas "moved" by Arthur Rothstein—because the structural intents of the New Deal were decidely unclear, at least to more than the few "brain trusters" (who were often in contradiction with each other) throughout the Depression.

It is now a commonplace of American history that the New Deal was not a wholesale restructuring of the American economy but an easing of certain social dislocations caused by structural changes already well in motion.[10] Like the situation of the Enclosure Act in England prior to the Industrial Revolution, people had to be moved off the land to emerging urban centers of manufacture. They had to understand that it was cities where they would live and work, that a return to their villages and their farms was impossible because it had slowly become impractical. (Tugwell openly stated this position before he became an FDR brain truster, while he was a brain truster, and after he left the FSA.) Where English social policy—seen two centuries later—destroyed the small farm and satisfied national needs through huge imports, American social policy of the 1930s had the similar effect of marginalizing the small farm by favoring, in a national crisis, mechanization and the creation of vast farms which, in addition to great quantities of food—far more than could be immediately consumed—also produced enormous surpluses: virtually an organic capital.

At this distance we acknowledge that government agencies implementing the Agricultural Adjustment Act (AAA) provided direct loans as well as a wide range of solid agricultural and social services to large- and middle-income farmers in order to keep them, and their expertise, on the land. Although there was grumbling from economically less sophisticated quarters, support for this massive governmental intervention continued throughout the 1930s and, by the decade's end, consolidation resulted in appropriately sprawling, industrially manageable tracts. Agribusiness was in place in almost every respect that we know it today. Small farmers, however, were not overjoyed. Lacking much capital and access to cost-saving finance, processing, and transportation networks, they rapidly joined the tenant farmers who had once rented their land, the hands and part-time farm laborers whom they had hired in the good years. Forced off the land, all took to the roads.

These were the Oakies, the Arkies, the black and white stream that would become in Robert Coles' apt phrase, "the South goes North."[11] And what was to be done with these millions? In no way could such numbers of the newly dispossessed be severed from the social fabric and then allowed to go their way. Sullen and fearful, they were also dimly aware of causes, certainly the local and to some extent the regional ones. Their frustration and anger were potential human dynamite whose explosion could easily provoke violent counter-explosions, in containment or in punishment. And then what? No doubt, went Tugwell and others' reasoning, some of these people could be retrained in sub-urban/urban centers for urban occupations, as in England. Others, the really stubborn ones, however, would have to be supported as farmers for a time.

The Resettlement Administration (RA), later the FSA, was given the task of picking up the pieces the AAA and parallel policies had left. Enter the historical section of the FSA, Stryker's FSA photographers, whose achievement needs to be assessed as the exceedingly complex, sophisticated propaganda it was, which Stryker agreed it was, and which he himself made clear to his photographers as he directed them to fulfill the two kinds of spoken and unspoken quotas mentioned earlier.

On the one hand, the condition of the dispossessed required dramatic presentation before the American public in order to build public support for innovative and costly relief programs, hence the search for images that condemned. Increased public awareness, properly organized (or orchestrated), validated a sweeping social policy that guaranteed the RA, among other agencies, funds to continue. The RA would continue to make loans to small farmers and support their health-care programs, as well as establish more government-supervised camps for migrants and medical-care clinics in these camps. But it was not enough to record the worn-out land or even the horrendous living conditions of those forced off their farms and on the road (the palpable reasons average men and women may be moved to revolt); FSA cameras also had to render the other side—that FSA programs could work and, later in the 1930s, were working. This would build public support for necessary long-term rehabilitation

I1

I2

I3

programs, also costly, which would retrain the men and women and revitalize (or withdraw and protect) the land. Cameras, then, were to defend FSA programs from critics on the left and the right.

This second role required that cameras also search out an ineffable but absolutely essential quality—character; hence the celebratory mode of visual representation, suggesting that, underneath the rags and the grime, was backbone capable of using what the government had given, of reestablishing a decent life. Given a helping hand, guided by New Deal experts, and sheltered from the more aggressive economic forces, these dispossessed would make a go of it. And the public would thereby be reassured that the world they knew had not gotten any worse, that millions of marginal citizens had once again settled down into unthreatening passivity.

The two kinds of classic photographs served an additional purpose which had its not-too-farfetched parallel a decade later. Just as dramatic anticommunism, stirred up at the bottom but, as some have argued, directed from the top, provided an ideological cover for the launching of the Marshall Plan and its subsequent by-product, the U.S. penetration of post-World War II prostrate European markets,[12] so dramatic images—such as Lange's "Migrant Mother" (Nipomo, California: 1936) [I1] and "Ditched, Stalled and Stranded" (San Joaquin Valley, California: 1935) [I2], or Russell Lee's "Christmas Dinner in Tenant Farmer's Home" (Southeastern Iowa: 1936) [I3]), could be seen as serving, on a smaller scale, to engage and then deflect public attention, keeping the fans watching the plays on the field, as it were, while the real game was back in the clubhouse.

The Beautiful Pictures

Knowing the maker is very nearly to know the process of making. More than most photographers of their time, more than many since, the FSA photographers were masters of the image: middle-class professionals who could deliver a particular image or group of images on demand. And they were directed by a man well tutored in the demand for congruence between idea and image and who well understood the technical aspects of making, processing, and distributing those images. Stryker may have lacked the social graces of the time or seemed to have affected a Mr. Smith-Goes-to-Washington suspicion, but, as no less than Robert J. Doherty, former director of the International Museum of Photography at George Eastman House, has argued, scanning Stryker's personal library and recalling his close friendship with artist Ben Shahn explode any naïve judgments as to "the aesthetic aspects of the Stryker projects."[13] This is not to imply that all were master technicians. Lange, by all accounts, was a notorious example of mechanical ineptitude, Evans openly scorned "technical tricks." Yet Lange also got exactly what she wanted, from skilled darkroom technicians to precisely the right image, as documentary filmmaker Pare Lorenz emphasized in his 1941 review of her pictures of the disposessed: "She has selected them with an unerring eye. You do not find in her portrait gallery the bindle stiffs, the drifters, the tramps, the unfortunate aimless dregs of the country. Her people stand straight and look you in the eye."[14] (In praising Lange's skills at selection, Lorenz has unwittingly revealed her skills of exclusion; but that, we have seen, is another matter.) And Evans, in his directions for printing the photograph "Winter Resorters, Florida" (1941–1942), could exhibit an astonishing ability to locate and insist upon the desired details:

NOTE FOR THE ENGRAVER:
Please note unsightly light triangles, seven of them, above the numbers. Could you simply black them all out, matching the black next to them. Also: try to get clearly the veins in the left leg of the woman, but without retouching. Also: we want the lettering on the newspaper at right to be as clear as possible, again, without retouching.

Yet even such demonstrable technical skill does not imply that all were aware of the ideological freight their work carried or the ideological uses to which their work would be put. Few of the FSA photographers, however, would have agreed that their photographs were without freight and, even after the passage of four decades, would bridle at any evaluation of their work or its impact that regarded their photographs as mechanical conveyors of neutral information. The flashy, contemporary, outrageously exploitative *Fortune* photographer, Margaret Bourke-White, would dissemble: "With a camera, the shutter opens and closes and only the rays that come in to be registered come directly from the object in front." In marked contrast, FSA photographers repeatedly acknowledged the aggressive implications of their profession and were sensitive to the personal dislocation their intrusions could create.[15] Moreover, for seven of the ten—Jack Delano, Carl Mydans, Marion Post Wolcott, John Collier, Evans, Lange, and Lee—there had been a formal association with the arts, and with the latter three experience including not only academic study and supervised making of photographs, but the commercial marketing of images to a discriminating clientele.[16] Even someone at the furthest remove from this "art industry" process, Gordon Parks, who was with the FSA marginally and briefly, was not immune to its ideological implications. Parks had had an initially unsophisticated interest in pictures suddenly mainlined by the wife of Joe Louis, "who asked him [for what might be characterized as a tutoring in developing middle-class attention] to come to Chicago to photograph a new line of ladies' fashion."

Biographers of artists unfailingly recite the "sacrifices" their subjects made in order to create art. Left unspoken is the fact that, as a function of their class, these artists had a choice. Had they chosen not to do art, they had the tangible option of doing something else and likely living quite well. FSA photographers were in a similar position and, though she was not one of them, what novelist Eudora Welty wrote of the pictures she took while with a Works Projects Administration (WPA) agency (*One Time, One Place*, 1971) illuminates these issues: "And had I no shame as a white person for what message might lie in my pictures of black persons? No, I was too busy imagining myself into their lives to be open to any generalities."[17]

A question is implicit in what Welty calls her need to "imagine" herself "into their lives," one she anticipates and then goes on to answer with a candor equal to Agee's:

Perhaps I should openly admit here to an ironic fact. While I was very well equipped for taking these pictures, I was rather oddly equipped for doing it. I came from a stable, sheltered, relatively happy home that by the time of the Depression and the early death of my father . . . had become comfortably enough off by small-town Southern standards. . . . I was equipped with a good liberal arts education [in Mississippi, Wisconsin, and New York]. . . . I was bright in my studies, and [yet] when . . . I returned home from the Columbia Graduate School of Business . . . of the ways of life in the world I knew absolutely nothing at all.[18]

A background that purported to allow her to know the world in reality allowed her to know only a fraction of the world. Like the FSA photographers of her time, Eudora Welty realized the real irony was that social privilege resulted in personal impoverishment. And, like her subjects, she realized that this experiential imbalance would be corrected only by bringing one's work closer to the "everydayness" of working people's lives, as they, not she, experienced those lives.

In the light of such self-awareness, it is more than unfair to regard the FSA photographers as "dupes" of either the left or right wing of the New Deal, irresponsibly naïve of the implications of their work, or as passive agents of an aggrandizing federal bureaucracy. The true situation was and remains far more complex and far more knotty than easy labeling will allow. But Welty's brief account suggests one reason the FSA photographers could never be entirely subservient to the ideological directives outlined earlier. Each were artists, challenged by the nature of their art as well as a personal, emotional calculus. True, the photographer's professional status meant that any encounter would begin as sharply asymmetrical, though two factors would quickly invite a balancing: their own unconscious needs ("I knew nothing at all") and the needs of their work ("imagining . . . into their lives"). These needs were so apparent that their subjects satisfied both by insisting upon an element intrinsic to any authentic relationship—the subjects' need for attention. So the meaning of Shahn's insight, his phrase "extraordinary manner," becomes clearer: nothing less than the same quality of attention must be paid to "invisible" people as those people, in the course of life, pay to the very visible people whom the social structure automatically rewards because of *their* privileged status.

The appeal of the FSA photographs becomes clearer too. Experiences denied by the confines of class were now available to that class, and if there was something slightly titillating and exotic about "how the other half lives," there was also the solid, four-square element of necessity, since these photographs stimulated the same feeling of incompleteness in the viewer that they did in the photographers, which, in turn, compelled attention.

Unfortunately, experiencing worlds through photographs cuts several ways. Susan Sontag writes about photographs as cheap knowledge. She warns that "they make us feel that the world is more available than it really is."[19] This is never more the case than with the classic photographs, the "beautiful" ones, because these photographs are made in such a way that they fulfill the viewers' need to be reassured that the world hasn't gotten any worse. The viewers get all they want—the aesthetic "feel"—which preempts, in crucial emotional and political ways, any further involvement. The experience these photographs occasion is not an absolute one, nor even a matter of a continuum. Elements of either the condemnatory or celebratory mode can be identified within them to some extent, and people are, after all, moved by them. The experience is at its most explicit and most extreme, however, with a third kind of classic photograph—the *artists' photograph*.[20] This third group, as exemplified by certain works by Evans, has been intensively appreciated by a narrow spectrum of photographers (who regard themselves as artists first) and art historians for their abstract, severely formal qualities. These images encourage instant identification as kinds, and they insist on a drill of concentrated, demanding analyses.

I4

Arthur Rothstein's variously titled photograph of the 1936 Dust Bowl in Oklahoma [I4] is a striking example of the first mode, the condemnatory.[21] Some versions have been printed as lighter or darker, sharper in focus than others, but all show a barren landscape where motion reigns supreme, where human life, in a not-too-distant background (a man, a youth alongside, a small child not far behind), is bowed by wind, where even solid man-made structures (a low plains house) readily demonstrate the abrasive, bleaching effects of this natural force. Obviously, what is being condemned here is less an "act of God" than a social structure (or lack of one) that allows human life so carelessly to be at the mercy of the elements.

I5

The celebratory mode is exemplified by Dorothea Lange's "Hoe culture, Alabama, 1937" [I5], a straightforward photograph of a black person holding a portion of a handle. While basic aspects of this mode can be located in photographs of the landscape or of man-made structures, the human presence is central and, if not directly present, usually implied: What is being celebrated here is not so much virgin landscape as an organic relationship of necessity between man and nature and, particularly during this period of time, between Americans and their land. The celebratory photographs reinforce the pastoral myth and revive the waning expectation that productivity must result from such a relationship, even as the nation becomes irrevocably urbanized and rural values are made inoperative—except as nostalgic longing—for lack of an appropriate arena.

Man prevails, the viewer is persuaded, though this is made possible only with the support of that indomitable spirit mentioned earlier; hence, photographs in this mode are essentially character portraits and borrow heavily for their construction from studio techniques.[22] So, in Lange's photograph, for example, we do not need to see either head and shoulders or below the thighs, as the direct close view we are given provides us with ample enough details to draw the intended conclusions. That weathered, sweat-stained handle is part weapon, part enemy, part old friend and, as such, has complex familiarity. Not exactly cradled, it is not held in a vise-grip either. The comfortable angle of the handle and the hands and arms, the quality of focus around such details as the badly worn denim field-jacket and the heavily patched denim pants are concentrated without clutter. The *quality* of contrast, rich softness rather than bleak glare, has the further effect of ennobling these honorably worn garments, these work-worn hands and muscled arms and, by implication, the entire enterprise beyond.

To sacrifice, in Greek, is to make sacred; these celebratory photographs assure us the ancient metaphysic lives by reassuring us that this labor has in effect sanctified the laborer, whatever the material outcome to him in this troubled time.

Virtually any of Evans' FSA photographs will do as an example of the third mode, though some, naturally, are better made than others. The first thing one notices is the surface polish and a sharpness of detail. For contrast, whites are very white and blacks, as we may recall from Evans' "Note for the Engraver" quoted earlier, are very black; in any case, all tones are matched. These points may be dismissed as simply a function of technical production, but the point is that it is a particular kind of production, one geared to following standards learned in producing portraits of important people or large industries, where each has a keen sense of the details he or she wishes to purchase.

I6

I7

I8

Evans' *Fortune* magazine work in the 1940s hardly brands him as a corporate toady but his multiple commissions from Lincoln Kirstein (if not the wealthiest, certainly the most discerning patron of the arts in American history), helps to define his audience with the added twist that, with the cold, hard art he made, Evans actually went further, was far more exacting than his exacting patron. His is also a production where detail and contrast are geared to demanding reproductive needs; if these images are to be rapidly and widely distributed in the mass media, they must be made in a certain way. (Evans' are so much the *artists' photograph* in this respect that few, if any, in the mass media have approached the model. This is particularly striking—and ironic—if one compares the quality of reproduction and printing of Evans' own photographs in the Museum of Modern Art's (MOMA) *Walker Evans* (New York Graphic Society, 1971) and *First and Last* (Harper & Row, 1978). MOMA's is luminous and deep, Harper & Row's imprecise and dull.) Then there are the classic elements of order, harmony, and balance, which, in these photographs, means that awkward angles, irrelevant or confusing details, unwanted objects or people are cropped, spotted, or otherwise banished—in the darkroom. Everything goes together, and the unity the overall composition approaches has an impressively dramatic but also oddly nonreferential quality.

It is a shibboleth of classic aesthetics that "great art" sends us back into the world, if not entirely refreshed, usually fortified to meet what may lie before us. Yet quite the opposite may be the case. Evans' interiors of Hale County, Alabama, sharecroppers' shacks [I6] or haunting frontal views of rural churches [I7], [I8] are designed to freeze moments in time. Emotions are so intensified— by careful positioning, enormous attention to the most minute detail, distinct, yet never too sharp a tone—such that something curious occurs. We don't so much see as experience the things of this world. And do so in such a way that the experience comes to take the place of the things of this world; we prefer the photograph of that church interior in Alabama to actually sitting at the keyboard of that dark, gleaming organ and pumping away at the big foot pedals.[23]

This would be well and good if the experience would finally send us back into the world ready to do something after our moment of contemplation. It does not, and the moment can be a long one. The photographs' clarity humbles, not the discrete "I" who will act but the "I" who, like billions of other discrete grains of sand, simply is. The beautiful pictures are so complete in themselves, that it is within them—emotionally—that we remain, during and after the time we view them. (The intensity of our involvement is fueled by the contrast between the pedestrian subject matter—peeling road signs or neat shelves of seed packets in a general store, in an Evans photograph—and the extravagant attention the photographer has paid to the subject matter.) We are rapt before the iconic image, engaged, then quite relaxed. The pressure is off, and should we return to the internal hum of the photograph repeatedly, gone is that other need—to understand the conditions that caused the peeling paint, or why the seeds sit unbought, why there is no money to buy them—much less the imperative to commit ourselves to a struggle that would address and then hopefully change those conditions.

Vernacular Pictures

In contrast, vernacular pictures are never cool and formalized. The poverty in them is rarely beautiful, in Whitman or anyone else's sense; the viewer, visually conditioned by the three previously discussed modes, is hard put to know how to respond to images of the ordinary, photographed in an "ordinary" fashion.

Perhaps this is because, like other common expressions of contemporary culture, they are all too often taken for granted or seen as the raw materials for a more compressed form of expression: art. Assuming art to be the higher form of expression because it is formally mediated by an artist—who is himself or herself technically competent and an inspired seer—and because the process of mediation releases potentialities (in materials or in words) not otherwise available, several questions arise: What should be the relationship between art and the vernacular? And, since the meaning of a made thing, especially a photograph, can in no way be separated from numerous factors in its making, not least of which is the relationship between the artist and his or her subject, what should *that* relationship be?

The vernacular as common, everyday expression of ordinary people is a well-established evaluative category in many areas, including the literary. There, learned, formalized patterns of speech or highly conscious, stylized modes of

construction (as in classical rhetoric, with its rigid insistence on appropriate occasions for particular figures or tropes) are frequently enough contrasted with
nonstandard expression that is native to a people or a region.

Romance philologist Erich Auerbach, in *Literary Language and Its Public: in Late
Latin Antiquity and in the Middle Ages* (1958, 1965), has traced the relationship
between formal speech and the vernacular in discovering, for example, that literary Latin was strongest (most inclusive and most flexible) when it was most
closely in contact with the vernacular. After the dissolution of the Empire in
400 A.D., however, Latin lost its richness; as a "dead" language tied to the in-
sular worlds of the Church, law, medicine and the court, Latin became "pomp-
ous and obscure," in Auerbach's judgment, so self-conscious that its form
became the primary element of interest to the near exclusion of its content. But
at the margins, something of the old vitality obtained. There, with the entry of
Christianity into the formal classical world—particularly the Latin tradition of
oration and writing—"Rhetoric," according to Auerbach, "gave the impression
of simplicity . . . the sentence structure sometimes verges on the colloquial."

By the Middle Ages, and as Christian preaching became the chief means of
public instruction, this "Sermo Humilus" drew upon classical eloquence and
ancient rhetoric even as it became more homely and utilitarian—concentrating
on its main purpose of drill and edification.[24] Auerbach did not presume to
judge the absolute value of this new, humble style but only to stress the importance of the new relationship between the classical past and the vernacular
present and to remind his readers that, when Latin separated from the vernacular, it was Latin that suffered most.

This mixing of styles and especially the infusion of the language of the people
(including slang) have been responsible for much of the energy in modern art
as well as in modern literature. *American Renaissance* (1941), the masterwork
interpretation of mid-nineteenth-century American culture, has F. O. Matthiessen noting that the rise of nineteenth-century English romanticism was consist-
ently attributed to Wordsworth and Coleridge's calls for a poetry whose
language would be brought "near[er] to the real language of men." Naturally
neither poet relied on the verbatim speech of the time so much as on their
own mediated sense of that speech and their rejection of the previous period's
shopworn "poetic" conventions. So, too, did Matthiessen's major American au-

thors, and he devotes an entire section of his book, "The Word One with the Thing," to demonstrate the fruitful connections between Emerson's theory of language and the mixed, distinctive productions of Thoreau, Melville, and Whitman. Emerson's theory included a critique of American literature that was produced in response to the formal conventions of a backward-looking literary elite rather than to the immediate, prospective demands of a new environment. New-world experience should give rise to new language, and Matthiessen quoted with approval from Emerson's journals of the 1840s:

The language of the street is always strong. What can describe the folly and emptiness of scolding like the word *jawing*? I feel too the force of the double negative, though clean contrary to our grammar rules. And I confess to some pleasure from the stinging rhetoric of a rattling oath in the mouth of truckmen and teamsters. How laconic and brisk is it by the side of a page of the *North American Review*. Cut these words and they would bleed; they are vascular and alive; they walk and run. Moreover, they who speak them have this elegancy, that they do not trip in their speech. It is a shower of bullets, whilst Cambridge men and Yale men correct themselves and begin again at every half sentence.

His approval was by no means absolute; Matthiessen cautioned that plain speech, the native idiom pursued mechanically, could "provide only another set of literary artifices."[25]

While Auerbach's is the most searching historical examination of the concept of the vernacular in literature and Matthiessen's among the most imaginative exploration of its imaginative uses in poetry and fiction, virtually any of Freud's papers on psychoanalytic technique can be seen to stress the centrality of common speech in psychotherapeutic transactions and the fact that something as common in constituent elements and form as the human dream is nothing less than the "Roman road" to an understanding of the human unconscious.

Architecture is another field where the vernacular has been an important category, encouraging the surge, most recently, of vernacular reconstructions in urban and rural, industrial and agricultural environments, and in encouraging the discovery and appreciation of what John Brinckerhoff Jackson has called "vernacular landscape." *Vernacular Architecture of the Lake Counties* by R. W. Brunskill contains the following useful distinctions:

The building types included [in this study] are, of course, vernacular rather than "polite" in quality, and predominantly domestic and rural. They are "vernacular"—the products of local craftsmen meeting simple functional requirements according to traditional plans and procedures and with the aid of local building material and constructional methods, rather than "polite"—the efforts of professional designers, meeting the more elaborate needs of a formal way of life with the aid of internationally accepted rules and procedures, advanced constructional techniques, and materials chosen for aesthetic effect rather than local availability.[26]

The literary, psychological, and architectural go a distance as analogues for conceptualizing vernacular expression. They have their limits, however. Introducing the vernacular as a category in the reading of photographs raises special difficulties because the central mediating device is nothing so simple as a typewriter, in the case of writing, transmitting words. There the writer constructs a sentence and by the typewriter transmits that sentence to paper. Marshall McLuhan notwithstanding, little is altered by this process of transmission. Yet the camera is a far more complex and much more centrally involved instrument; in the process of making a picture, the camera alters the image in ways in which the typewriter does not alter the word.

The parallels between the vernacular in speech—especially syntax and diction—and the vernacular in images would require another book, though here one can say that with photographs the vernacular may well be both intrinsic to the subject (intrinsic in the sense of pictures including vernacular objects as well as persons, places, regions) *and* part of a vernacular process, a certain manner of commissioning, making, reproducing, and distributing photographs.

Someone wed to a formalist literary aesthetic misses this entirely, as when Alan Trachtenberg argues in a letter to the authors, that

any definition of vernacular which excludes those of the FSA pictures which have become famous (or classic) simply because they have become famous, seems strange—especially since there seems no more important way of understanding what Evans at least was doing than by viewing his pictures as deliberate attempts to incorporate vernacular things into a vernacular vision.

Trachtenberg's "simply" negates or ignores what fundamentally distinguishes photographs from literature or art and, in particular, what distinguishes these vernacular FSA pictures from any other group of the period. Evans' vision from first to last, moreover, was an elite, not a vernacular vision, and commentators from Kirstein in the 1930s to Szarkowski three decades later perceptively identified Evans' use of popular materials—commercial art, home implements, hand-painted signs, makeshift furniture, auto junkyards, small-town storefronts, everyday clothing, children's dolls—as *expropriation* for Evans' "somber," "puritanical," "pure" conception of art, not *incorporation* into a new, mixed, democratic form.

Like much of high modernist art and despite implicit or explicit references to Whitman's democratic perorations, Evans' conception of art was openly parodic. Kirstein characterized his vision as a means by which Evans "cauterized" his origins ("the naked, difficult, solitary attitude of a member revolting from his own class," wrote Kirstein), a stab at the bourgeoisie, not a gesture of solidarity with the workers. And Szarkowski saw in it "those tendencies which flourished in painting around the 1960s under the label of Pop Art," hardly the kind of image one wanted to give back to the people, except in condescension.

Just as it would be an error to assume that all snapshots—with their often stereotyped expectations, formats, executions, and responses—are vernacular, so it would be an error to accept the single, carefully selected frame as the vernacular format rather than, say, entire groups of pictures. (Again, Evans often took multiple exposures of a single location, individual, or group, yet allowed only one version to be seen in print: his.) In this respect, Stryker was onto something essential when, later in the 1930s, he firmly instructed portraitists such as Russell Lee to "keep moving" about the total environment of their subjects. Like the licensed, university-trained architect sent "out" to labor under local conditions with local materials, Stryker felt it necessary to reeducate this kind of individual in the field as to the unexplored possibilities of the field.

One such lesson, in a letter of January 1937, makes specific the content, even though it is couched as "advice":

There are some oustandingly fine things among them [recent pictures Lee made and sent to Stryker]. In general, I have one criticism to make, namely, that perhaps you have not told as full a story as you might have. . . . Would it not be better to have taken fewer families and spent more time with each?

After underscoring further limitations in what Lee had done, Stryker moved directly to correction, with the following, significant suggestion: "You have done many pictures of the families standing in front of their house or shack. They appear a bit stiff taken in this manner. These would be all right, provided we could show members of the same family in the house and doing various things."[27] Lee had made a static "document"; his boss, Stryker, knew that other contexts, over time, could provide other documents, and he wanted them.

That formal art gives us valuable knowledge of the world as well as pleasure is not in doubt. It is an insult to common sense and very likely self-defeating, however, to assume that the material with which that art mixes or from which it often arises (what Matthiessen called the "loamy subsoil") should callously be dispensed with once the artifice is complete.

In *Artworlds* (1983), sociologist Howard S. Becker observes that the more commercially valued the work of art the worse (more exploitative) its relation to its subject; given the nature of images and mass culture, relations between photographers and their subjects have scarcely provided exceptions. In "Let Us Now Revisit Famous Folk," Howell Raines, a *New York Times* reporter and Alabama native, has reviewed if not the most celebrated photographer-subject relationship certainly a photographic case that most celebrates the fragility and importance of photographer-subject relations. James Agee, to his credit, more than foresaw Raines' excoriating findings, though it would be Evans who would bear the brunt of criticism in the years that followed.

Almost a half-century after the encounter between northern artists and southern sharecroppers, Raines found the three west Alabama families Agee and Evans came to know a summer month in 1936 still in place: "[They] abide there yet," wrote Raines, "still worked to the bone, still, by the standards of their nation, poor and undereducated, and still, many of them, mad as hell at Walker Evans." Why?

In the first place, the actual content of the photographs in *Let Us Now Praise Famous Men* (1941) reflected Evans' sense of his subjects rather than his subjects' sense of themselves. "These pictures are a scandal on the family," Ruby Fields told Raines. "How they ever got Daddy's picture without a shirt on and

barefooted, I'll never know." The Fields, Burroughs, and Tingle families believe they were promised that these images "would never be seen in the
South" (certainly not from the front cover of a mass-market paperback) and
"only upon that promise were [Agee and Evans] given the run of the shacks."
Yet in terms of control and distribution Agee and Evans obviously promised
what they could not deliver, given their contractual arrangements with both
Fortune magazine and the FSA, or they willfully deceived people whom they
might have more than placated if they had taken the time to explain the true
situation and maintained that relationship of trust (as Robert Coles has with
those he got to know in his *Children of Crisis* series). The subjects were never
given the choice. Thus objectified, left to be treated as *things* by museums, col-
lectors, and visiting anthropologists, they find it is impossible," writes Raines,
to see such self-images "as art or to be glad for having a Place in History."
The images' high visibility and ease of access in the current culture (over the
printed word) makes these subjects angrier at Evans than at Agee; he is more
the villain because Agee's words sat in enormously qualified context, whereas
Evans' images, austere and isolated, sat up front in *Let Us Now Praise Famous
Men*, before Agee's text.

Then, there are other issues. Photographs are also good investments, and their
stock these days keeps rising. Raines records a conversation with a photograph
collector who, like a high-tech doctor in a busy urban hospital referring to a
patient as a disease entity, casually tosses around prices for these individuals'
images in the thousands of dollars, an "Allie Mae [Burroughs]" or "a Floyd
[Burroughs]." Understandably, the Fields, Burroughs, and Tingle families, unaware of the history of their portraits and uninformed about art markets but
knowledgeable as to the worth of their only possessions—their privacy and
their suffering—consider themselves exploited, deprived "of a fair share of the
profits [on the book and the photographs] which they imagine to be
enormous."

Having opened his revisitation with an understated review of the Southern
tenant-landlord system, Raines bitterly concludes:

Of course to suppose that this farmer [Floyd Burroughs] who happened to be
chosen to pose for a great photographic artist has some claim on the proceeds
from "a Floyd" rests on a misunderstanding of the economics of art. The artist

provides the genius, takes the risks and reaps the rewards. Those who pose for him provide, as it were, only the raw materials of the process. It is a relationship in some ways similar to that between the landlord and his tenants.[28]

Raines's last sentence is telling, and an anticipation of just this kind of exploitative relationship may explain, in part, other qualities of vernacular pictures. Unlike the classic FSA photographs, they present a bland and often somewhat confusing exterior, one that is not immediately engaging. And vernacular pictures are not easy to be "in" once the viewer has managed, through the careful reconstruction of context and intent, to define and then to gain a point of entry. This is because the "subject matter," without that reconstruction, seems easily exhausted and as a consequence generates no intellectual or affective need on the part of the viewer. Absent as well, as we shall see, are the formal elements of classic photographs that might pump up emotion and enhance memorability. Trained on stunning surfaces and sharp, clean edges, the viewer wonders about the undifferentiated grayness of the vernacular image, is annoyed by the seeming inarticulateness of a construction that requires, as part of its vehicle as well as its content, specific captions, detailed, explanatory texts, maps, and diagrams below or alongside the image. Are they weak? Can't these photographs stand alone? What was it that engaged the photographer in the first place? Wasn't the photographer as puzzled as the viewer that the "essence" of the subject didn't turn up in the developing tray or, at least, under the enlarger?

The point is that vernacular pictures exist in and refer to another world of discourse. Just as vernacular pictures presuppose a photographer-subject relationship substantially other than the classic case we have reviewed (and embodied in photographs of plain doctoring to be read), so it cannot be assumed that such relations have gained much attention or are easily documented.[29] Moreover, given the prevailing ideology that permeates high art and the self-aggrandizing, fast-buck society of which it is a part, vernacular pictures may be seen as necessarily offensive, even hostile and unrevealing to the photographer or viewer whose way of responding to them trivializes them almost reflexively.[30]

In an oppressive social and political environment, vernacular language often throws up the vulgar and the obscene, as Leo Marx has suggested by entitling his essay on dissident American writers, "Noble Shit." More than merely quirky or faddish, use of normally "forbidden words" has served as defense and offense, means of protest and vehicles for liberation for what Marx calls "saving visions."[31] On some level, the FSA photographers must have understood this immense power and vulnerability. Reprinting a negative shortly before her death, a negative she had made while with the FSA in 1936, Dorothea Lange began to cry. "The print is not the object," she said aloud, turning to her darkroom assistant after she had composed herself. "The object is the emotion the print gives you."[32] She had gotten close to people's lives. For an instant she had remembered the meaning of those lives again, as they must have flooded over her, decades before, in the midst of the Great Depression.

5
Reading the FSA Medical Photographs

79
Farmersville, Tulare County, Calif. May 1939.
Farm Security Administration camp for migratory
workers. Sons, migratory workers, bringing their
father who is sick and old to the camp clinic.
DOROTHEA LANGE.

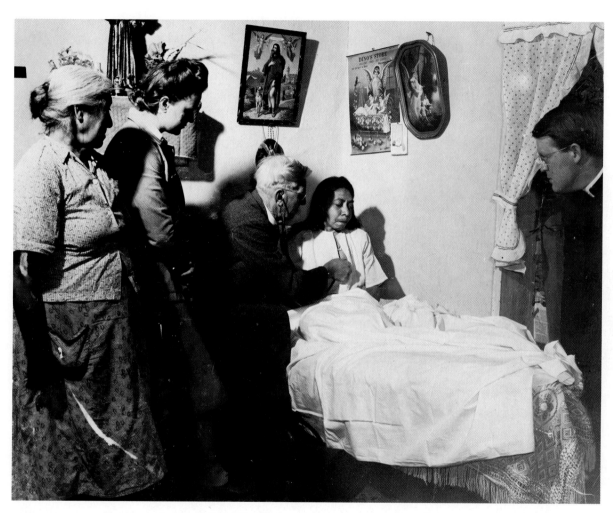

80
Questa, N.M. Jan. 1943.
Doctor Onstine, of the clinic operated by the Taos
County Cooperative Health Association, and
Father Smith, the parish priest, at the bedside of a
tuberculosis patient.
JOHN COLLIER.

Having taken such care with the making of their images, their distribution, and presentation, both Dorothea Lange and Walker Evans, above all the other FSA photographers, would have understood the order and placement of these doctor-patient photographs. Each would have understood that a book (or exhibition) that opens with a photograph of a black woman with a small black bag leaving a cabin and closes with a doctor and priest attending a Chicano woman with TB, is making a statement. They would also know that a different statement was being made by the picture that follows the first—of a well-dressed company doctor walking before a row of unpainted houses—and by the penultimate photograph—of a bent old man in front of an officious woman in a clinic listening, it appears, while two younger men (his sons?) stand to the side and look away; and that each pair of photographs is certainly saying things in different ways than does the close-up of a black doctor in Chicago with a "CASH ONLY" sign on a large, wooden desk in front of him . . . that sign a reminder of our present-day "Doc-in-a-box" supermarket medicine.

Looking at the photographs, the viewer will undoubtedly learn something of medical practice a half-century ago, but by *reading* them, not only as a text in the manner suggested in the four previous chapters, but with respect to their selection and placement in this book, much more may be learned. The viewer, however, quite reasonably may ask us how these eighty "plain pictures" were selected and organized. What aspects of them were seen as of particular interest, given the various historical, medical, and photographic background presented, and what ideology do these vernacular pictures embody?[1]

Stryker's File

A decade ago we discovered that the collection of FSA photographs we had so admired—for many wrong and, we slowly came to see, some of the right reasons—also contained a small number of photographs documenting the 1930s roots of the primary care movement. We began to assemble these, acquiring the images in necessarily a piecemeal fashion; "necessarily" not because the photographs were expensive (they were not), but because they were organized under a system not conducive to categorization schemes other than Roy Emerson Stryker's scheme. Even if we had known, for example, that Walker Evans was unlikely to have taken any medical photographs—given his style but also given the fact that only the 1937 Arkansas-Tennessee flood would have been a possible assignment source—photographs filed under the other photographers were not otherwise identified in the Library of Congress FSA photographer index as to content.[2] Then there was the "File."

Stryker's file was a repository, a goal, and a rule almost as controlling as St. Benedict's. Early in the historical section's work, Stryker indicated his desire to gather an all-inclusive range of images of American life—alongside the bureaucratically required condemnatory and celebratory images—and to gather them around what he believed was the nation's central, organizing myth: the land. (Stryker's pastoral ideology was not unique; no less than President Roosevelt and millions of other citizens shared it, and millions still do.) As a consequence, although estimates vary widely, as many as 450,000 and as few as 250,000 images were actually made, but also, in the course of this effort, Stryker reduced the total number some 100,000 by punching holes through those he judged inadequate for the File.[3] This was a winnowing process, and the reasons given were purely technical, in that certain images were said to be blurred, duplicates, or badly made. But the true reasons, others asserted, were also ideological in the sense that images that didn't conform to Stryker's notion of what the File should contain were destroyed.

Confusing, because once the RA had become the FSA, Stryker set out covertly—though explicitly to anyone within earshot—to make a documentary about *everything* in America. Yet if this were true, why, as Stu Cohen has wondered,

are there virtually no pictures of the upper class in the file, except for Marion Post [Wolcott]'s stunning work in Florida (which she was only allowed to do because Stryker had ordered her to take some R & R time in Miami while she was photographing migrant workers in Belle Island)?

It was not that images of the privileged were automatically destroyed; nothing so crude. Stryker believed the Jeffersonian vision of the yeoman farmer to be the true vision and urbanized, industrialized, corporatized, wealthy America the aberration. The well-off had their own programs, the marginal and the dispossessed had the FSA crumbs from the table. Stryker did not need to edit images of the privileged from the File because he had already pre-edited them by not assigning them in the first place. Were justification demanded, he knew he could always fall back on the assertion that he had not been paid a million dollars over eight years to document a class of Americans who were capable of amply documenting themselves. Besides, and more personally, adds Cohen, "he came from an Old Progressive Party family and the upper class was anathema. He told me that he could still, in advanced age, remember his father preaching nightly and concluding with: 'And Lord, damn the banks, damn the railroads, and double damn Standard Oil!'"

Stryker pointed out the obvious irony himself, that he worked for a Standard Oil documentary project after the FSA, Cohen says, but such self-awareness did not alter his conception of what he was then shaping or the process of documentation he was stolidly evolving.[4] But, because he was not a photographer and therefore could provide little in the way of technical directives or advice on composition, was he merely a passive recipient of images that he then either included or excluded? John Tagg's "The Currency of the Photograph" argues just the opposite; the truth was more complex and, introducing another perspective, "in some senses . . . the photographers were only co-authors of the pictures, for Stryker, whose original conception was to go beyond his narrow [FSA] brief . . . issued regular detailed shooting scripts to all his photographers."[5]

Certain critics have said that these scripts were meant to be suggestive,[6] but Russell Lee, who tended to follow Stryker's suggestions more than most, stayed with the FSA through budgetary reductions until its end (and was invited by Stryker to join a subsequent documentary project funded by Standard Oil); Walker Evans, who rather outspokenly did not, was let go in 1938. Stryker could admire the personal discipline and attention to detail of an Evans, although he said he could not keep him because Evans had not produced enough images. Despite Evans' relatively small output, posterity has judged him to have captured an extraordinarily resonant tone as well as the quintessential details; the overriding demand at the time, however, was not for the unique, slowly crafted, precious-object art image, as Walter Benjamin's would make the distinction, but for images that could and would be mass-produced, which was quite another matter. While specially illustrated and finely printed publications were presented to congressmen and others who could be influential, Stryker cultivated close ties with large and small newspapers; his FSA pictures reached millions as a result, and, when *Look* magazine began in 1936, he successfully courted that seminal-mass market image purveyor too.[7]

Stryker's file,[8] then, begins with the American land, and the photographs it contains follow the land's shape, its seasons, and the way it is situated with respect to other natural forms such as rivers, mountains, lakes, and hills. Division after division, subsection after subsection follows organically the life that flows from the land: the way the land is worked and the implements that work it, what it gives up and the times it gives them up, where that harvest goes, how it goes, who takes it, and who distributes it when it gets to where it is going. Here is a representative Stryker script on the subject, dated February 19, 1942, and addressed to Russell Lee and Arthur Rothstein "in particular":

I. Production of foods—fruits, vegetables, meat, poultry, eggs, milk and milk products, miscellaneous products.
a. Packaging and processing of above.
b. Picking, hauling, sorting, preparing, drying, canning, packaging, loading for shipping.
c. Field operations—planting; cultivation; spraying.
d. Dramatic pictures of fields, show 'pattern' of the country; get feeling of the productive earth, boundless acres.
e. Warehouses, filled with food, raw and processed, cans, boxes, bags, etc[9]

Where Are Doctors and Patients?

Where did doctors and patients fit into this? Where were health in general and medical care in particular in Stryker's scheme? The answer, more a surmise from the File, would be: fairly far down the list. Stryker knew from first hand experience that the health of farmers was essential to getting their tasks done and maintaining their land. But doctors were city folk, small-town based at best, and the urban life was something to be dealt with, not celebrated. This attitude may be gained from an undated script of Stryker's entitled "The Small Town" and reprinted in *Ohio: A Photographic Portrait: 1935–1941*. In it Stryker has twenty-two large Roman numeral headings (e.g., I. On the Street, II. Stores, III. Theatres, IV. Banks, etc.; the ninth is "The People of the Town at

Their Work," subtitled "Pictures of the people of the town and what they do."
There are thirteen subdivisions under this Roman numeral, plus "And others,"
and although we cannot be certain, the first item suggests priority ranking
from top to bottom:

Editor of the local paper
Lawyer (and his office)
Postman or rural mail carrier
Plumber
Druggist filling prescriptions
Filling station attendant
Clerks
Doctor (and his office)[10]

With his usual thoroughness, Stryker, in numerous sections, directs his FSA
photographers to restaurants, pool halls, barbershops, saloons, beer parlors,
bus terminals, schools, churches, lodges, local industries and shops—but not to
clinics or hospitals. (In Stryker's schema, the doctor is an institution because he
is a person, quite unlike the present when individuals cluster around institutions in the hope of gaining personal identity from them. Similarly, photos in
the past were seen to "document" what was there—it really was there—
whereas in the present, photos or moving pictures, as in Walker Percy's novel,
The Moviegoer, "certify" existence because a thing or person has appeared in a
movie.)

Fascinating as these Stryker taxonomies may be for sociologists and social historians, as regards medical photographs and the File, the situation is clear, if
slightly deflating: Medical photographs were not central to the mission of the
FSA as it has come to be understood by historians or, until recently, by those
in medicine looking for antecedents. What was central was documentation of
the land's destruction, of desperate rural conditions, and of success in trans-
forming them; medical care—good, bad, or indifferent—was deemed to be a
marginal component of those conditions. Moreover, as we have seen, hardly
any of the victims of the Depression felt they "deserved" comprehensive
health care and doctors (few in number for this segment of the American population, to begin with) lacked capital or facilities, or, perhaps more important,

an ideological flexibility that would have translated into an institutional flexibility. Medical practice and its financing required radical reorganization; these physicians could not or would not do it.

Therefore we did not find the several thousand FSA medical photographs under any single heading as convenient as "medical care"; rather, we had to follow the twists and turns of the File. In practice, this meant searching under the headings of "health care," "doctors," "nurses," "clinics," "hospitals," and a half-dozen other separate headings, along with following each of those headings under the half-dozen *regions* (e.g., North East, South, Far West), all of which were organized under the general pattern of the land. The several thousand medical photographs we did locate, after a search that was likely the equivalent to what sociologist Howard S. Becker has called "paying one's dues,"[11] did not appear to have been subjected to Stryker's critical punch; a third were either of poor technical quality or unfocused. This may have been the case because so many of the other kinds of photographs were already in the File by 1938–1939 (none of the medical photographs is a classic, and only one, the doctor examining the little girl before the worn "organ" in Oran, Missouri [41], has ever been reprinted in either a general FSA collection or an individual FSA photographer's collection) and because, by the early 1940s, FSA photographers were being "farmed out" to other agencies, such as the Public Health Service and the Office of War Information (OWI); and, although these agencies paid well and on time, they paid on the basis of bulk, not quality.

41

Stryker, it has been said, was deeply concerned with the content of photographs and, toward that end, according to Arthur Rothstein, "operated the photographic section more like a seminar in an educational institution." In addition to the scripts we have seen, James Borchert notes that Stryker

assigned books for photographers to read before assignments and had long talks with them prior to leaving. While in the field photographers made contact with FSA employees or other experts to guide their work. In addition, Stryker carried on a rich correspondence with photographers in the field, praising completed work, giving detailed instructions for the kinds of photographs needed by the section, urging more complete captions, and critiquing work in terms of content.[12]

But not, so far as can be determined, for the areas he felt unimportant or about which he was uninformed, like medicine. Clearly, one must prepare for fieldwork, and James Borchert's study of the inner world of alley life, as rendered over the decades in photographs, demonstrates that limited access and poor data result from not knowing enough at the start. Like the doctor-patient relationship, access is a function of trust, and trust is built over time. On the other hand, while other areas of FSA inquiry—such as the making of crops—demanded extensive preparation, it is probable that all the FSA photographers had been patients prior to their work and had had family who had been patients. Indeed, in few other sectors of American life would they encounter situations as humanly basic and emotionally complex where they could draw upon their own experiences in order to gain perspective. And perhaps this is what we really see when we look at these medical photographs: the FSA photographers' encounter with their own mixed feelings.

Although we acquired these medical images over half a dozen years, selecting and reselecting as we went, there were several continuous selection principles.

Once it was evident that the bulk of this grouping embodied notions of primary care now considered significant, images that did not were excluded. Given the FSA's orientation, few institutional images had been made, and, given the 1930s, few instances of high technology had made it into the File either. In any event, isolated images of monumental medical structures or Flash Gordon-type medical machinery, which were unrelated to the tasks of care, were excluded. Three subject categories, useful for organizing, emerged: the doctor's office, patients waiting for the doctor, and the doctor attending (attending infants, children, adults, and the elderly).

I9

I10

Later excursions through the File followed these categories even though this meant the further exclusion of photographs of high visual interest; two of the more striking were "quack" photos ("Motion Picture Show Billboard, Yuma, Arizona, Feb 1942, Russell Lee: ARE YOU FIT TO MARRY. California Law Says You must Have a Certificate of Health to Get Married. SEE THIS VITAL PRODUCTION!" [I9] or "Sign Along U.S. Highway 99, between Tulare and Fresno, California, May 1939, Dorothea Lange: MAKES REDDER BLOOD. DR. PIERCE'S GOLD MEDICAL DISCOVERY" [I10]). Also excluded were photographs that illustrated medically related subjects but subjects that were distant from either the doctor-patient relationship or tasks of care, such as ("Schenectady, N.Y., June 1943 Charts at the Elmer avenue elementary school showing the progress made in the corrective exercise class. Pictures are taken three times a year" or "Portsmouth, Ohio. Jan 1942, John Vachon Doctors of the medical service committee under the civilian defense program, meeting to discuss organization").

Two other issues—geographical distribution and photographer distribution—proved especially difficult to resolve. Two-thirds of the FSA medical care projects may have been in the South, but the FSA photographers went everywhere, and, like them, we wished to represent the entire country. Regrettably, the File could not oblige, though its limitations were instructive: no medical photographs were available for nearly half the states (21). After cataloging under the three subject headings for the exhibition total of 56, we found that Missouri, New Mexico, and West Virginia accounted for a third of the images (18); and six additional states—Arizona, California, Georgia, New Jersey, New York, and North Carolina—added another third (20). More than two-thirds of the medical photographs chosen were coming from less than one-fifth of America. For the book, expanding the total number of images to 80 and making many thematic and technical compromises allowed us to add six new states, but still, three-fifths of the images came from only one-fifth of the country. Representing the photographers became an increasing priority with us, particularly in attempting to represent styles of the photographers and the variety of equipment and processing they used. In the end, this became less important than adequately representing minorities and women and searching out examples of primary care in small towns and urban areas. Because the FSA was the kind of agency it was (class conscious and racially sensitive), this latter task was easier, with the added complication that, as a function of the FSA's progressive attitudes, the photographs may appear more contemporary and less representative, in any absolute sense of "representative."

Looking at the Doctor's Office

While the interior of the doctor's office is a private space for private transactions, these first FSA photographs [3 through 21] render the office's public face and provide clues to the organization of the doctor's day during the 1930s. In West Virginia or Louisiana, New Mexico or Illinois, the activities within the

9

16

5

1

doctor's office are no secret. The purpose and, often, the identity of the practitioner are announced outside, though not, as with "SPECIALIST: MEN'S DOCTOR," so crudely put. (These latter are tainted by old-city urban associations—Baltimore [9] and Pittsburgh [16]—and, as if this were not sufficiently corrupting, Rothstein juxtaposed within a single frame the doctor's sign within the shade, as it were, of his seedy neighbor's "RELIABLE CUT RATE" Rubber Goods shop, placing the other practitioner behind an equally shoddy facade. Both doctors remain anonymous, treating "social diseases" upstairs.) Any breaks in the rural doctors' posted schedules are for house calls (surgery, as the British would call office hours, then as now, was in the mornings) and, in the case of Tygart Valley [5], one of three innovative homestead projects in West Virginia,[13] our (German extraction) physician shows himself party to an innovative form of medical organization by splitting his time between two locations, the second on Thursdays and Sundays.

The initial picture from Greene County, Georgia [1], presented the medical reality of southern rural conditions: oppressive heat, grinding poverty, and midwives who keep things going. This black woman's shack was weathered but her kit (in another photograph) was neat—as her person. Pretty flowers before such dwellings, whether hers or a patient's, required more cultivation and care than the demands such an environment allowed. Tygart Valley Health Center (a modern term, "health," not "medical care"), closer to Washington in more ways than one, perhaps, shows its relative affluence in a well-painted frame structure on an attractively landscaped site. Enhanced by the photographer's elevated camera angle, multiple power lines overhead are evidence that labor-saving electrification has come to this formerly impoverished West Virginia lumbering area. Automobiles before the offices in two pictures remind us that doctors in small communities may have been the ones who had the automobiles—if indeed these are their cars—so that they could make house calls with them. In any event, the heavily mud-splattered car in Louisiana (see p. 173) tells us precisely what the doctor drives through, though the contrast with the very white shoes of the black woman walking up the stairs of the office makes us wonder how she keeps them so white. We wonder too at the elegant sedan parked alongside the well-used Taos County Cooperative Health Association [7] station wagon (is its owner in any way connected to this practice?), even as we notice the thin white layer upon the ground. Yes, snow comes to the Southwest, disabusing us of yet another fiction.

4

7

19

6

Lettering also can inform. Of a piece with these exteriors (and suggestive of the interiors we shall soon view), the doctors' signs are modest and unassuming. Their aim is to instruct, not distract or impress or advertise; if anything, their form understates what can be promised to those who enter.[14] The sign in Merigold, Mississippi [19] seems the least presentable, the least permanent. A made-over storefront office with large, uncurtained windows reflects, perhaps, a lack of concern for privacy as well as the hard times we might infer from the location and the date. Perhaps, too, the issue of accessibility has overridden the issue of privacy, as is often the case where cash is tight, though the black man in the middle of the frame, before the front door, sports a dapper three-piece suit, and the groups of almost-as-well-dressed men and women near him seem to belie such a situation. Dr. B. R. Bale's Circleville, Ohio, office at 149 Main and Court streets (see p. 20) has a nice curtain, undercut, unfortunately, by the peeling paint beneath the molding and the fact that the lettering in "DOCTOR" and "B.R. BALES" do not match one another by a central Ohio country mile. While he was photographing in this area, Ben Shahn recorded many farm foreclosures,[15] so the molding was not likely to have been scraped and repainted for a time, even as the concern for property and the proper use of space is made explicit by a small sign in the lower right-hand corner, in curt, architect-neat lettering: "PRIVATE ENTRANCE. DO NOT SIT ON THESE STEPS." Is the doctor strapped for space too? Are the steps his waiting room, like the porches in other pictures? Back in a moment.

Glancing inside the doctor's office, appearances also seem given over to the demands of practice. The uniform clutter presented by two different photographs of doctors' desks, as far apart as Missouri [6] and Texas [20], confirms the true nature of solo practice in those days: solo meant solo; no secretary, minimum assistance from the wife (she had everything else to do), and no nurse, unless there was a part-time one from the Public Health Service, who had to be paid by the PHS because this doctor, like most others, couldn't afford to pay her or a secretary, even in flush times, much less in the middle of the second Depression, when this photograph was taken. To save time, everything had to be close at hand; hence the high visibility in these and other doctors' offices of clipboards, stethoscopes, clocks, hats, and the doctor's black bag.[16] The telephone, seldom out of sight, is in the same room as the examination because, naturally, who else would be there to answer it, should it ring, except the doctor? These and the other Texas doctor's office [8] show huge rolltop desks, not so much for style as for function; without modern suspension files to hold and staff to stuff all the paperwork and documents, the rural general practitioner had a problem the rolltop solved: all those unread journals, flyers, bills, notes, records, and coffee cups could be stored and locked at a moment's notice.

20

8

Private Spaces

Moving inside, we see small, unadorned open spaces congruent with their exterior. Nothing fancy, no surprises. Before the twentieth century, classically trained and classically oriented senior physicians would lecture their younger colleagues on the "proper decor" for the consulting room. Tasteful furnishings went arm in arm with the piety due to one's instructors (in the form of posed portrait photographs, of course), and we have only to call to mind the interior of Freud's *Berggasse 19*, and his consulting room at that address with its extraordinary collection of ancient statuettes and artifacts, to say nothing of its couch, to have an image of what that world was like. Clinic spaces and charity hospitals rooms were another matter entirely, to judge by period photographs alone.

In spite of its obvious importance, public or private, however, few have written about this place in the twentieth century. One who has, about the effects that the physical layout of the doctor's office may have on doctor-patient communication, is Paul Goodman, in an essay entitled "The Meaning of Functionalism."[17]

Looking only at seating Goodman observes that, throughout history, it has varied enormously, depending on the type of public or private function, from the semicircular Greek theater to the psychoanalytic couch. The patient on Freud's couch, the analyst seated out of sight, is the setting meant to promote free associations in the patient; in the Sullivanian school for treating psychotics, the doctor and patient sit in chairs, face to face, across a desk—an arrangement meant to facilitate discussion of current reality problems within strict limits. In standard medical practice, seating is like Goodman's description of the Sullivan school, but with variations in the position of the desk, which reflects differences in emotional closeness between doctor and patient, and issues of control.

30

10

The small dimensions of the room in these photographs, here a function of economic necessity, are paradoxical since they also encourage just the kind of intimate communication specialists in these matters, like Robert Sommer and Edward T. Hall, stress.[18] Doctor and patient in this Oran, Missouri, encounter [30] are certainly close. With the sparse office furnishings and the few other items in place (which can be seen in other negatives of this assignment), the two are seldom more than five to six feet apart and, when seated, they are invariably closer, only three feet apart, which is considered optimal for personal exchange. This view and the others show the rolltop desk on the side of the room, out of the way and unimposing. Placement in the black surgeon's room [10], by contrast, reinforces his specialty's authority, as do the Rodin "Thinker" bookends and the dozen tall surgical tomes in the glass bookcase behind him. Doctor-patient communication in this tiny room is to be had across the heavy desk's highly reflective glass top, between the black upright typewriter and the "CONSULTATIONS: CASH" sign noted earlier—a straight and narrow passageway.

In recent studies, the size of the desk and its placement in the consulting room seem far less important to the patient than closing that door. Other medical photographs will show it shut—a visible sign of privacy intended to encourage communication by guarding the confidentiality of the relationship. But in this one [30] we are given what we must assume is, by mutual consent, a privileged view. We are looking at another straight and narrow passageway but, easily apparent without the side view, the encounter is scarcely as distanced as the other. The physician is in a dark business suit rather than a stark, white hospital top, and we observe that his attentiveness corresponds to the patient's serious, back straight-in-the-chair stance and that the man's clean pea jacket (over his spotted overalls and mud-caked boots) is matched by the doctor's clean shirt and neat tie. Mutual respect is communicated through correspondences in clothing and posture. The woman beyond the doorjamb—the patient's wife? a stranger?—is not crucial to the information to be conveyed, and she does not wish to acknowledge this violation of personal space. They may pose, she will not. And yet, as studies have shown, the privacy guarantee is less than certain. Even with the door closed, poor acoustics (worse now, lacking those thick oak doors) often allowed the patient's complaints and the doctor's advice to seep out into the waiting room.

Like the classic photographs, a view of these vernacular pictures will show that they are neither candid nor spontaneous. But the openness of the relationship exists to an even greater degree than posed photographs would suggest because, it seems, the majority of the subjects are in open collusion with the FSA photographers. This implies the existence of a shared motive: both photographer and subject are aware of the immediate purposes of these images, and they want to give the appearance of a "real good thing," or at least they want to do their part for the FSA.

Waiting for the Doctor

Classic photographs are discrete visual objects, whereas vernacular pictures are collective, participatory events. The classic photographs do not tolerate anomaly; in them, order is the order of the day, whereas vernacular pictures tap deep into the richness of life, as most actually live it, by refusing to limit the subject or rigidly control details.

29

The location of the doctor's office in this southern image of a woman and children waiting is, without the Irwinville, Georgia, caption [29], unspecific, though the scene is busy and fairly throbs with pathos and melancholy at first glance, from the tall, isolated, shadowy man in the background to the little boy in the foreground who hasn't a clue as to what he should be doing before a camera. The man's white hat oddly corresponds to the bewildered, staring face of the boy, and background and foreground are flattened, almost compressed. Yet small joys abound between, around, alongside when we look closer, and a larger truth is suggested. Earlier, we heard country people tell of their anxiety and concern while waiting. Here, we can see the relaxed way the mothers, young and old, are standing and holding their children, their smiles, exaggerated poses, even their flirting with the camera.

Such comparisons and contrasts are the process by which vernacular pictures convey meaning, and here the subtle truth is worth having: if the former im-

33

26

28

15

age (and subsequent views of several western clinics, Arizona [33] and California [26], for example) showed one response to waiting space, this Irwinville Farms Resettlement Project show us another and answers the question whether illness separates us from others or opens us to new communities.

The classic photographs strain toward the timeless stasis of Art; before them, we learn to keep our distance. The vernacular picture is, we have seen, in constant motion, between itself and the authenticating caption, between itself and the participating viewer, who is, as Alan Trachtenberg has said of the experience of Lewis Hine's photographs, as much agitated as informed.[19] Every picture in this selection has its awkwardness or anomaly, as if to say that on this click, at least, the professional wasn't much in control—a rough parallel to the work we have to do in order to use Stryker's file and having done it, we find ourselves curiously instructed in the process. In the waiting room of a Penasco, New Mexico, clinic [28], for example, the patients display an all-too-common wariness of the professional (in this case, the government picture-maker from Washington). Unlike the boy in Georgia, however, they know what's coming and look down or away from the lens, even as an unspotted observer from the street looks in on them and on our FSA photographer. The theme of *avoidance*, a clue to failure in the doctor-patient relationship, is sounded at still another level by this picture because we are forced, by careful examination of the waiting room's background, to reconsider the patient's response.

That is, while waiting for that doctor in Oran [30], a patient could read the ten (framed) thoughts entitled "How to Treat Your Physician," all put in easy, comfortable language. Elsewhere across the land, mingled with conventional warnings in big letters about V.D. ("DON'T GIVE SYPHILIS"), posters on waiting-room walls informed patients and their escorts about proper diet, posture, inoculations, personal hygiene, the need for regular examinations, the importance of X rays, and the usefulness of a sound body for the war effort—all characteristic, it would seem, of good preventive medicine. And they are, except that the message of several of the posters is oblivious to the resources available to these FSA patients. In Taos, Chicano babies are to be examined once a week, children once a month; in Gee's Bend, Alabama [15], a black man "shows interest," we are told by the caption, in an attractive food chart that lays out, bar-graph fashion, the protein content of various foods . . . but they are foods he has never seen, for the most part, nor would the condition of his life allow him to purchase them even if he knew what they were. Who wrote, designed, and printed these posters? Who put them up?

So, given a background that announces itself unaware of patients, perhaps the patients' avoidance is understandable, even justified. Compliance does not automatically follow from the provision of adequate information, in the 1930s or in the 1980s, and building the primary care relationship, we are reminded by these images, requires constant attention to the congruence between the doctor's advice and the everyday reality—and limitations—of patients' lives. Tucked into many of these vernacular pictures, then, are their own stringent self-criticism: despite the sponsor, the FSA, a medical patient or an informed viewer would observe that the pictures in question give the lie to a practice that separates medical care from an appropriately supportive social and political milieu.

32

33

26

Another example: Chicago. Like the aging Chicano in Penasco, the men in this all-black clinic waiting room [32] also have their hats off. The traditionally deferential gesture here, however, seems grudging, more form than acquiescence, and certainly not the respect one finds in a sound relationship. Of all those waiting, only one is looking at the camera (slipping a glance at a friend next to her?). The rest are stiff, still, simply not "making waves." Had black photographer Gordon Parks made this picture rather than Jack Delano, would its general tone be warmer? Possibly, though it is more likely that the controlling element is the constricting context: there is literally no space between the seats. Eleven Mile Corner in Arizona [33] and Woodville in California [26], even the New Mexico waiting room, are spacious by comparison with this place: a quick count shows us no less than twenty people jammed together in unpadded card-playing chairs, knees touching backs—undoubtedly waiting one to two hours for a visit. If amenities such as coat racks existed, these well-dressed and dressed-up patients have resisted them. Were they in heavy coats because the clinic was cold that April? Were they "dolled up" because the OWI wanted an image of Southsiders in jackets and ties, in dresses, nylons, patterned scarves, and earrings in order to reassure black members of America's (segregated) armed forces about life back home? Were they buttoned up because they were, after all, mere transients, not meant to be comfortably at home in a clinic presumably for them? Such is power of the waiting room.

More than simple irony, the image is in fundamental contradiction, it would seem, with whatever conventional purpose lay behind its making. We wonder whether this constricted quality carried over into the doctor-patient relationship. Similar, though far more unhappy in appearance, are those waiting for the doctor some thousand miles away in Arizona [33]. Hats on or off, these men stare into space too; they are aware of the camera's presence, they do not wish to meet it face-to-face. Not in service and away from their work (if they have it), the "WELL BABY CLINIC" sign behind them does not reassure, and they seem particularly out of place during this time of day, with the women and their children in the same waiting space. One fellow with his black hat on gives the camera a measured look, while another—an older, grizzled fellow—cradles a battered hat in the lap of his battered overalls, as though holding his breath until these people and their flashguns go away.

55

Attending: Home Visits

Perhaps this sort of passive resistance and whatever adverse effects it had upon medical care were lessened when the doctor met the patient on his or her home ground. The house call has been judged an inconvenience at best and an inefficient anachronism at worst, but these arguments are oblique to the point that John Vachon's picture, "Country doctor examining child in farm house" [55], makes. Dispensing with home visits was a time-saver for the physician, and it allowed more patients to be seen closer to that new testing equipment; but this Scott County, Missouri, picture reminds us that also dispensed with was intimate knowledge of the patient's living space. With the visit, one learned how patients organized their lives and, as was often the case, how they related to other members of the extended family who were frequently present and part of the problem, if not the solution.

58

Later we will see visiting the doctor or the doctor visiting as an occasion, a ceremony in those days for which the family prepared. They not only cleaned up but, as in Box Elder, Utah [58], dressed up too. An attractive family comes to see their FSA doctor: four girls and their little brother are lined up, sister is checked first. Mother is watching in her smart print dress and father is attentive with his tie on, hat off, arms folded, standing tall in his knee-length laced boots. Daughter #2, in another version of this examination scene [51], has a

51

I11

52

53

pretty dress on, but, should we notice, this second shot allows us to see her worn T-strap shoes, thereby disclosing the true nature of this family's condition. While there was no dressing up in that Scott County farmhouse, still, we must acknowledge that our window into their home offered the view of only a single room, and a portion of that room, at that, on a single day in their lives. Although farm clothing is timeless and meant to be frayed, would an office-based history of this family have told us the same things as the worn curtains and the unpolished furniture tell us? The vulnerable little girl's lesions and the mother's obesity would reveal themselves anywhere, but, without the home visit, would we know the distance this family has traveled between the time the organ in the background was new and where they are in 1942? Has World War II's urban expansion passed these rural folk by?

Medical surveys of the Depression told us what illnesses people had but not how they were treated. Several of the FSA pictures suggested how they treated themselves [I11] (see p. 17), while these of the doctor attending confirm what patients came for, and what they actually received when they got there. The organs the public knew best were the lungs, heart, and stomach. Most complaints, therefore, were either "upper" or "lower." And we can see that the FSA photographers accurately recorded the range of what the doctor did in the 1930s because they have him listening, testing, looking into ears (sometimes, though rarely, at eyes), drawing blood, making injections, taking blood pressure and temperature, bandaging (Doctor Goodson once billed the assailants of a patient for stab wounds), giving information (that "advice"), and writing prescriptions.

Most familiar to us, even today, are many of the pictures in this grouping that show the doctor with his stethoscope, attending to those upper and lower complaints by "looking" into the body, sounding those "hidden" places. Certain of the pictures, in Blanch, North Carolina [52] and Maricopa County, Arizona [53], are badly (because inauthentically or carelessly) posed; with the former nothing could be accurately heard by the doctor through the child's clothing, and with the latter the instrument is positioned by the carotid artery and is therefore too high to be of use.

Still, this simple piece of technology, as Stanley Joel Reiser details for us, had (and has) its extremely practical as well as deeply magical uses. Along with the black bag (and the white coat in the clinic or hospital), it was a portable, visible symbol of the doctor's authenticity; before it, all conversation ceased, while the doctor listened. And listening, the doctor could authoritatively decide the seriousness of the complaint aided, but not dissuaded, by the patient's testimony. Was the chest congested (the most common complaint of the times) because of "croup" or pneumonia? Was the pain in the chest an attack or merely indigestion? Murmurs and irregularities of the heart could, with a skillful practitioner, be accurately diagnosed, and serious lung diseases could be differentiated from another bad bout of "flu." In either case, prescriptive action took the form of habit alteration: the doctor acted upon the patient by recommending an enhanced diet and bed rest or moderating the pattern of exertion. These attending pictures are congruent with 1930s statistics because they show us not only fewer interventions, but less aggressive interventions. Yet, as we shall see, context can be everything because so-called "doing nothing" then was tantamount, for many farmers on the edge of physical exhaustion in the face of daily demands, to serious intervention by the doctor—prescriptive lessons we could stand to learn again.

Attending: Infants and Children

The very young and the very old cannot come alone nor, when the doctor attends, are they able to make their needs known by themselves. Labeling the nonpatients in this next subgroup [35–62] *escorts* obscures the fact that they are not only responsible for transporting and "keeping an eye" on the patient, but that they (parents in these cases) often have complaints or information about the patient that may also require attention: How shall the patient be managed after the doctor's intervention? what, if the doctor knew it, would make him or her want to see the patient again immediately? In addition to these elements of their role and physical restraint, parents "translate" their youngsters' concerns to the doctor much as, roles reversed, children-become-adults and in-laws will translate the concerns of their aged parents (sometimes poorly, as in [79]) in years to come. Or, as those of any age with language, cultural, class, or racial differences, may need their complaints translated to the doctor and the doctor's advice translated in return.

79

36

37

54

46

What becomes, in effect, a triadic rather than a dyadic encounter, requires our reading here to be especially sensitive to the movement between the actors. Emotional triangles are inherently unstable, and we know that children and adolescents pose special problems in the encounter because lines of authority are constantly shifting, even as the young are constantly testing them. Should parents be absent from the actual encounter, as in Klamath County, Oregon [36] or Dailey, West Virginia [37], doctors must assume the role of *in loco parentis*, in which the acceptable authority of a trusted adult may easily become the unacceptable authoritarianism of a distrusted stranger. That paternalism was not always a pejorative term may be seen in these pictures where naked children (rarely shown in the 1930s) are comfortably looked after by the doctor. One little boy in Bridgeton, New Jersey, appears absolutely terrified [54]. However, another frame in the sequence of shots (not used) shows the black physician snatching victory from defeat by role reversal: the child is allowed to listen to the doctor's "interior" with the same stethoscope used on him.[21] All smiles are the result.

Recalling some of what each party had to say of the other in chapter 2, we should be aware that transference and countertransference issues are at least as primitive with the young as with adults. Parents in the consulting room—and nurses as above—may provide additional support for the doctor's work in the form of modeling ("Here's how mother does it") or straight sympathy. In the picture of the tiny girl being treated for hydrophobia [46] in Chaffee, Missouri, father helped to hold her during the painful treatment; in another, prior frame (not used), however, he sat alongside her in the waiting room, looking just as glum as she did. Parents may also provide support for quite another kind of behavior, and in the picture at the Aqua Fria FSA camp for migratory workers in Maricopa County, Arizona (see p. 183) the mother's weight comes down, we think, on the side of her son: through body posture, the placement of her hand across her chest, and an expression of doubt on her face (the "DON'T GIVE SYPHILIS" sign directly behind her), she supports the boy's wariness; the doctor will be forced to prove himself in the face of a traditional alliance he cannot hope to modify, much less break, for the patient's benefit.

Like the stethoscope on one's bare skin, the laying on of hands by the physician has both practical and magical effects. Doctors must touch to palpate and to sound, even as patients implore to the doctor, "Look me over." But they mean "make contact" and often feel disappointed, cheated, if their physician hasn't touched them during the encounter. Doctors in all the previous pictures made physical contact with the young they were attending. This Reedsville, West Virginia, encounter [59] seems no different, is straightforward and even more no-nonsense than the others. Yet another look at the examination taking place will show that doctor and patient are expending considerable effort at making the encounter a success. How so?

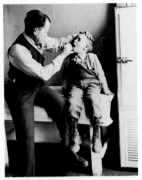

59

In an early FSA photograph (1935), an RA subsistence homestead is on trial. While neither doctor nor patient has wasted much time presenting himself to the other (the boy is in overalls, the doctor is without suit coat, and his stethoscope is stuck into his back pocket; both are in workboots), each has had to situate himself awkwardly in order to have this encounter *and* to satisfy Arthur Rothstein. The boy is on the very edge of the table but braces himself with his arms, while the doctor is off balance but holds the boy in a firm, protective manner, and, not incidentally, conducts a throat examination: a metaphor for the reciprocity a good relationship requires.

53

Attending: Adults and the Aged

Although these pictures are decades away from a relationship wherein medicine is a commodity that one party consumes and the other provides (or worse, where medicine is an "industry," and for-profit hospitals grow even faster than the computer and drug industries),[22] still, they document a transition point. With them, we can see not only the medical home visit coming to an end and hospital- (or at least clinic-) based health care on the rise, but we can see health becoming a general, societal responsibility rather than an individual and private choice.

Children were brought to the FSA clinics for advice on those many acute infections they always seem to get. The photos of youngsters remind us that it was during the 1930s when parents began to seek out the doctor more frequently because they no longer trusted themselves to treat their children themselves and because the state was finally assisting them in this health care measure by

39

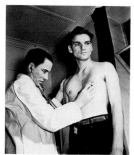

72

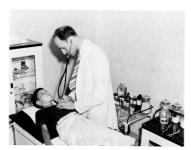

49

providing greater access at a lower or an affordable cost. (Those who grew up during the years these photos were taken can remember that it was during the Depression years when "Health" became a category on their report cards and an "Unsatisfactory" might have stood for anything from bad habits, like nail-biting and poor posture, to bad teeth or eyes in need of "corrective" lenses.)[23]

World War II changed many things in American society, and from the later photos, those in 1942–1943, we can see that medical care was one of them. If the war demonstrated that women could do any task—even heavy, dangerous industrial work—it also demonstrated that the "war effort" demanded a healthy population. "Your First LINE OF DEFENSE is a HEALTHY BODY," read the poster in that Bridgeton, New Jersey, clinic, and the barrel-chested black man had the stars and stripes behind him should the babies and their mothers have missed the point [39]. And the series of adult examinations—whether listening to the heart in Brooklyn [72], palpating the abdomen in Wilder, Idaho (see p. 134), giving an examination for work in Washington, D.C. (see p. 130), or taking blood pressure in Brooklyn [49]—were a clear indication that the state was "taking care" of industrial workers needed for its war production.

Of course this was no small distance from the creation of comprehensive social services and the demand for comprehensive health care as a right of every citizen, but the pictures nevertheless embody a situation that is in marked contrast to the one in earlier decades.

Preventive medicine had entered American culture with Flexner's medical re-forms and at the insistence of Progressives in politics and society. Individuals were having regular examinations at the turn of the century, to be sure, but, except for the well-off, the regular "checkup"—with its combination of physical examination, information exchange, advice, and relation-building—was out-side the average American's budget. Acute, not regular, interventions were the norm. Yet at the same time, the need for preventive medicine, along with fundamental changes in societal and personal hygiene, was wholly necessary. Tenants, sharecroppers, and migrants, we know, suffered the most by its ab-sence. Working from dawn until dusk, from "can to can't" like the small farmer, there was nothing between them and the inexorable ravages of their up-bringing and environment, what David Eugene Conrad has called "the diseases of malnutrition, filth, and immorality." Indeed, "their diet of cornbread, molasses, and sowbelly (fat salt pork), eaten three times a day, caused pellagra, their lack of sanitation led to malaria, typhoid, and many other diseases, working in the fields barefooted gave them hookworms."[24] And as VD was a constant presence, numerous FSA clinics, for small farmers as well as migrants, attacked it and TB head-on by isolating the tubercular patient and openly warning and aggressively treating those with VD [Maricopa County, Arizona (see p. 98, and p. 137), and Bridgeton, New Jersey (p. 101)].

Talk was not cheap, relative to the average American's ability to pay for it from a professional, though (we may recall Doctor Goodson's several consultations with the woman experiencing marital difficulties) patients sometimes compromised their budgets in order to talk with someone, even as doctors sometimes compromised their fees and time schedules in order to listen when the occasion demanded.

71

The effects of the prepaid health-care plans can be seen to some extent simply by the variety of average, preventive medical encounters they made possible for adults—for lice in Kempton, West Virginia, for prenatal care in Woodville, Georgia [71], and for maintenance for the elderly in Penasco or Questa, New Mexico. Although many of these encounters show adults approaching the doctor in the old manner, passively being acted upon, whether as supplicants in Corpus Christi, Texas ("DON'T SPIT" in the background—one more order), head hung, waiting for the injection in New York, or seemingly "cooled out" with a prescription in Culp, Illinois [76], others give a sense of abandoning this stance, to the point that, in several encounters, patients are part of the exchange, and not only by virtue of the FSA photographer's attention. The intrinsic asymmetry of the doctor-patient relationship remains unchallenged. The doctor, after all, has the skills, and the people in the 1930s came to get some *thing* from him, if only the confirmation of illness and its seriousness. Yet in picture after picture we see patients acknowledged as partners in the healing process.

76

Certainly, the doctor could have been forced into this risky mutuality by the FSA photographer, just as recalcitrant or adamant physicians were forced to accept the FSA medical program in their area because they had to charge less than their urban counterparts, collected less than they charged, and had still

61

74

79

80

less social distance with which to prop up their self-esteem; and the FSA paid their bills regularly. The possibility also exists that individual physicians, in response to this medical new deal, like Dr. Tabor in Dailey, West Virginia [61], became vulnerable because they saw the admission of their own limitations as, ultimately, in their patients' best interest too. The FSA patient handbook mentioned in chapter 2 underscored patients' *duties* as well as their *rights*. The man bandaging the woman's forearm in New York City [74] has earned her beaming gratitude, but the image also suggests that she, by more than her illness, has earned his beaming attention. Such reciprocity, these images argue, is the by-product of a process: systematic attention to each partner's needs rather than one-way streets of overwhelming distress and aggressive, irregular diagnosis and treatment.

Primary care focuses upon prevention, support, maintenance, and relief over time, rather than on a short-term cure. Re-viewing the order of these pictures persuaded us that the last two needed to be reversed.

Having argued for attention to unconscious and ideological directives beneath the surface of things, our original ordering ended on a sour note. Each of the two pictures renders the greatest test of the doctor-patient relationship: last things. Dorothea Lange's shot of the old man in a California clinic [79] is austere though also enigmatic to the point of noncommunication. Rather than introducing beneficial uncertainty, the image introduces an ever-deepening series of questions that provide less wisdom than bafflement. What is being said is as uncertain as the identity of the woman who is saying it. If there is no clear statement as to diagnosis and treatment, there is even less evidence as to whether or not she is a doctor or even a helping person. The two younger men—hats in hands like the aging man to their side (their father? we wondered)—have withdrawn from his need into their own sense of shame and/or impotence: his presumed illness, even if he is a complete stranger, encourages a regression, activating our worst fears about dependency and weakness. His suffering becomes an embarrassment and of no use to him, them, or us.

In measured contrast, this New Mexico image of a woman in an advanced stage of TB [80] is surrounded by a proper community of sufferers. To the circle of family, friends, and priest is added her physician, who is a patient in the sense that he is being long-suffering with her. It is he, ironically, who is far closer to death—chronologically speaking—than the woman he dutifully treats. And what gift does she give to him? She holds up her end of the relationship; she tries to be brave.

Captions, Propaganda, Identity

In "The Work of Art in an Age of Mechanical Reproduction," Walter Benjamin observed that "the camera introduces us to unconscious optics as does psycho-analysis to unconscious impulses."[25] Less by adding—save by the manipulative processes of framing, selection, and altering proportion by enlargement—photography enriches the viewer by the static equivalent of TV's instant re-play: what we only glanced at a moment ago can be re-viewed, at leisure, again and again. But if "it enables the original to meet the viewer half-way . . . the cathedral leaves its locale to be received in the studio of the lover of art,"[26] the techniques already mentioned, as well as the close-up, cropping, and the ease with which details may be removed from negatives, simultane-ously undermine the photograph's *authenticity*. Perhaps this is what Benjamin had in mind when he noted, "For the first time captions [to a work of art] have become obligatory."[27] Why? Because, according to Benjamin, they anchor the image in time and space, and thereby validate it for the viewer.

However important captions are to documentary photographs—and these plain pictures especially—it must also be acknowledged that there are no fewer problems with them, they are no less open to error and manipulation, than the ones attached to any of the general body of FSA images. (There are possibly more problems, given the frequently technical nature of the medical informa-tion they attempt to convey.)[28]

The other FSA captions may often have understated the Depression, but, un-like these doctor-patient ones, the affective dimension was not so entirely ab-sent. Their reportorial style mimics the extreme facticity of the medical model. No single caption reveals, for example, anything like Lange's charged verbatim accounts of bewildered and pained dislocation or Lee's relentlessly accumula-tive rolls of data, which can amount to an accusal or an indictment, as with

62

46

34

112

the family of Mr. De Buis, a Cajun farmer, and his wife and six children. They own 20 acres of ground on which there is a small, plainly furnished, but comfortable house. He raises cane and some corn for feed, has about 200 chickens, 2 cows and several hogs. He is very pessimistic about farming and says, "What we gonna do if they keep on cutting us down?" (New Iberia [vicinity], La. Oct 1938; LC USF 34 31787-D)

The doctor-patient captions faithfully answer who and what, not how and why. We can see hungry people obviously suffering the immediate ravages of disease or we can reasonably infer the slower though inevitable horrors of diseases undiagnosed, untreated, unprepared for—but the accompanying captions take no license, provide us with none of the subjective content of their subjects' lives. They do not lie in that what they do tell is incontrovertibly true, but they do not tell the whole truth either and in their selectivity, their extreme subservience to bureaucratic need (i.e., Washington), they speak in a governmental rather than a humane vernacular.

Nevertheless, like the doctor-patient pictures, the contradictions and anomalies these captions contain allow an informed reader to get behind their dumbness with a few simple questions: Why is a doctor giving typhoid inoculations in a public school in the USA in 1941? [62] Given the nature of typhoid, the unstated implication is that we have a serious public health problem. Why is a little girl being subjected to rabies injections? [46] More then than now, this was an extremely painful series, to begin with, and the medical outcome from the seriously compromised vaccine was so uncertain as to be marginal. And those "Japanese-Americans" so anxiously "patroniz[ing] the camp clinic" [34]—implying they have the run of the land, free to come and go at will. Aren't they from the nearby internment camp?

In trying so hard to show the FSA health-care program to advantage, in piling noun upon noun without qualifying (and possibly introducing offensive or revealing adjective or adverb), these doctor-patient captions announce themselves as selected and edited as the photographs they accompany and although surely anchoring the latter in "time and space," they forewarn the reader as to their official purposes just as surely as a prizefighter who telegraphs his punches.

Yet here is Arthur Rothstein, who said,

I13

I15

I16

I14

There is no question that these [FSA] photographs were taken with great honesty, in spite of all attempts of political opponents of the program to say it was propaganda. It wasn't propaganda. It was just the way things were. The style and approach of the photographs, the idea of being unobtrusive, and of allowing people to act naturally, unposed and unmanipulated, give the photographs credibility.[29]

Rothstein, the other FSA photographer who went with Lee to Stryker's post-FSA Standard Oil documentary project, who later became photography editor of *Parade* magazine, still might not be expected to offer much insight into an earlier project with which he was so deeply identified and which provided him with his initial orientation. On the other hand, to so completely skirt questions of selection and composition, especially since two of his most celebrated images (to say nothing of the overly bleached skull he moved around the South Dakota Badlands in 1936 [I12])[30] are masterful precisely because of the way in which the images were composed and selected from the dozen similar images in the series Rothstein shot, seems odd. Or instructive.

"Plantation owner's daughter checks weight of cotton, Kaufman County, Texas, August 1936" [I13], was the first picture, and "State highway official moving sharecroppers, New Madrid, Missouri, 1939" [I14], was the second. The little girl with the cotton field sweeping away behind her is, needless to say, a Texas version of Shirley Temple—white, with pretty curls, a smart sun dress—primly going about her father's duties while dumbfounded blacks in attendance watch in simple amazement . . . another implication being this emasculating sweetheart is checking on *them*. Should we examine other versions of this picture, say [I15] or [I16], we can see what statement Rothstein was working toward. A side view of the scene entitled "Cotton Pickers" [I15] and frontal view, "Cotton pickers who receive fifty cents a hundred pounds" [I16];, have Shirley Temple blocked by a black boy in the first and by part of the weighing arm in the second. In either case, the relationship in this social drama is visually less explicit and lacking in the intensity [I13] provides. With the second Rothstein picture, the viewer would be hard pressed to come up with much sympathy for the white state trooper supervising what amounts, it seems, to an eviction of black sharecroppers. They are hefting furniture, the piteous side view of it all shows the trooper's jackboots to his disadvantage and his cigar at a particularly arrogant tilt. The trooper is carrying out *his* tasks with pleasure too. Yet, strictly speaking, this is not an eviction. The original, full caption mentions the area to which these sharecroppers are being moved as *between* a levee and the Mississippi River. The background is that there is flood danger; despite Rothstein's visual positioning, despite the trooper's posture, the displacement is for their safety and not one more act of oppression.

Dorothea Lange, we know, did not feel the need to defend the FSA photographs against charges of propaganda. She openly admitted to deleting an offending thumb from the corner of the famous "Migrant Mother" print and, moreover, complained that the Library of Congress "never reproduced 'Migrant Mother' the same way twice," despite her creating a *guide print* to act as a control in the printing process.[31]

Stryker had his thoughts as to how the authenticating captions were to be made; but we know the photographers also had preferences, even demands.[32] Nothing was to be made up for Lange. Milton Meltzer quoted the following account from Ron Partridge, Lange's driver/helper while she was photographing in the Imperial Valley, California, in those momentous months in 1937:

She would walk through the field and talk to people, asking simple questions—What are you picking?—and they'd answer, tossing her whatever fruit or vegetable it might be. She'd show interest in their clothing, their knives, their bins, their trucks. How long have you been here? When do you eat lunch. . . . Every hour or two she'd go sit in the car and write down verbatim what people had said.[33]

Meltzer noted that certain captions Lange used with her photographs would come directly from what she had heard; it is possible that Lange was able to take the position she took with respect to captions because, unlike the others, she had the images *and* the text and could be certain about both.

"The way things were . . . ." And then we think of Stryker's scripts, which must have taken dedicated searching on the part of the photographer to locate those specific things at that moment in time. Example One: "While Delano was still photographing the happy faces and well-kept farms of Green County [Georgia]," writes Hurley (and thanks to the FSA farm assistance program that had been operating there for a time, it might be added, "a letter from Roy [Stryker] indicated that the agency was taking new directions. He wanted Jack to take a few days off and go over to Fort Benning [Georgia] to photograph the soldiers." Why? to "show the effect of the military buildup on the surrounding area. 'Try to get a picture [Stryker wrote Delano] of a soldier, lonely, trying to pick up a date.' "[34] Example Two: John Collier was exploring the movement of the urban wealthy to then-rural Westport, Connecticut. He was told to get "healthy" defense industry workers. "Back he went," writes Hurley, "to Pratt and Whitney [aircraft engine manufacturer], complaining that it was almost impossible to get pictures of typical workers because 'typical' workers ('strong and grim') did not exist. . . ."[35] They had been drafted away to World War II, but Collier, in true "documentary" fashion, was to locate them anyway.

If Walker Evans allowed his images to speak for themselves (through the articulate critics they aroused) while Arthur Rothstein was defensive about the obviousness of his superb constructions, if Russell Lee confronted the essential reality of people's lives and, like Dreiser, overwhelmed the viewer with the unavoidable weight of facts while Dorothea Lange listened to her subjects and photographed her listening and used image and word to deepen the meaning of the other, our reading of their work is enhanced by knowing their actions and limitations, knowing what they could control and did control, along with what they could not control and what they did not know they were controlling.

These glancing remarks, almost asides when one considers how much could be said and needs to be said about previously ignored background and technique, nevertheless begin to illustrate the manifold ironies and paradoxes, the latent energies, rich content, and unanswered questions even the slightest reading of vernacular pictures can yield. All of them are radically incomplete and, as a result, almost completely referential, and what they refer to is a country that has not yet begun to be explored, though, in social and local history, vernacular architecture, and poetry, work is in progress. From a political point of view, the current status of vernacular pictures demonstrates the acceptance, in analysis, of the status quo and all the ideological implications of that position, which necessarily follow. As art, they are another example of what happens to local or regional materials when they are inappropriately subjected to international "standards." Their neglect is an indication of the priorities that have dominated the American Studies movement since its expansive, European excursions in the late 1940s and early 1950s. And from a medical perspective, recent interest in them suggests an attempt to deflect the course of American medical training which is heading toward scientism and the organization of American medicine which is heading toward overspecialization, increasing reliance on high technology, and mega-hospital domination. It is in an almost entirely overlooked area, however, that of the *craft* of photography, that perhaps the greatest mystification has occurred, and perhaps it is in this area that future reconsiderations of vernacular photographs and these FSA pictures might begin.

For too long photographers, historians, and critics of photography have attempted to put images into frames, as it were, as though they were taxonomists plopping bugs and butterflies into kill bottles, when the task has been not dissection and labeling—separation and isolation—but seeing the underlying unity and then telling others how all the pieces are connected. Ben Shahn communicates some of what can happen to an artist—though for the ultimate benefit of all—when these connections are made:

I remember the first place I went . . . one of the resettlements FSA built. I found that as far as I was concerned, they were impossible to photograph. Neat little rows of houses. That wasn't my idea of something to photograph at all. But I had the good luck to ask someone, "Where are you all from? Where did they bring you from?" And when they told me I went on to a place called Scott's Run, and there it began. From there I went all through Kentucky, West Virginia, down to Arkansas, and Mississippi, Louisiana, in other words, I covered the mine country and the cotton country. I was terribly excited . . . did no painting at all in that time.[36]

Notes

Introduction

1.

Vernacular means something native to a place or region, something that is common and generally understood by the average person without reference to learned sources. Although, as a concept, it may be applied to numerous areas, such as architecture and photography, it is most frequently employed in literary analysis.

With respect to twentieth-century medicine Sir George Pickering used the concept—unwittingly—while addressing himself to what he took to be medicine's decline as a learned profession. Weakening language skills—primarily physicians' writing—were a clue, but Dr. Pickering was quick to trace this to a decline in classical education. Latin was important once, but no longer. Just as important, perhaps, was what Latin symbolized. In the past, Dr. Pickering asserted,

it was a knowledge of Latin which distinguished the learned professions from other vocations. [More particularly] the goldsmiths, the mercers and other [medieval] guilds. . . . might have developed skills and an understanding and familiarity with the materials of their craft in no way inferior to that of doctors, lawyers, and priests, but they did not command the same respect or social status because they did not write in Latin.

In the event non-classically trained doctors were listening, the point was underscored: "They could not communicate with learned folk, nor were they able to match the scholars in their disputations." ("Medicine at the Crossroads: Learned Profession or Technological Trades Union?" Nuffield Lecture, *Royal Society of Medicine*, Vol. 70 [January 1977], pp. 16–17.) Dr. Pickering quite rightly opposed the dangerous implications of narrowly trained physicians but, in the process, seemed unaware of the dangers of another process—not only the historic gate-keeping function of formal speech and the institutions where it might be learned, which only a glance at Thomas Hardy's *Jude the Obscure* would readily furnish, but the ac-

tual weakening of learning by lack of contact with the vernacular.

By contrast, a century and a half earlier on this side of the Atlantic, Ralph Waldo Emerson, excited with what such contact might mean for an emerging American culture, could write:

The literature of the poor, the feelings of the child, the philosophy of the street, the meaning of household life, are the topics of the time. It is a great stride. It is a sign—is it not?—of a new vigor when the extremities are made active, when currents of warm life run into the hands and feet . . . what would we really know the meaning of? The meal in the firkin; the milk in the pan; the ballad in the street; the news of the boat; the glance of the eye; the form and gait of the body ("The American Scholar," in *The Writings of Ralph Waldo Emerson*, edited by Brooks Atkinson [New York: The Modern Library, 1940, 1950], p. 61).

Emerson saw new possibilities in the fact that, rather than the "sublime and beautiful," in literature and in life "the near, the low, the common" were being explored and celebrated. The concept of the vernacular, as it relates to both medical care and photography, will acquire greater definition as this book progresses; a specific, fuller discussion may be found in chapter 4 and in the notes to chapter 4.

2.

Franklin Delano Roosevelt, *Second Inaugural Address of the President of the United States* (20 March 1937).

3.

H. Jack Geiger, M.D., "An Overdose of Power and Money" [Review of *The Social Transformation of American Medicine* by Paul Starr], *The New York Times Book Review* (9 January 1983), pp. 1ff.

4.

Paul Starr, *The Social Transformation of American Medicine* (New York: Basic Books, 1983), p. 3.

5.

George Abbott White, "Primary Care in the 1930s. Working People Consulting the Doctor,"

Harvard Medical Alumni Bulletin (April 1980), p. 26. For the Kaiser Plan, see E. W. Saward, "The Relevance of Prepaid Group Practice to the Effective Delivery of Health Services," *U.S. Department of HEW* (Washington: GPO, 1969). A still earlier period is examined by J. L. Schwartz, "Early History of Prepaid Medical Care Plans," *Bulletin of the History of Medicine* (39, 1965), pp. 450–475.

6.
Leo Marx, "The Vernacular Tradition in American Literature," in *Studies in American Culture*, edited by Joseph J. Kwiat and Mary C. Turpie (Minneapolis: University of Minnesota Press, 1960), pp. 109–122. Marx's interest in the vernacular has been a continuing one, as evidenced throughout his valuable study, *The Machine in the Garden. Technology and the Pastoral Ideal in America* (New York: Oxford University Press, 1964), and in other articles cited in these notes.

7.
The point is a commonplace of art criticism although it is very skillfully developed with respect to photography by Susan Sontag in *On Photography* (New York: Farrar, Straus and Giroux, 1977), p. 28. See also what is likely the most incisive political reading of photographs and film, her piece on the Nazi, Leni Riefenstahl, "Fascinating Fascism," *New York Review of Books* (6 February 1975), pp. 23–30.

8.
Paule Marshall, *The New York Times Book Review* (9 January 1983), p. 3. Marshall goes on to discuss the implications of common speech not only for contemporary women writers but for the modernist movement as well.

1. Context of the Photographs: FDR, FERA, AAA, RA, FSA
1.
Was FDR's concern an unexamined nostalgia for the land but one which masked a politician's desire for power? Was it his notorious realpolitik, articulated through a vast infrastruc-

ture of agencies the reigning Democrats controlled? Or was it part of a complex pastoral tradition he inherited, affirmed, and used? The first of these possibilities was put forth, brilliantly but cynically, in Richard Hofstadter's essay, "Franklin D. Roosevelt: The Patrician as Opportunist," in *The American Political Tradition* (New York: Alfred A. Knopf, 1948), pp. 311–347. The most recent examination of the second is Albert U. Romansco's *The Politics of Recovery: Roosevelt's New Deal* (New York: Oxford University Press, 1983). And pastoral, as it relates to the development of American technology and political power, may be seen in Leo Marx's previously cited book, *The Machine in the Garden.* There has been a long-standing tradition of dialogue between pastoralism and the urban environment, one of the more recent installments being Raymond Williams's fine study *The Country and the City* (New York: Oxford University Press, 1973). And worth exploring is Leo Marx's essay-review response, "Pastoral and Its Guises," *Sewanee Review*, Vol. 82, No. 2 (Spring 1974), pp. 351–362.

2.
Paul Fussell, *The Great War and Modern Memory* (New York: Oxford University Press, 1975). A thorough, bitter, eloquent testament to those who were battered in World War I's trench warfare.
3.
For the most interesting and humane account of this movement and what it meant in terms of personal transformations, see Robert Coles's *The South Goes North* (Boston: Atlantic-Little, Brown, 1972).

4.
"The Dangers of the Road," in *The Great Depression*, edited by David A. Shannon (Englewood Cliffs, New Jersey: Prentice-Hall, 1960), pp. 58–59.

5.
Charles Kindleberger, *Manias, Panics and Crashes: A History of Financial Crises* (New York: Basic Books, 1978).

6.
Quoted in many places, but seen to best advantage in Richard Hofstadter, "Hoover and the Crisis of American Individualism," in *The American Political Tradition*, p. 295.

7.
John M. Blum, et al. *The National Experience* (New York: Harcourt, Brace and World, 1963), p. 632.

8.
Dixon Wechter, *The Age of the Great Depression* (New York: Quadrangle Books, 1948, 1971), p. 17.

9.
William E. Leuchtenburg, *Franklin D. Roosevelt and the New Deal, 1932–1940* (New York: Harper & Row, 1963), p. 1.

10.
John Kenneth Galbraith, *The Great Crash* (Boston: Houghton Mifflin, 1954, 1961), pp. 182–183.

11.
Paul K. Conkin, *The New Deal* (New York: Thomas Y. Crowell, 1967, 1975), p. 37.

12.
Paul K. Conkin, *The New Deal*, p. 37.

13.
Michael Ross Grey, "Primary Care in the Great Depression: The Medical Care Program of the Farm Security Administration" (Senior Honors Thesis, The Committee on History and Science, Harvard University, 1980), p. 19.

14.
Arthur M. Schlesinger, Jr., *The Crisis of the Old Order, 1919–1933* (Boston: Houghton Mifflin, 1957), p. 458. Re-reading Schlesinger's detailed, often passionate account of the events leading to the Depression is a bracing antidote to the "crackpot realism" (to borrow a phrase from sociologist C. Wright Mills) of the 1980s, regarding the need for federal retrenchment in the face of a shifting national economy. Schlesinger's barely concealed outrage at the plight of

the dispossessed is especially striking when one considers he was writing during the anesthetized 1950s.

15.
Arthur M. Schlesinger, Jr. *The Crisis of the Old Order*, p. 3. Along the same terrifying lines, William E. Leuchtenburg quotes one A. N. Young, president of the Farmers' Union of Wisconsin, who told a Senate committee,

They [the farmers in his union] are just ready to do anything to get even with the situation. I almost hate to express it, but I honestly believe that if some of them could buy airplanes they would come down here to Washington and blow you fellows all up. . . . The farmer is naturally a conservative individual, but you cannot find a conservative farmer today. . . . I am as conservative as any man can be, but any economic system that has in its power to set me and my wife in the streets, at my age—what can I see but red? (*The Perils of Prosperity, 1914–1932* [Chicago: The University of Chicago Press, 1958], p. 262).

16.
Arthur M. Schlesinger, Jr., *The Crisis of the Old Order*, p. 3.

17.
Arthur M. Schlesinger, Jr., *The Crisis of the Old Order*, p. 453.

18.
Albert U. Romasco, *The Politics of Recovery*, p. 54.

19.
Albert U. Romasco, *The Politics of Recovery*, p. 57.

20.
Albert U. Romasco, *The Politics of Recovery*, p. 63.

21.
President Hoover, acting out an old pattern, had relied upon existing (private) social welfare agencies to provide relief. According to Richard S. Kirkendall, Hoover firmly believed that "this was the American way." Even after the Crash and as the crisis deepened, "he was confident

that the local agencies could succeed with only a small amount of help from the federal government." Reluctant to rely on state agencies (because it would suggest the problem was larger than isolated, local difficulties?), and fearful that a large federal relief effort would shake business confidence, Hoover's bottom line was that, in Kirkendall's judgment, "he feared the destruction of the American character by federal action" (*The United States, 1929–1945* [New York: McGraw-Hill, 1974], p. 25).

22.
William E. Leuchtenburg, *The Perils of Prosperity, 1914–1932*, p. 15. Also,

When municipal lodging houses became overcrowded, men huddled in empty freight cars or in shutdown factories. . . . In Arkansas, men were found living in caves. By the Salt River in Arizona, miners camped under bridges. In the great cities, girls slept on subways. Thousands of Americans wandered the country, aimlessly, in search of a job, or relief, or just a sense of motion. . . . By 1932, there were from 1 to 2 million men, including a few hundred thousand young boys, roaming the country. . . . In the St. Louis dumps, small groups of men, women, and children dug for rotten food. In Chicago, they stood outside the back doors of restaurants for leavings or scoured the market districts for spoiled fruit and vegetables. In the coal hills of Pennsylvania, families were fed on weeds and roots (pp. 253–254).

23.
Denial could go to great lengths during this desperate period, Leuchtenburg observes, as when "the President's own relief experts reported that unemployment was mounting to incredible levels, he [Hoover] would not believe them. Because of 'an aroused sense of public responsibility,' Hoover claimed, 'those in destitution and their children are actually receiving more regular and more adequate care than even in normal times.'" Quoted by William E. Leuchtenburg, *The Perils of Prosperity*, p. 255.

24.
Strongly contesting recent attempts to rehabilitate Hoover's reputation, Arthur M. Schlesinger,

Jr., questioned Hoover's "philosophy of voluntarism" on two points. First, that Hoover, though experienced as a large-scale engineer and planner, never took the time to think through whether his version of voluntarism (what has been characterized in that historical context as "guild capitalism") could work in the mass society America had become by the late 1920s. And second, that Hoover's voluntarism itself was a function of an equally particular reading of America and its history. Answering Hoover's 1932 speech that the "so-called new deals . . . would destroy the very foundations of our American system," Schlesinger replied, "Or, at least his American system: the system based on the principle of voluntarism, by which it was left to each individual to choose whether or not he would perform his social duty." Quoting one of those "unforgettable lines" from Hoover's memoirs ("Many persons left their jobs for the more profitable one of selling apples."), Schlesinger excoriated: "His voluntarism amounted to little more than defense of business syndicalism against social control—a defense delivered with an engineer's dogmatism and packaged in Quaker cant" ("Hoover Makes A Comeback," *New York Review of Books* (8 March 1979), pp. 12–14.

25.
Albert U. Romasco, *The Politics of Recovery*, p. 64.

26.
See Otis L. Graham's essay, "The Planning Ideal and American Reality: The 1930s," in *The Hofstadter Aegis*, edited by Stanley Elkins and Eric McKitrick (New York: Alfred A. Knopf, 1974), pp. 257–299. On Wallace, see other citations below and Arthur M. Schlesinger, Jr.'s analysis in *The Crisis of the Old Order*, previously cited, and in his *The Coming of the New Deal* (Boston: Houghton Mifflin, 1959). Three of Tugwell's books, cited in the bibliography, are particularly useful in this conection, as is Bernard Sternsher's *Rexford Tugwell and the New Deal* (New Brunswick: Rutgers University Press, 1964).

27.
"As a social worker," wrote Richard S. Kirkendall, "he [Hopkins] was convinced that the loss of a job was usually the result of forces beyond the individual's control and that the person on relief must not be made to feel like a pauper" (*The United States*, p. 51). Striking even harder at the worst of the Protestant work ethic which demanded that the unsuccessful be shamed if they sought public assistance, Hopkins argued for cash dispersal rather than commissary and, thereafter, for jobs rather than cash. A fascinating figure, see also Robert E. Sherwood's *Roosevelt and Hopkins* (New York: Harper & Brothers, 1948), Searle F. Charles's *Minister of Relief: Harry Hopkins and the Depression* (Syracuse: Syracuse University Press, 1963), and Paul A. Kurzman's *Harry Hopkins and the New Deal* (Fair Lawn, New Jersey: R. E. Burdick, 1974).

28.
See Paul K. Conkin's *FDR and the Origins of the Welfare State* (New York: Carvcle, 1967) and Donald S. Howd's *The WPA and Relief Policy* (New York: Russell Sage Foundation, 1943).

29.
Arthur M. Schlesinger, Jr., *The Coming of the New Deal*, p. 35.

30.
Arthur M. Schlesinger, Jr., *The Coming of the New Deal*, p. 35.

31.
Arthur M. Schlesinger, Jr., *The Coming of the New Deal*, p. 39.

32.
Arthur M. Schlesinger, Jr., *The Coming of the New Deal*, p. 71.

33.
David Eugene Conrad, *The Forgotten Farmers: The Story of Sharecroppers in the New Deal* (Urbana: University of Illinois Press, 1965), p. 1.

34.
Dwight Macdonald, *Henry Wallace: The Man and the Myth* (New York: Vanguard Press, 1948), p. 46.

35.
David Eugene Conrad, *The Forgotten Farmers*, chapter 1, "The American Peasants."

36.
Sidney Baldwin, *Poverty and Politics: The Rise and Decline of the Farm Security Administration* (Chapel Hill: University of North Carolina Press, 1968), p. 78.

37.
David Eugene Conrad, *The Forgotten Farmers*, p. 36.

38.
Dwight Macdonald, *Henry Wallace*, p. 47.

39.
"A farm," wrote Henry Wallace in 1930, "is an area of vicious, ill-tempered soil with a not very good house, inadequate barns, makeshift machinery, happenstance stock, tired, over-worked men and women—and all the pests and bucolic plagues that nature has evolved . . . where ugly, brooding monotony, that haunts by day and night, unseats the mind," as quoted in Sidney Baldwin, *Poverty and Politics*, p. 88. One must keep in mind that it was what Rexford Tugwell represented, as much as who he was as an individual, that made him so attractive in the Washington of the early 1930s. Large-scale federal planning was seen as the wave of the future then, and Tugwell was its cutting edge.

40.
Bernard Sternsher, *Rexford Tugwell and the New Deal*, p. 150.

41.
Bernard Sternsher, *Rexford Tugwell and the New Deal*, p. 194.

42.
Dwight Macdonald, *Henry Wallace*, p. 48.

43.
Richard S. Kirkendall, *Social Scientists and Farm Politics in the Age of Roosevelt* (Columbia: University of Missouri Press, 1966), p. 73.

44.
What it looked like from the standpoint of a tenant farmer, albeit an extraordinarily perceptive and articulate one, can be seen in a remarkable autobiography of the period, as told to Theodore Rosengarten, *All God's Dangers: The Life of Nate Shaw* (New York: Alfred A. Knopf, 1974). Shaw [Ned Cobb] describes land in an idiom deeply congruent with the brutalities that have been visited upon it by man and nature alike.

45.
Tugwell Rugwell was critical of the homestead and self-contained concept because he believed each looked to the past rather than to the future, to the individual rather than to cooperative units of social organization. Kirkendall quotes him making this point in a letter to FDR: "We need to be more cooperative," he wrote the President, "all of us, if we need anything in the world" (*Social Scientists and Farm Politics in the Age of Roosevelt*, pp. 129–130).

46.
Michael Ross Grey, "Primary Care in the Great Depression," p. 25.

47.
Richard S. Kirkendall, *Social Scientists and Farm Politics in the Age of Roosevelt*, pp. 110–111.

48.
Paul S. Conkin, *the New Deal*, p. 58.

49.
Sidney Baldwin, *Poverty and Politics*, p. 122.

50.
Pressing domestic difficulties also made resignation a necessity, given that Tugwell was highly visible and increasingly under fire. He did not desert the RA; rather, he pressed Wallace to make a 2000-mile trip through the South in order to see conditions for himself, thereby reinforcing the need for the RA's work. "The Secretary," wrote Arthur M. Schlesinger, Jr., of the journey, "returned . . . badly shaken." And Wallace himself wrote soon after that, "I have never seen among the peasantry of Europe poverty so abject as that which exists in this favorable cotton year in the great cotton States from Arkansas to the East coast." Wallace continued, "I am tempted to say that one third of the farmers of the United States live under conditions which are so much worse than the peasantry of Europe that the city people of the United States should be thoroughly ashamed" (*The Coming of the New Deal*, pp. 375–376).

51.
Baldwin suggests that the attacks, which were couched in terms of administrative critiques, masked the fundamental ideological disagreements critics would not voice. *Poverty and Politics*, p. 114.

52.
Sidney Baldwin, *Poverty and Politics*, p. 117.

53.
Sidney Baldwin, *Poverty and Politics*, p. 117.

54.
Calvin Kytle, "Roy Stryker: A Tribute," in *Roy Stryker: The Humane Propagandist* (Louisville, Kentucky: University of Louisville Press, 1977), p. 4.

55.
F. Jack Hurley, *Portrait of a Decade: Roy Stryker and the Development of Documentary Photography in the Thirties* (Baton Rouge: Louisiana State University Press, 1972), p. 12.

56.
F. Jack Hurley, *Portrait of a Decade*, p. 14.

57.
Judith Mara Gutman, *Lewis W. Hine and the American Social Conscience* (New York: Walker & Company, 1967), p. 9. The first to repossess Hine for more than straight historical reasons and opening with numerous useful questions about the nature of Hine's work and its making, Gutman's study disappoints the reader primarily because its subsequent rambling, episodic commentary never adds up to a consistent analysis.

58.
John R. Stilgoe, *Metropolitan Corridor: Railroads and the American Scene* (New Haven, Yale University Press, 1984). Stilgoe's study bypasses the period of the railroad's inception and focuses, instead, upon what Leo Marx has called "its glorious heyday, the half-century (1880–1930) between the effective completion of the national rail system and the beginning of its decline." During this period the railroad was the way to go; during most of it, the railroad was the *only* way to go, and Stilgoe makes concrete how, beyond the attractive, urban-influenced depots in small towns and in the countryside, not much else existed. Indeed, that the rail line remained a corridor, a strip of prosperous, citified, back-East environment, tells us much about the farm life with which it so starkly contrasted.

59.
Walter Rosenblum, foreword to *America & Lewis Hine, Photographs 1904–1940* (Millerton, New York: Aperture, 1977), p. 13.

60.
Alan Trachtenberg, essay in *America & Lewis Hine, Photographs 1904–1940*, p. 127. Anticipating the kind of reading of photographs that would increase over the next decade, Trachtenberg's excellent analysis weaves biography, history, politics, influences, and conventions with an attention to minute detail and larger symbol not dissimilar to his study of the Brooklyn Bridge. Dealing with the criticism of Hine's work photos as "weaker" than Hine's earlier investigations of children in factories and slums, however, Trachtenberg confuses his reader by retreating to the literary equivalent of achieved form. That is, he defends Hine's photographs of workers on the job by classifying them as "affirmative" (P. 133), in contradistinction, one supposes, to the "negative" but "stronger" images of Hine's earlier period. Rather than regard these as the complementary half and value their informational and other contributions, Trachtenberg has chosen to justify them aesthetically as well. Judged as art,

their formal characteristics may well represent a lesser achievement. But the point Trachtenberg appeared on his way to making was that the aesthetic dimension was only one of several important dimensions a viewer must consider in the evaluation of Hine's achievement. Prior to these statements, Trachtenberg quite properly rotated Hine's photos through a very large context; by suddenly suggesting that the aesthetic dimension constitutes the overarching evaluative criterion—the all-encompassing context—Trachtenberg not only undercuts his own argument but weakens his reader's appreciation for and understanding of Hine's work. Given the split in the American Studies movement between so-called highbrow evaluations (intellectual history and forms of the New Criticism as applied to literature) and lowbrow evaluations (the new social history and popular culture view of women's, black, and minority literature), such a rapid shift becomes more understandable.

More helpful is Trachtenberg's review of the Gutman and similar books in "Through the Lens of Social Vision," *The Nation*, 10 June 1968, pp. 766–768.

61.
F. Jack Hurley, *Portrait of a Decade*, p. 14.

Primary Care in the 1930s
Our informants on medical practice in the 1930s are by no means a representative sample, rather medical colleagues who willingly reminisced about their early practice years, as well as supplying us with notes. Thus, we are indebted to Drs. Lewis Dimsdale, now of Fort Lauderdale, Florida, for his account of practice in Sioux City, Iowa; Salvatore Lima for Boston's North End; John Angley, Max Pearlstein and Harriet L. Hardy for Pembroke, Northfield, and Braintree, Massachusetts, respectively; and William H. Goodson, Jr., for Kansas City, Missouri. Mrs. Mary Manningham, Winchester, Massachusetts, let us read letters to her children which detailed family medical problems in Wisconsin during those years.

1.
Robert A. Caro, *The Years of Lyndon Johnson. The Path to Power* (New York: Alfred A. Knopf, 1983), p. 508.

2.
F. Carleton Chapman, "The Flexner Report," *Daedalus*, Vol. 103, No. 1 (Winter 1974), p. 107.

3.
F. Carleton Chapman, "The Flexner Report," p. 107.

4.
Robert and Helen Merrell Lynd, *Middletown* (New York: Harcourt, Brace and Company, 1929), p. 435.

5.
Robert and Helen Merrell Lynd, *Middletown*, p. 435.

6.
O. L. Peterson, "Vanishing Physicians," *Annals of Internal Medicine*, 76:141 (1971). See also, *Health in the U.S., 1981* (Hyattsville, Maryland: U.S. Department of Health and Human Services, 1981) and *National Ambulatory Medical Survey, 1977*, Summary Series 13, No. 44, DHEW PH 5, 80, 1975 (DHEW, 1980).

7.
Committee on the Costs of Medical Care (CCMC), *Medical Care for the American People* (Chicago: University of Chicago Press, 1932).

8.
Robert and Helen Merrell Lynd, *Middletown*, both quotations p. 436.

9.
Charles S. Johnson, *Shadows of the Plantation* (Chicago: University of Chicago Press, 1934), p. 196.

10.
Charles S. Johnson, *Shadows of the Plantation*, p. 196.

11.
Charles S. Johnson, *Shadows of the Plantation*, p. 196.

12.
Charles S. Johnson, *Shadows of the Plantation*, p. 196.

13.
Charles S. Johnson, *Shadows of the Plantation*, p. 192. See also, Peter H. Wood's "People's Medicine in the Early South," *Southern Exposure*, VI, No. 1 (1978).

14.
Arthur F. Raper, *Preface to Peasantry: A Tale of Two Black Belt Counties* (Chapel Hill: University of North Carolina Press, 1936), p. 49.

15.
Rosemary Stevens, *American Medicine and the Public Interest* (New Haven, Connecticut: Yale University Press, 1971), p. 187.

16.
Arthur F. Raper, *Preface to Peasantry*, p. 48.

17.
Arthur F. Raper, *Preface to Peasantry*, p. 48. Raper continues: "The writer has seen a tenant farmer enter the store, explain to the storekeeper the ailings of his wife, and walk out with medicine. In one instance the man behind the counter asked whether the last bottle seemed to have helped; upon being told, 'Why not much, at any rate,' he turned to another shelf with, 'Well, John, you try this kind this time.'"

18.
Robert and Helen Merrell Lynd, *Middletown*, p. 437.

19.
Robert and Helen Merrell Lynd, *Middletown in Transition, A Study in Cultural Conflicts* (New York: Harcourt, Brace and Company, 1937), p. 397.

20.
Federal Writers' Project, *These Are Our Lives* (Chapel Hill: University of North Carolina Press, 1939), p. 32.

21.
Federal Writers' Project, *These Are Our Lives*, p. 82.

22.
Lewis Thomas, M.D., *The Youngest Science: Notes of a Medicine Watcher* (New York: The Viking Press, 1983), p. 21.

23.
Lewis Thomas, M.D., *The Youngest Science*, p. 21.

24.
CCMC, and note 31.

25.
Arthur E. Hertzler, M.D., *The Horse and Buggy Doctor* (New York: Harper Brothers, 1938), p. 61.

26.
Arthur E. Hertzler, M.D., *The Horse and Buggy Doctor*, p. 63.

27.
From office records, William Hammack Goodson, M.D., Liberty, Missouri, through the courtesy of his grandson, John D. Goodson, M.D., The Clinics, Massachusetts General Hospital.

28.
From office records, William Hammack Goodson, M.D. This note is exactly as it was written, not in the interest of embarrassing the writer but as an example of communication between doctor and patient in those times.

29.
B. K. Harris, "Plow Beams for Pills," in *These Are Our Lives*, p. 269.

30.
B. K. Harris, "Plow Beams for Pills," in *These Are Our Lives*, p. 269.

31.
Personal communication from physicians in practice during the 1930s: John Angley, Lewis Dimsdale, Salvatore Lima, Harriet L. Hardy, Max Pearlstein, and William H. Goodson, Jr.

32.
For this change, see Rosemary Stevens and Paul Starr cited earlier.

33.
William H. Goodson, Jr., M.D., letter to the authors, c. 1982.

34.
Arthur E. Hertzler, M.D., *The Horse and Buggy Doctor*, p. 131.

35.
Arthur E. Hertzler, M.D., *The Horse and Buggy Doctor*, p. 132.

36.
Arthur E. Hertzler, M.D., *The Horse and Buggy Doctor*, p. 253.

37.
Arthur E. Hertzler, M.D., *The Horse and Buggy Doctor*, p. 132.

38.
Lewis R. Tryon, M.D., *Poor Man's Doctor* (New York: Prentice-Hall, 1945), p. 124. Gayle Stephens, in *Continuing Education* (November, 1984), adds, "I even heard of two doctors [during the Great Depression] who carried guns for each other," p. 607.

39.
Robert and Helen Merrell Lynd, *Middletown*, p. 443.

40.
Robert and Helen Merrell Lynd, *Middletown*, p. 443.

41.
Thomas Neville Bonner, *The Kansas Doctor, A Century of Pioneering* (Lawrence, Kansas: University of Kansas Press, 1959), p. 223.

42.
Benjamin J. Gordon, M.D., *Between Two Worlds* (New York: Bookman Associates, n.d.), p. 319.

43.
Charles S. Johnson, *Shadows of the Plantation*, p. 196.

44.
Charles S. Johnson, *Shadows of the Plantation*, pp. 196–197.

45.
J. C. Furnas, *How America Lives* (New York: Henry Holt, 1941), p. 166. Not surprisingly, this *Ladies Home Journal* survey of "America" did not touch the wealthiest, even as it probed the lives of the poorest. And those of the upper middle class, who had high earnings rather than wealth, were not required to break down their budgets for *Journal* readers in anything like the detailed manner of the lower middle class or the working people who were set up as representatives of their group. These attitudes, interesting in and of themselves, also may be found in the way in which the camera recorded (or did not record) the doctor-patient relationship in private practice as opposed to hospital clinics—matters treated in chapter 3.

46.
J. C. Furnas, *How America Lives*, pp. 196–197.

47.
Lewis Thomas, M. D., as quoted by Stephen Jay Gould in "Calling Dr. Thomas," *New York Review of Books* (21 July 1983), p. 12.

48.
CCMC.

49.
Arthur F. Raper and I. D. Reid, *Sharecroppers* (Chapel Hill: University of North Carolina Press, 1941), p. 37.

50.
National Committee for the Defense of Political Prisoners, *Harlan Miners Speak* (New York: Harcourt, Brace, 1939), p. 86.

51.
B. K. Harris, *These Are Our Lives*, p. 270.

52.
Joseph A. Jerger, *Doctor—Here's Your Hat!* (New York: Prentice-Hall, 1939), p. 11.

53.
B. K. Harris, *These Are Our Lives*, p. 270.

54.
B. K. Harris, *These Are Our Lives*, p. 271.

55.
Charles S. Johnson, *Shadows of the Plantation*, p. 197.

56.
Frederick D. Mott and Milton I. Roemer, *Rural Health and Medical Care* (New York: McGraw-Hill Company, 1948), p. 217.

57.
As quoted in Michael Ross Grey, "Primary Care in the Great Depression," p. 15.

58.
Don Marquis, "Country Doctor," edited by N. Fabricant and H. Werner, *The World's Best Doctor Stories* (New York: Garden City Books, 1951), p. 3.

59.
Helen Ashton, *Doctor Serocold: A Page from His Day-Book* (New York: Doubleday, Doran, 1930), p. 168.

60.
Helen Ashton, *Doctor Serocold: A Page from His Day-Book*, p. 169.

61.
CCMC.

62.
CCMC.

63.
Annual Report of the Chief Medical Officer, FSA, July 1, 1940–June 30, 1941. U.S. Department of Agriculture, FSA (Washington: GPO, 1941).

64.
Michael Ross Grey, "Primary Care in the Great Depression," p. 16.

65.
Michael Ross Grey, "Primary Care in the Great Depression," p. 17.

66.
Michael Ross Grey, "Primary Care in the Great
Depression," p. 26.

67.
Michael Ross Grey, "Primary Care in the Great
Depression," p. 26.

68.
As quoted in Michael Ross Grey, "Primary Care
in the Great Depression," p. 37.

69.
Thomas Neville Bonner, *The Kansas Doctor, A
Century of Pioneering*, pp. 229–230.

70.
See tables 40 and 41, *Statistics, Encyclopedia of
Social Work*, Seventeenth Issue, edited by John
B. Turner (Washington, D.C.: National Associa-
tion of Social Workers, 1977), Vol. 2, pp. 1659,
1660–1661.

71.
As quoted in Michael Ross Grey, "Primary Care
in the Great Depression," Appendix 1.

72.
Michael Ross Grey, "Primary Care in the Great
Depression," p. 38.

3. Medical Photographs and the Doctor-Patient Relationship

Everyone has snapshots, and a considerable
literature in the form of collections, large and
small, has grown up around the formal portrait.

For a sound overview of the nation's images,
see Jonathan Green's *Critical History of
American Photography* (New York: Abrahms,
1984). Then look to Ben Maddow's *Faces: A
Narrative History of the Portrait in Photography*
(Boston: New York Graphic Society, 1977),
which may well outweigh all the others put
together—in actual pounds—and in numbers of
useful images. See especially these sections:
"Class and Conscience: Europe," pp. 228–257;
"America," pp. 258–307; and "The Studio
Portrait in the Twentieth Century," pp.

372–407. The socialization of the well-off is
only one of the subjects treated in the most
recent volume of Robert Coles's *Children of
Crisis* series, *The Privileged Ones* (Boston:
Atlantic-Little, Brown, 1977), one of the most
important psychological and political studies of
class as a process; and Coles contributes a
valuable introduction to Mary Lloyd Estrin's
laconic collection of middle-western wealthy, *To
the Manor Born* (Boston: New York Graphic
Society, 1979). Handsomely printed and well-
annotated, the "famous and infamous" fill 216
pages of diplomats, scientists, businessmen,
artists, sports greats, and outlaws, in Wesley
Maren's *Sincerely Yours* (Boston: New York
Graphic Society, 1983). An immodest word
from the professional photographer and a view
from the inside of that relationship may be had
with *In Search of Greatness: Reflections of Yousuf
Karsh* (New York: Alfred A. Knopf, 1962) and
also *Karsh Portraits* (Toronto: University of
Toronto Press, 1976) Karsh helps to define the
multiple motivations and multiple maneuvers of
sitter and portraitist, as Richard Avedon's
Portraits (New York: Farrar, Straus & Giroux,
1976) demonstrates the dominance of
photographer over subject. More sensationally,
we get the structure of the formal portrait
relationship in John Krobal's *The Eye of the
Great Hollywood Portrait Photographers,
1925–1940* (New York: Alfred A. Knopf, 1980),
and, more commercially, see Nancy Hall-
Duncan's *The History of Fashion Photography*
(New York: Alpine Book Company, 1979). Any
collection of Alfred Stieglitz, Paul Strand,
Edward Weston, or Edward Steichen
photographs will amply demonstrate changes in
the way "artists" have handled the portrait,
and an extremely interesting perspective on the
artist's studio a century earlier can be found in
Alan Trachtenberg's essay, "Brady's Portraits,"
The Yale Review (Vol. 73, No. 2, January 1984),
pp. 231–253.

As snapshots taken by industry and
government (or individual connected to either)
are increasingly becoming a part of serious

sociological studies of nineteenth-century industrialization, so snapshots of "domestic" life are gathering interest, either by cultural historians like Martha Banta (whose forthcoming book on images of women in the late nineteenth and early twentieth centuries utilizes snaps from her mother's album) or students of photography such as Jonathan Green, who organized and edited an issue of *Aperture* devoted to the so-called casual picture, "The Snapshot," *Aperture Monograph* (Vol. 19, No. 1, 1974). In his introduction, Green claims that "the word snapshot is the most ambiguous, controversial word in photography since the word art." Several collections by Michael Lesy plumb this ambiguity in the attempt to explode stereotypes or in the attempt to illuminate one or another aspect of American life, perhaps the most relevant here being his *Time Frames: The Meaning of Family Pictures* (New York: Pantheon Books, 1980).

The collection of medical photographs discussed in this chapter were part of Dr. Richard C. Cabot's classic, *Physical Diagnosis*, a text that was first published in 1900 and went through eleven editions in thirty-four years. A colleague, Dr. F. Dennette Adams, undertook the revision of Cabot's book in 1937, and Dr. Adams's version went through three more editions. That photographs of the doctor and patient together in the office were extremely uncommon before the 1930s is apparent in viewing a recent historical collection, *Illustrated Catalogue of the The Slide Archives of Historical Medical Photographs of Stony Brook* (Center for Photographic Images of Medicine and Health Care), compiled by Rima D. Apple (Westport, Conn: Green Wood Press, 1984). Some 2% of the 3016 photographs assembled showed doctor and patient together outside the hospital, and of these over half were of doctor and child—again suggesting that convention, or other reasons cited, prevented the camera's intrusion on adults. Though there are few medical photographs in collections other than the strictly medical for reasons cited in this essay, images of the doctor and patient together may

be found in works of art. An example would be *Medicine and the Artist, 137 Great Prints*, Selected with Commentary by Carl Zingrosser (New York: Dover, 1970). The photographer Eugene Smith made a fine photo-essay of this relationship in the late 1940s for *Life* magazine, "Country Doctor" (20 September 1948), pp. 115–126, and a thoughtful meditation along this line twenty years later was John Berger and Jean Mohr's, *A Fortunate Man: The Story of a Country Doctor* (London: Penguin Press, 1967), also published in the United States by Pantheon Books.

1.
Quoted in "Living in a Snapshot world," John A. Kouwenhoven, *Half a Truth Is Better than None* (Chicago: University of Chicago press, 1982), p. 147.

2.
John A. Kouwenhoven, "Living in a Snapshot World," p. 149.

3.
Dan Schiller, "Realism, Photography and Journalistic Objectivity in 19th Century America," *Studies in the Anthropology of Visual Communication*, Vol. 4, No. 2 (Winter 1977), p. 87.

4.
John A. Kouwenhoven, "Living in a Snapshot World," p. 154.

5.
Erving Goffman, "Gender Advertisements," *Studies in the Anthropology of Visual Communication*, Vol. 3, No. 2 (Fall 1976), p. 68.

6.
Karin Becker Ohrn, *Dorothea Lange and the Documentary Tradition* (Baton Rouge: Louisiana State University Press, 1980), p. 11.

7.
Erving Goffman, "Gender Advertisements," p. 70. See also his work, *The Presentation of Self in Everyday Life* (Garden City, New York: Doubleday, 1959).

8.
Erving Goffman, "Gender Advertisements,"
p. 102.

9.
Janet Mills Ragan and Albert D. Smouse, "Pose
Preference in Social and Business Photographs," *Studies in Visual Communication*, Vol.
7, No. 3 (Summer 1981), pp. 76–82. The authors assert on p. 76 that, given the choice,
"the particular photograph that each individual
chooses from an array of proofs is likely the
one that most closely approximates his or her
ideal self."

10.
Karin Becker Ohrn, *Dorothea Lange and the Documentary Tradition*, p. 11.

11.
Alison Gernsheim, "Medical Photography in
the Nineteenth Century," *Medical and Biographical Illustration*, 50 (London, 1961), pp.
147–156.

12.
Alison Gernsheim, "Medical Photography in
the Nineteenth Century," p. 150.

13.
The extent to which an artist remains committed or uninvolved, relative to his or her work
and its context, is no trivial question. Just what
relation an image-maker should maintain is explored by F. O. Matthiessen in his masterwork
interpretation of our culture, *American Renaissance*, where the daguerreotypist, in *The House
of the Seven Gables*, Clifford is slowly drawn
into a wealthy and powerful family. See "Hawthorne's Politics," *American Renaissance* (New
York: Oxford University Press, 1941), pp.
322–335. "His mind became a camera obscura,
a dark room which sensitively registered the in-
filtration of light from outside," observes Harry
Levin, comparing Hawthorne to yet another
brilliant moralist recluse, Marcel Proust. See
Harry Levin, *The Power of Blackness* (New York:
Vintage, 1958), pp. 36–42.

14.
Science as a discipline generally drew two different types of nineteenth-century Americans to
it, according to historian of science, Charles E.
Rosenberg. Scientific research was, he says, "a
means for achieving status and individual
achievement," for some, and for others it con-
firmed, in a less positive manner, their own
marginality, their own oddness with respect to
society as a whole. In Rosenberg's *No Other
Gods: On Science & American Social Thought*
(Baltimore: Johns Hopkins University Press,
1976), see especially "Science and Social Values
in Nineteenth-Century America: A Case Study
in the Growth of Scientific Institutions," pp.
135–152.

15.
Daniel M. Fox and James Terry, "Photography
and the Self-Image of American Physicians,
1880–1920," *Bulletin of the History of Medicine*,
52 (1978), p. 443.

16.
As quoted in Daniel M. Fox and James Terry,
"Photography and the Self-Image of American
Physicians," p. 442.

17.
Alison Gernsheim, "Medical Photography in
the Nineteenth Century," p. 150.

18.
Charles E. Rosenberg, "The Bitter Fruit: Hered-
ity, Disease, and Social Thought," in *No Other
Gods: On Science & Scientific Thought*, pp.
25–53. See also, Stephen Jay Gould, *The Mis-
measure of Man* (New York: W. W. Norton,
1982) as well as essays in *Ever Since Darwin:
Reflections in Natural History* (New York: Norton, 1977).

19.
Stu Cohen, "Letter to the Editor," *Radical
America* (July–August, 1977), p. 59. For a related discussion, see, *Truth & Falsehood in Visual Images*, Mark Roskill and David Carrier
(Amherst: University of Massachusetts Press,
1983). They are particularly skillful in rehears-

ing similar questions with respect to E. H. Gombrich's discussions of images.

20.
Mick Gidley, *American Photography* (London: British Association for American Studies, 1983), pp. 9–10.

21.
Daniel M. Fox and James Terry, "Photography and the Self-Image of American Physicians, 1880–1920," p. 453.

22.
Daniel M. Fox and James Terry, "Photography and the Self-Image of American Physicians, 1880–1920," p. 437.

23.
Although Roland Barthes's contributions are more appropriately discussed in chapter 5 when we deal with FSA captions [or texts, in Barthes's sense], his three relevant essays may be cited here: from the collection *Image, Music, Text: Essays Selected and Translated by Stephen Heath* (Glasgow: Fontana/Collins, 1977); "The Photographic Message," pp. 15–31; "Rhetoric of the Image," pp. 32–51; and "The Third Meaning," pp. 52–68.

24.
For Brady's photographs, see R. Meredith, *Mr. Lincoln's Camera Man: Mathew B. Brady* (New York: Scribner's, 1960) and James D. Horan, *Mathew Brady: Historian with a Camera* (New York: Crown, 1955). Precisely which Civil War photographs Brady made and which were made by his associates—under his direction or autonomously—is not at issue here.

25.
Walt Whitman, *Specimen Days*, with an introduction by Alfred Kazin (Boston: David R. Godine, 1971), p. 20.

26.
Walt Whitman, *Specimen Days*, p. 35. Group photographs, of surgeons from Finlay and Harewood hospitals, may be seen on p. 37; tra-

ditionally posed, what is immediately interesting about the two is that the doctors are in service dress in one, civilian dress in the other.

27.
Walt Whitman, *Specimen Days*, p. 42. This edition of Whitman's book contains not only Whitman's descriptions of how the field hospitals and convalescent camps were organized but accompanying photographs as well: "fancy to yourself a space of three to twenty acres of ground, on which are grouped ten or twenty very large wooden barracks, with, perhaps, a dozen or twenty, and sometimes more than that number, small buildings, capable altogether of accommodating from five hundred to a thousand or fifteen hundred persons. Sometimes these wooden barracks or wards, each of them perhaps from a hundred to a hundred and fifty feet long, are ranged in a straight row, evenly fronting the street; others are planned so as to form an immense V; and others again are ranged around a hollow square. They make altogether a huge cluster, with the additional tents, extra wards for contagious diseases, guardhouses, sutler's stores, chaplain's house; in the middle will probably be an edifice devoted to the offices of the surgeon in charge and the ward surgeons . . . " (p. 28).

28.
Specimen Days is, like that other Whitman monument, *Leaves of Grass*, a whole built from segments composed over time. Whitman describes his use of notes and diary, his methods of composition and revision, throughout *Specimen Days*; in this edition see, especially, pp. 3, 10, 17, 19, 31, 39, and the memorable phrase, "The real war will never get in the books," as he explains it on p. 60.

29.
John A. Kouwenhoven, "Living in a Snapshot World," p. 180.

30.
L. J. Henderson, M.D., "Physician and Patient as a Social System," *New England Journal of Medicine*, Vol. 212 (1935), pp. 819–823. Likely a

horror in Dr. Pickering's eyes, Henderson saw medicine as applied science, and Henderson's concern was not that physicians were in danger of being narrowed by science so much as they were in danger of being overwhelmed by it; science was a good thing, and if personal relations had become less important "relative," he noted, "to the new technology," the answer was not more of the humanities but a stiff dose of "the science of human relations" (p. 819). A biochemist by training, Henderson nevertheless had a genuine concern for the affective side of human experience and, believing that the valuable empirical and intuitive experience the physician gained in the course of his or her life seemed die with them, this was his alternative. Like many Americans of his time, Henderson had been exposed to European thought, but the exposure was scientific, not cultural or philosophical, and so it is understandable that his psychological modeling came from the mathematician Gibbs at Yale rather than the psychoanalyst Freud in Vienna.

31.
L. J. Henderson, M.D., "Physician and Patient as a Social System," p. 820.

32.
L. J. Henderson, M.D., "Physician and Patient as a Social System," p. 821.

33.
L. J. Henderson, M.D., "Physician and Patient as a Social System," p. 822.

34.
L. J. Henderson, M.D., "Physician and Patient as a Social System," pp. 822–823. Freud's remark, to be found in "On Beginning the Treatment" (1913), *The Standard Edition of the Complete Psychological Works of Sigmund Freud* (London: Hogarth Press, 1958, 1978), p. 139, belongs to that extremely useful series of papers on technique he wrote between 1911 and 1914. It is with this handful of essays—"The Handling of Dream-Interpretation in Psycho-Analysis" (1911), "The Dynamics of the Transference" (1912), "Remembering, Repeating and Working-Through" (1914), and "Observations on Transference-Love" (1915 [1914])—that the most direct sense of psychoanalysis as a practical treatment can be gained. Others, such as John Bowlby more recently, have explored the important implications of attachment itself.

35.
Harry Stack Sullivan, M.D., *The Psychiatric Interview*, edited by Helen Swick Perry and Mary Ladd Gawel (New York: Norton, 1954, 1970). The title for this particular compilation of Sullivan's work is unfortunate because the impression given is static. Sullivan details the interview, but for him it is part of a continuing process of interpersonal psychotherapy; therefore, the interview is a paradigm for that process and as such, dynamic.

36.
Harry Stack Sullivan, M.D., *The Psychiatric Interview*, p. 57.

37.
Jay Haley, "Symptoms as Tactics in Human Relationships," *Strategies of Psychotherapy* (New York: Grune & Stratton, 1963), pp. 9–10.

38.
Jay Haley, "Symptoms as Tactics in Human Relationships," p. 10.

39.
Psychoanalyst William F. Murphy told us that audio recording of doctor-patient interviews for the teaching of psychiatric residents began in the Boston area in 1945 when a wire recorder was made available to him and his colleagues at the Veterans' Hospital (Conversation, August 1984). See his oft-cited study, with Felix Deutsch, M.D., *The Clinical Interview, Volume One: Diagnosis, A Method of Teaching Associative Exploration* (New York: International Universities Press, 1955). The video camera was introduced into medical clinics for teaching and research purposes in the 1970s; see this traced in "Learning Medicine by Videotaped Recordings," John D. Stoeckle, Aaron Lazare, Charles Weingarten, and Michael McGuire, *Journal of Medical Education* 56: (1971), pp. 518–520.

4. Ideology and the Vernacular

1.

Walker Evans, *First and Last Photographs* (New York: Harper & Row, 1978); F. Jack Hurley, ed., *Russell Lee, Photographer* (Dobbs Ferry, New York: Morgan and Morgan, 1978); Milton Meltzer, *Dorothea Lange. A Photographer's Life* (New York: Farrar, Straus and Giroux, 1978); and Arthur Rothstein, *the Depression Years, As Photographed by Arthur Rothstein* (New York: Dover, 1978). Other FSA books have since appeared, though the situation described has remained the same. See, for example, *Dorothea Lange. Photographs of a Lifetime. An Aperture Monograph* (Millerton, New York: Aperture, 1982).

2.

Morris Dickstein, who should know better, opens his full-page review of *The Great Depression* (framed by FSA photographs top and bottom) with: "Thanks to Walker Evans, Dorothea Lange and other great photographers who worked for the Farm Security Administration, we have a collective dream of what the Great Depression looked like . . . " ("Poverty, Shame and Self-Reliance," a review of Robert S. McElvaine's *The Great Depression, The New York Times Book Review* [22 January 1984] p. 9.)

3.

Karl Mannheim, in his classic study, *Ideology and Utopia* (New York: Harvest Books, 1936, 1968), categorized ideas that defended the social order as "ideological" and those that sought to change it as "utopian." An all-inclusive, comprehensive account of reality—which was an admixture of passion, belief, and idea—was considered a total ideology, whereas a similar thought system which, in the Marxist sense, represented an explicit party, faction, grouping, or institution, was considered a partial ideology.

The concept of ideology emerged late in the eighteenth century in France as a positive means of clarifying, intellectually, the political landscape. Napoleon gave ideology its negative connotation, however, by blaming his fall from power on the intellectuals of the Institut National, whom he scorned as *ideologues*. Karl Marx rejected this reactive labeling as a kind of idealism, arguing that ideas were neither autonomous nor neutral, that they always served one material interest or another and that, by definition, accepting any idea apart from the particular context of history and the particular class that produced it resulted in "false consciousness" rather than anything like objective truth. Heir to the previous world-explanatory system—religion—ideology to Marx was freighted with what he considered religion's necessarily irrational trappings: dogma, ritual, and revelation. The priest had given way to the intellectual, and instead of serving the Church he now served the State.

Marx insisted that instead of clarifying reality, intellectuals mystified it; the task of any critical thinking individual, whether intellectual or not, was to unmask these ideologies by examining their *function*, not their *content*. A half-century later, the New Deal may be said to have institutionalized federal intervention in local affairs as well as in an enormously larger state. While the content of its ideology was and remains a matter of considerable disagreement, it is the functions of the New Deal we refer to in this book when we are using the term "dominant" ideology.

See Norman Birnbaum's "The Sociological Study of Ideology, 1940–1960," *Current Society*, Vol. IX, No. 2 (Oxford, 1960), as well as the first part of Daniel Bell's controversial *The End of Ideology* (Glencoe, Illinois: Free Press, 1960) and George Lichtheim's "The Concept of Ideology," in *The Concept of Ideology* (New York: Vintage, 1967). An excellent gathering of the rich arguments on ideology, its political, religious, and psychological dimensions, may be had from *The End of Ideology Debate*, edited by Chaim I. Waxman (New York: Clarion Books, 1968). Applied to a major work of cultural explication, see George Abbott White's "Ideology and Literature: F. O. Matthiessen's *American Renaissance*," in *Literature in Revolution*, edited by

George Abbott White and Charles Newman (New York: Holt, Rinehart & Winston, 1972), pp. 430–500.

4.
John Collier, as quoted in Hank O'Neal's *A Vision Shared: A Classic Portrait of America and Its People, 1935–1943* (New York: St. Martin's Press, 1976), p. 293. See also Collier's *Visual Anthropology* (New York: MacMillan, 1958).

5.
Roy Stryker Collection, University of Louisville Photographic Archives, Louisville, Kentucky.

6.
Ben Shahn, as quoted in *The Photographic Eye of Ben Shahn*, edited by Davis Pratt (Cambridge, Massachusetts: Harvard University Press, 1975), p. x.

7.
For all the assembled information, this is in sum the reformist message one finds in William Stott's *Documentary Expression and Thirties America* (New York: Oxford University Press, 1973). Stott's examination of documentary is primarily an aesthetic one, uninformed by either a critical history or a critical politics. As a result, the book's moral judgments become the very strain of document they claim to discredit: manipulative moralizing. Leaving aside the argument that all documentary is by nature manipulative, it is as if the reader is made to "feel bad" about certain economic and social conditions in the United States in the absence of any solutions or, worse, any substantive explanations. An impressive close analysis of Walker Evans's photographs, which sharply delineates the difference between Evans's intentions and those of his subjects (the ones we know from *Let Us Now Praise Famous Men* [1941]), redeems an otherwise misleading excursion through the genre.

8.
It should go without saying that the following historical reconstruction is of the sort that can only take place at a very great distance, and only after information and arguments from numerous sources have been carefully sifted, discussed, and resifted. Even then, it cannot be assumed that all parties will agree, not only on what happened or what did not happen but what it meant that X happened and Y did not. Sadly, partisans of individual historical actors or institutions will routinely treat such macroanalyses as nothing less than the imputation of "conspiratorial" motives toward their favorites, insisting that no one knew what was occurring, or that A did not know what was occurring, or that A did, and that it is the analysis that has misunderstood or distorted A's true motives. The necessity of the Russian Revolution is a good example of this category of historical work, and Lenin's role, as seen by Trotsky, is a good example of this subsequent partisan inquiry.

9.
A description of the sophisticated forms of "information" distribution may be found in Sidney Baldwin's *Poverty and Politics*, pp. 118–119. Reading this, one can see that, from its inception, the Historical Section was explicit about its role, even if Stryker also had plans of his own for it.

10.
These are available in several casebooks on the 1930s, for example, *The New Deal*, edited by Morton Keller (New York: Holt, Rinehart & Winston, 1963), *The Great Depression and American Capitalism*, edited by Robert F. Himmelberg (Boston: D. C. Heath, 1968), and *The New Deal: The Critical Issues*, edited by Otis L. Graham, Jr. (Boston: Little, Brown, 1974). Perhaps the single most illuminating essay is Barton J. Bernstein's "The New Deal: The Conservative Achievements of Liberal Reform," in *Towards a New Past: Dissenting Essays in American History* (New York: Pantheon Books, 1968), pp. 263–288. For additional material, consult the bibliographical note below.

11.
As cited above.

12.

Less commonplace though no less well argued, this position may be founded at the center of the large literature on the Cold War that was produced during the 1960s and 1970s. D. F. Fleming's early work, *The Cold War and Its Origins* (in two volumes, Garden City, New York: Doubleday, 1961), does not suffer by comparison with later, more intimately informed European studies such as Andre Fontaine's *History of the Cold War* (in two volumes, New York: Pantheon Books, 1968, 1969), see pp. 321–329; or later American scholarship such as Joyce and Gabriel Kolko, *The Limits of Power* (New York: Harper & Row, 1972), see pp. 359–383, 428–452, and 453–476; and, also in this context, Michael Paul Rogin's *The Intellectuals and McCarthy* (Cambridge, Massachusetts: MIT Press, 1967), especially pp. 216–260.

13.

Titles that suggest deep as well as broad aesthetic study on Stryker's part were in his library, books such as *Vision in Motion* by Moholy Nagy, Doherty notes, and Kepes's *Language of Vision*. He continues, "These weren't just accidents in the library of an economist who thought all artists were a little peculiar . . . there seems to be evidence that [Ben] Shahn personally undertook the art education of Roy Stryker." Moreover, Doherty writes that Stryker authorized a chapter for the third edition of the Leica Manual in 1938, surely one of the more sophisticated pieces of photographic equipment then and now. See Robert J. Doherty's "The Elusive Roy Stryker," in *Roy Stryker: The Humane Propagandist* (Louisville, Kentucky: University of Louisville Press, 1977), p. 11.

14.

Pare Lorenz, as quoted in Milton Meltzer, *Dorothea Lange*, p. 105.

15.

Perhaps the most self-conscious, self-critical form this has ever taken may be found in James Agee's *Let Us Now Praise Famous Men* (Boston: Houghton Mifflin, 1941). There, typical of what is scattered throughout, is the following: "When they saw the amount of equipment [Walker Evans's camera equipment] stowed in the back of our car, they showed that they felt they had been taken advantage of, but said nothing" (p. 25). The most recent biographical account of this is Laurence Bergreen's *James Agee: A Life* (New York: Dutton, 1984), in chapter 8, appropriately enough titled, "Spies" (pp. 158–182). See Walker Evans's comment on the experience in *Remembering James Agee*, edited with an introduction by David Madden (Baton Rouge: Louisiana State University Press, 1974), pp. 104–107, and chapter 4, "A Way of Seeing," in Alfred T. Barson's *A Way of Seeing* (Amherst, Massachusetts: University of Massachusetts Press, 1972), pp. 71–105.

Although Bergreen describes Agee's means of gaining access to the center of the three sharecroppers' lives as a mixture of "chance and cunning" (p. 170), this was nothing as compared to invasions of privacy by other photographers of the times. Agee and Evans's caustic attitude toward Margaret Bourke-White in this regard is conveniently available in the form of a third "note" to *Let Us Now Praise Famous Men*, which simply reprints portions of a *New York Post* column on her that manages to be chic, bouncy, breathless, and savaging simultaneously. " 'You can't possibly miss her,' Miss Bourke-White's secretary told me [the *Post* author], 'because she's wearing the reddest coat in the world.'. . . A superior red coat, Miss Bourke-White called it, and such fun. It was designed for her by Howard Greer, and if you're as little up on your movie magazines as I am, you'd better explain that the Greer label is some pumpkins." More to the point, " . . . this is the young lady who spent months of her own time in the last two years traveling the back roads of the deep south bribing, cajoling, and sometimes browbeating her way in to photograph Negroes, share-croppers and tenant farmers in their own environment." After a sampling of her technical "ingenuity," such as intruding into black and white worship services with "exploding flashlights" and "bribing" subjects with "Buttercup and Rooster snuff," the *Post* writer records Bourke-White expounding on the white fundamentalist church: " 'The Negro churches are not, somehow, so shocking, because you think of Negroes as being actors and emotional, but with the white people the whole business is so sordid and desperate and out of place. It isn't as though their church played any role, as we know religion. It's just a place where people go to shout and scream and roll on the floor.' " Two decades did nothing to inform Bourke-White's monumental insensitivity, as she repeats virtually the same tone and diction in her autobiography, *Portrait of Myself* (New York: Simon & Schuster, 1963); see p. 134 especially.

16.
For each, the world of high-pressure, high-budget, high-income image manufacture was nothing new; Evans's father had been an executive with Lord & Thomas, a Chicago-based advertising firm of national stature. The son received art training at, in his words, "expensive private schools" and, after dropping out of Williams College, spent a year at the Sorbonne in 1926 which, he later remarked, allowed him "a revolutionary eye education" in that he was able to directly view the School of Paris painters. Lange's first marriage was to the professional painter and muralist Maynard Dixon, and she followed an apprenticeship in commercial (photographic) portrait work in New York City with the establishment of a West Coast studio that, like her husband's murals, catered to San Francisco's well-off. Lee began as a chemical engineer and advanced to plant manager in Kansas City, where the combination of a first marriage to a painter and an inherited income from several of his grand-uncle's farms encouraged/allowed him to move to what he termed "the world of West Coast art" in 1929 and, then, an "artist's colony" at Woodstock, New York, in 1931. There, like the others, Lee learned who bought what and what they were looking for in what they bought.

17.
Eudora Welty, *One Time, One Place* (New York: Random House, 1971), p. 6.

18.
Eudora Welty, *One Time, One Place*, pp. 6–7.

19.
Susan Sontag, *On Photography*, p. 24.

20.
The term is ours, the designation photographer Christopher Seiberling's, though neither he nor we are entirely satisfied with the actual word. A considerable debate has raged, of course, among those who make photos as to whether they are artists or photographers. As can be imagined, each term carries considerable freight. Until a more apt word comes along, the controversy is acknowledged, but the word is retained because of its useful association with formal, aesthetic properties.

21.
It is "Dust storm, Cimarron County, Oklahoma, 1936," in *The Depression Years*; "Dust storm, Cimarron County, 1936. Arthur Rothstein," in *Portrait of a Decade*; "Rothstein. Fleeing a dust storm; Cimarron County, Oklahoma, 1936," in Roy Emerson Stryker and Nancy Wood's *In This Proud Land: America 1935–1943 as Seen in the FSA Photographs* (Boston: New York Graphic Society, 1973); and "Father and sons walking in the face of a dust storm, Cimarron County, Oklahoma, April 1936, Rothstein," in *A Vision Shared*. The latter comes closest to the titling on the copy of the print in the files at the Prints and Photographs division, Library of Congress.

How the FSA photographs received their captions in those files is as interesting and difficult a question as how they have received their captions elsewhere. Historians of the FSA photographs have made many suggestions but have not sorted out precisely either the process or the participants, and it may well be an impossible task at this late date. But we do know that the photographers themselves had preferences, even demands—especially Dorothea Lange—

and that Stryker played a role in the caption process as well (all to be at least discussed as we read the medical photographs in chapter 5).

23.

Little wonder, then, that these are among the most emotionally satisfying photographs of the FSA photographers, or that the photographs that are more explicitly portraits are almost without exception extraordinary with respect to elements of composition, selection, finish, etc. Those by Lange ("Migratory laborer's wife near Childress, Texas, June 1938"; "Woman of the Plains" and "Ex-slave, Alabama, 1937") and Lee ("Negro Crossing himself and praying over grave in cemetery. All Saints Day, New Rocks, Louisiana, October 1938" and "Former Sharecropper, New Madrid, Missouri, 1938"), for example, are so superior as formal portraits that they cross the boundary into Evans's domain, discussed later.

23.

Evans's notes, separated from his photographs in *First and Last*, neglect to say *where* in Alabama. This nonreferential quality makes captions irrelevant, since the emotion generated routinely overwhelms the caption's intended specificity, short-circuits, in one sense, the caption's attempt at dialogue with the image. This kind of contradiction is especially harsh with a photographer like Lange, whose style the more she worked with her social policy/sociologist husband, Paul Taylor, was to wed word with image, was to get down "their exact words" and then to carefully use those words as an "extension" of the photograph. In collaborative works with Paul Taylor, either for state/national agencies or state/national legislative committees, this caption material is a rich resource, but a classic portrait like her "Migrant Mother," for exmaple, simply sweeps it away as the composition of mother and child (children) whisks the viewer from California to Rome, to the Vatican's *Pieta* rather than Gallo's grapes.

24.

Erich Auerbach, *Literary Language and Its Public in Late Latin Antiquity and in the Middle Ages* (New York: Pantheon Books, 1965).

25.

F. O. Matthiessen, *American Renaissance. Art and Expression in the Age of Emerson and Whitman* (New York: Oxford University Press, 1941), "The Word One with the Thing," Book One, Chapter One, Section 4, pp. 30–34. The Emerson quote is on page 35.

26.

R. W. Brunskill, *Vernacular Architecture of the Lake Counties* (London: Faber and Faber, 1974), p. 15. See also, John Brinckerhoff Jackson's *Discovering the Vernacular Landscape* (New Haven, Connecticut: Yale University Press, 1984) and *Landscapes* (Amherst, Massachusetts: University of Massachusetts Press, 1970).

27.

Roy Emerson Stryker letter to Russell Lee, January 1937. Roy Emerson Stryker Collection, University of Louisville, Photographic Archive, Louisville, Kentucky.

28.

"Let Us Now Praise Famous Folk," *The New York Times Magazine* (25 May 1980), pp. 31, 32, 34, and 36. See also, "Emma's Story: Two Versions," as told to Bradford L. Jenkin, *Southern Exposure*, Vol. VII, No. 1 (1979), pp. 8–26.

29.

Vernacular pictures should not be understood as somehow immune to the forces of ideology in a given culture that press on the other modes of visual representation; nor is their superior status, with respect to the other modes, a given. Leo Marx has written perceptively about this problem with Mark Twain's *Huckleberry Finn* as example. He has argued that while the imaginative use of the vernacular may be that novel's distinctive feature, the novel's success— as a novel—should not be entirely attributed to the use of the vernacular. "It means nothing," writes Marx, "to contend that the novel is great because it is written in the native idiom unless, that is, we mean to impute some intrinsic or absolute value to the vernacular. That would be ridiculous" ("The Pilot and the Passenger: Landscape Convention and the Style of *Huckleberry Finn*," *American Literature* [XXVII, May 1953], reprinted *Mark Twain, A Collection of Critical Essays*, edited by Henry Nash Smith [Englewood Cliffs, New Jersey: Prentice-Hall, 1963], p. 48). Whether the vernacular has no intrinsic value or whether its value is always a function of the skill with which it is utilized, its skillful contrast with other modes of discourse, is a nice question. In the psychoanalytic tradition, however, a central aspect of a successful treatment—an index of the patient's relative health—is the patient's ability to cut beneath successive layers of abstraction and adopted speech and to speak in his or her own language.

30.
These are all defenses and mobilized with good reason because they ward off the central problem of power. Take a psychoanalytically informed and politically liberal critic like Lionel Trilling, who could still write of *Let Us Now Praise Famous Men* soon after it was published, "[The one failure] . . . is not a literary failure . . . it is a failure of moral realism. It lies in Agee's [but not Evans's too?] inability to see these people as anything but good. . . . What creates this falsification is guilt . . . despite Agee's clear consciousness of his guilt, he cannot control it" ("Greatness with One Flaw in It," *Kenyon Review*, IV, i, 1942). The operative word here is, of course, *control*, and Trilling's concern was that intellectuals should explore their own privilege relative to others' oppression but not lose control while doing so. Whether Evans read Trilling or not, he certainly demonstrated his annoyed disregard for such critiques when it came time for a second edition of *Let Us Now Praise Famous Men*. Perfectly aware that he had his version of their lives, Evans now added their version—their posed presentations of self—this time around.

31.
Leo Marx, " 'Noble Shit': The Uncivil Response of American Writers to Civil Religion in America," *The Massachusetts Review* (Autumn 1973), pp. 709–739.

32.
Milton Meltzer, *Dorothea Lange*, p. 153.

5. Reading the FSA Medical Photographs

1.
Dorothea Lange put it fairly strongly when she said, "Everything is propaganda for what you believe in actually. I don't see how it could be otherwise. The harder and more deeply you believe in anything, the more in a sense you're a propagandist. Conviction, propaganda, faith. I don't know. I never have been able to come to the conclusion that that's a bad word" (*Dorothea Lange. Photographs of a Lifetime*, p. 153. See also John D. Stoeckle, M.D.'s introduction and forthcoming collection of essays on the doctor-patient relationship, *Encounters: Doctors and Patients* (Cambridge: The MIT Press, 1985).

2.
Within the main room of the Department of Prints and Photographs, Library of Congress, is a set of files in which all the FSA photographs are kept on positive microfilm chronologically (in the order in which they were made) and indexed by photographer. A card catalogue orders this material and gives the assignments (locations and duration) of each photographer while making the photographs. One uses the photographer, under this system, to get the negative series numbers, and it is therefore possible to view the entire series a photographer shot while on a particular assignment. Another file of FSA photographs exists in a separate location, the National Archives, and this includes photographs shot by FSA photographers while on loan to various other government agencies during this period, agencies such as the Department of Agriculture, the Office of War Information (OWI), and the Public Health Service. Sometimes these latter photographs turn up in

the large-format stand-up files in the Department of Prints and Photographs, but sometimes
they do not, and a researcher must call them
up from the negative series cards. Recently, another extremely interesting series of FSA photographs has come to light: color. A little over
600 of these images have been located, and in
addition to being catalogued in the card catalogue described above, they are also on a
videotape viewer. See Sally Stein's article, "FSA
Color: The Forgotten Document," *Modern Photography*, Vol. 43, No. 1 (January 1979).

3.
Personal communication to us, 3 March 1978.

4.
Personal communication to us, 30 October
1979.

5.
John Tagg, "The Currency of the Photograph,"
in *Thinking Photography*, edited by Victor Burgin
(London: Macmillan, 1982), p. 126.

6.
James Borchert, "Analysis of Historical Photographs: A Method and a Case Study," *Studies
in Visual Communication*, Vol. 7, No. 4 (Fall
1981), p. 39. The case of Evans's tenure with
the FSA is discussed in Hank O'Neal's *A Vision
Shared*, pp. 61–62. This latter is a situation
where people cannot help but choose sides.
Given the fact that Walker Evans could only
work in a certain slow, methodical manner,
making discrete, high-quality images, and that
the FSA required many, many photographs on
a continuous basis, what other outcome was
possible?

7.
"Shortly after Gardner Cowles brought out the
first issues of *Look*, Stryker wrote him a letter
that almost guaranteed the publisher's good-
will. He promised an exclusive scoop of the
government's photographs in exchange for possible publication" (Sally Stein, "FSA Color: The
Forgotten Document," p. 94). Stein's perceptive,
well-written account of the FSA's use of Koda-

chrome adds one more facet to our estimate of
Stryker's marketing distribution skills by answering the question as to how it was the FSA
was not as uncolored as people have believed.
According to Stein, the relatively expensive and
complicated-to-use color film was introduced by
Stryker in anticipation of a color market. She
writes, "Color was part of Stryker's strategy of
anticipating the future and radically different
requests that would be made upon the FSA
file" (p. 95).

8.
The actual construction of the "new" filing system was begun in 1942 while the FSA photographs were under their most severe
congressional attack and while Stryker was ar-
ranging, with Archibald MacLeish, to have
them transferred to the Library of Congress and
housed there permanently. A professional ar-
chivist, Paul Vanderbilt, was hired especially
for this task. That Vanderbilt conceived the system for the File out of what he found suggests
Stryker's underlying organization, which Stryker undoubtedly discussed with Vanderbilt as
the cataloguing process was under way. That
Stryker did not himself set up the system seems
obvious: Running the Historical Section and
trying to save the File from its critics inside and
outside the government, he had nothing like
the time such a project demanded.

9.
Roy Emerson Stryker and Nancy Wood, *In This
Proud Land*, p. 188. Other shooting scripts and
relevant correspondence may be found in Stryker's papers at The University of Louisville and
in the papers of the FSA in the National
Archives.

10.
Carolyn Kinder Carr, ed., *Ohio: A Photographic
Portrait* (Akron, Ohio: Akron Art Institute,
1980), p. 93.

11.
Howard S. Becker, "Photography and Sociol-
ogy," Studies in the *Anthropology of Visual
Communication*, Vol. 1, No. 1 (Fall 1974), p. 6.

This essay, like all of Becker's writings on photography, repays rereading.

12.
James Borchert, "Analysis of Historical Photographs," p. 39.

13.
Workers of the Writers' Program of the Works Progress Administration (WPA) of West Virginia, *West Virginia, American Guild Series* (New York: Oxford University Press, 1941), pp. 376–377. This extraordinary series of guidebooks, for all the states and including many major cities and some areas of particular interest (*Skiing in the East* and *Virginia's Negroes*, for example), is as great a national resource as the FSA photographs. In production at about the same time, WPA guidebooks were used by the FSA photographers, and FSA photographs found their way into many WPA guidebooks. It is no accident, therefore, that more than a few FSA projects and project towns are thoroughly described in the books.

14.
Christopher Seiberling informs us that, as late as 1976, the sign for the Taos clinic still stood.

15.
The Photographic Eye of Ben Shahn, edited by Davis Pratt.

16.
The black bag, along with the white coat, stethoscope, and other objects used to depict the doctor and the doctor's authority, is discussed in Dan W. Blumhagen's "The Doctor's White Coat. The Image of the Physician in Modern America," *Annals of Internal Medicine*, Vol. 91 (1979), pp. 111–116.

17.
Paul Goodman, "The Meaning of Functionalism," *Journal of Architectural Education*, Vol. 14 (1959) p. 32. For the photographs and the lengthy, informative introduction by Peter Gay, as well as the valuable comments by the photographer, see *Berggasse 19. Sigmund Freud's Home and Offices, Vienna, 1939. The Photographs of Edmund Engelman* (New York: Basic Books, 1976).

18.
See Robert Sommer, *Personal Space, The Behavioral Basis of Design* (Englewood Cliffs, New Jersey: Prentice-Hall, 1969) and, among others, Edward T. Hall, "Proxemics," *Current Anthropology*, 9:83 (1968) and Norman Ashcraft and Albert E. Scheflen, *People Space: The Making and Breaking of Human Boundaries* (Garden City, New York: Doubleday, 1976).

19.
Alan Trachtenberg, "Camera Work: Notes toward an Investigation," *The Massachusetts Review* (special issue on photography), Vol. XIX, No. 4 (Winter 1978), p. 838.

20.
Stanley Joel Reiser, "The Stethoscope and the Detection of Pathology by Sound," *Medicine and the Reign of Technology* (Cambridge: Cambridge University Press, 1978), pp. 23–44. Reiser guides us through major instruments and elements of modern medicine from a historic perspective.

21.
As noted earlier, here, and toward the end of this chapter, the "documentary" quality of documentary photographs must always be taken with a grain of salt. The viewer must constantly ask, What is this saying? and avoid inferences not supported by what can be seen in the photograph, aided by the accompanying text. A number of these medical photographs demonstrate how mercurial emotional states can be. The boy who is surly to the doctor in Maricopa County, Arizona, for example, in a shot later in the sequence is shown smiling to the nurse who hands him, we might infer, some medication.

22.
Gwen Kinkead, "Humana's Hard-Sell Hospitals," *Fortune* (17 November 1980), pp. 68ff. As this book goes to press, another chapter is

being written in the health-for-profit saga which threatens to undercut what little claim remains in medicine's altruistic philosophical underpinnings. Attitudes regarding profit and advertising promoting medical care are current in ways that would have been unthinkable, much less publishable, during the Depression. The Massachusetts General Hospital in Boston put its flagship psychiatric unit, McLean Hospital, up for sale to the Hospital Corporation of America, mentioned in Kinkead's article. After an internal struggle of some proportions, the sale was ultimately defeated by the faculty of the Harvard Medical School. For a measured response to the sale in the initial stages of that struggle, see Dr. Francis D. Moore's letter to the editor in the *Boston Globe* (22 August 1983), p. 13.

23.
Christopher Lasch and others have bemoaned the cult of the "expert" in American society and his/her intervention in the contemporary American family which, admittedly, has had its horrific aspects. On the other hand, the increase in hair lice and the reappearance of certain childhood diseases in public and private schools has recently encouraged a number of intellectuals and their essentially middle-class followers to rethink their positions on certain public human service interventions. Curiously, few of these examinations of experts have begun with what the bulk of the American population might actually need in the way of health and human services and what social policies might provide them in decent and timely fashion. For a thoughtful discussion of American social policy and social change in the twentieth century, see Ann Withorn's *Serving the People* (New York: Columbia University Press, 1984).

24.
David Eugene Conrad, *The Forgotten Farmers*, p. 15.

25.
Walter Benjamin, "The Work of Art in an Age of Mechanical Reproduction," in *Illuminations*, edited with an introduction by Hannah Arendt (New York: Schocken Books, 1969), pp. 217–251. This fascinating essay is justly celebrated for its then and still fresh view of the implications of reproduction in art, and not merely mechanical reproduction. Benjamin begins with the observation that a works of art have always been copied—by the artists themselves for models, by the artists' students as teaching aides, and by crooks. The difference now, which Benjamin elaborates, is that the process of reproduction is open to a larger and larger public, whereas in earlier times it was an entirely private operation.

26.
Walter Benjamin, "The Work of Art in an Age of Mechanical Reproduction," p. 221.

27.
Walter Benjamin, "The Work of Art in an Age of Mechanical Reproduction," p. 226.

28.
Examples abound, but historians of medicine and internists in the early 1940s may wonder about the caption for photograph [37], which has a child inoculated with measles vaccine years before it was available. Outright errors and general difficulties with the FSA captions are discussed in other works, notably the excellent catalogue of Walker Evans's FSA photographs, *Walker Evans. Photographs for the Farm Security Administration, 1935–1938* (New York: Da Capo Press, 1973). Unfortunately, the pages in this book are not numbered; but the discussion may be found on the page immediately following the "Catalogue of Photographs."

29.
Arthur Rothstein, as quoted in *Hank O'Neal, A Vision Shared*, p. 122.

30.
F. Jack Hurley, *Portrait of a Decade*, pp. 86–88. The flap over the Badlands skull occurred at a politically sensitive time, since FDR was running for reelection and was not pleased to be

31.
Milton Meltzer, *Dorothea Lange, Photographer*,
p. 134. In spite of Stryker's notion of what was
acceptable and unacceptable with documentary
photographs, the photographers naturally
enough had their own ideas on the subject, and
the point, of course, is that they were all
correct.

32.
Karin Becker Ohrn's excellent study of Lange
and documentary has much useful information
on the other FSA photographers and Roy Stryker. Concerning captions, she notes that Rothstein's and Lee's were inadequate as far as
Stryker was concerned; Rothstein's were too
spare and lacked essential data, Lee's belabored
the obvious. The correspondence between Stryker and Rothstein and Stryker and Lee, along
with various remembrances of conversations,
shows that Stryker felt his photographers were
not above doing homework on the writing of
captions. A good essay remains to be written
on the range of captions affixed to the FSA
photographs in the Library of Congress.

33.
Milton Meltzer, *Dorothea Lange*, p. 19. Given
Lange's marriage to Paul Taylor and the fact
that they often did extensive field work together, the several accounts of Lange's gathering of this kind of oral as well as visual
material makes perfect sense. Here is what she
recalled of ''Migrant Mother'':

It was raining, the camera bags were packed,
and I had on the seat beside me in the car the
results of my long trip, the box containing all
those rolls and packs of exposed film ready to
mail back to Washington. It was a time of relief. Sixty-five miles an hour for seven hours
would get me home to my family that night,
and my eyes were glued to the wet and gleaming highway that stretched out ahead. I felt
freed, for I could lift my mind off my job and
think of home. I was on my way and barely
saw a crude sign with pointing arrow which
flashed by at the side of the road, saying PEA-
PICKERS CAMP. But out of the corner of my
eye, I did see it. . . . Having well convinced myself for 20 miles that I could continue on, I did
the opposite. Almost without realizing what I
was doing, I made a U-turn on the empty highway. I went back those 20 miles and turned off
the highway at that sign, PEA-PICKERS
CAMP. I was following instinct, not reason; I
drove into that wet soggy camp and parked my
car like a homing pigeon. I saw and approached the hungry and desperate mother as
if drawn by a magnet. I do not remember how
I explained my presence or my camera to her,
but I do remember she asked me no questions. . . . She told me her age, that she was 32.
She said they had been living on frozen vegetables from the surrounding fields, and birds that
the children killed. She had just sold the tires
from her car to buy food. There she sat in that
lean-to tent with her children huddled around
her, and seemed to know that my pictures
might help her, and so she helped me. There
was a sort of equality to it. (Dorothea Lange, as
quoted in *Dorothea Lange. Photographs of a Lifetime*, p. 76).

Would that we could locate similar accounts of
the photographer's encounters with doctors and
their patients.

34.
F. Jack Hurley, *Portrait of a Decade*, p. 150.

35.
F. Jack Hurley, *Portrait of a Decade*, p. 152.

36.
Ben Shahn, as quoted in Hank O'Neal, *A Vision
Shared*, p. 46.

Bibliographic Note

The text and footnotes contain a good many specific references, especially to photographic material that directly relates to the FSA photographs and their reading. Because the New Deal context of the photographs draws upon such a large literature on the one hand and because the reconstruction of medical practice during the 1930s draws upon such a smaller and relatively more specialized literature on the other, we thought it useful to indicate to readers in a note what we found useful in each.

1. History of the Photographs

The literature on the Depression in general and the New Deal in particular is vast and grows still larger each year. Among the major surveys that detail origins, we have found the most useful to be William E. Leuchtenburg's *The Perils of Prosperity, 1914–1932* (Chicago: University of Chicago Press, 1958) and the first volume of Arthur M. Schlesinger, Jr.'s three-volume *Age of Roosevelt, The Crisis of the Old Order, 1919–1933* (Boston: Houghton Mifflin, 1957).

More particular studies of the earlier Progressive politics are John Morton Blum, *The Republican Roosevelt* (Cambridge, Massachusetts: Harvard University Press, 1954) and Arthur S. Link, *Woodrow Wilson and the Progressive Era* (New York: Harper & Row, 1954), though the most influential description of that world as well as a critique of its Populist and liberal values is Richard Hofstadter's *The Age of Reform: From Bryan to F.D.R.* (New York: Alfred A. Knopf, 1955). Persuasive challenges to Hofstadter's interpretation, his discrediting of mass movements and perhaps misleading emphasis upon personalities, are Robert H. Wiebe, *Businessmen and Reform: A Study of the Progressive Movement* (Cambridge, Massachusetts: Harvard University Press, 1962) and Gabriel Kolko, *The Triumph of Conservativism* (Glencoe, Illinois: The Free Press, 1963). An even more comprehensive and suggestive analysis of social structure and ideology prior to the Depression is Wiebe's *The Search for Order, 1877–1920* (New

York: Hill & Wang, 1967) and a searching account of the limits of the welfare state approach, within the parameters of industrial capitalism, is Theodore J. Lowe's *The End of Liberalism: Ideology, Policy, and the Crisis of Public Authority* (New York: Norton, 1969). For thoughtful perspectives by British Americanists, see Frank Thistlethwaite's *The Great Experiment* (Cambridge: Cambridge University Press, 1955) and Maldwyn A. Jones's *The Limits of Liberty: American History 1607–1980* (New York: Oxford University Press, 1983). One of the most fascinating commentaries on the New Deal may be had from the hand, more or less, of Sir Isaiah Berlin, who headed the section of the British Embassy in Washington responsible for preparing weekly reports for the Foreign Office in London (which went directly into the hands of Prime Minister Winston Churchill): *Washington Despatches, 1941–1945*, H. G. Nicholas, Ed. (Weidenfeld and Nicholson: London, 1981). Robert S. and Helen Merrell Lynd's *Middletown* (New York: Harcourt, Brace, 1929) was the pioneering sociological examination of the way in which issues and ideas entered middle class and working people's lives, in this case, in the 1920s, and John Kenneth Galbraith's account of the stock-market collapse, *The Great Crash, 1929* (Boston: Houghton, Mifflin, 3rd ed., 1972) marks the end of that era in clear, chilling detail.

Schlesinger's second and third volumes of *The Age of Roosevelt, The Coming of the New Deal* (Boston: Houghton Mifflin, 1958) and *The Politics of Upheaval* (Boston: Houghton Mifflin, 1960) provide a thorough narrative of New Deal actions which followed upon the heels of the desperate, confusing stasis of the early 1930s; *The Politics of Upheaval* comes to a halt as FDR begins his second term, and the outstanding complement is William E. Leuchtenburg's *Franklin D. Roosevelt and the New Deal, 1932–1940* (New York: Harper & Row, 1963). Of the five volumes of biography to date (1952–1977), Frank Freidel's *Franklin D. Roosevelt: Launching the New Deal* (Boston: Little,

Brown, 1973) adds the most important information to both Schlesinger and Leuchtenberg for critical reappraisals. Several such possibilities may be seen in Richard Hofstadter's early essay, "Franklin D. Roosevelt: The Patrician as Opportunist," in *The American Political Tradition* (New York: Alfred A. Knopf, 1948), and, with less cynicism and more attention to social policy implications, Howard Zinn's introduction to *New Deal Thought* (Indianapolis, Indiana: Bobbs-Merrill, 1966), pp. xv–xxxvi, and Barton J. Bernstein's "The New Deal: The Conservative Achievements of Liberal Reform," in *Towards a New Past: Dissenting Essays in American History* (New York: Pantheon, 1968), pp. 263–288. Zinn's is a collection of primary documents, articles, and speeches of the period by the principals and their critics.

Conditions on the American land immediately before and during the Depression are best represented in Southern period studies, classics such as Charles S. Johnson, *Shadow of the Plantation* (Chicago: University of Chicago Press, 1934); Arthur Raper, *Preface to Peasantry: A Tale of Two Black Counties* (Chapel Hill: University of North Carolina Press, 1936); John Dollard, *Class and Caste in a Southern Town* (New Haven, Connecticut: Yale University Press, 1937); Margaret Hapgood, *Mothers of the South: Portraiture of the White Tenant Farmer Woman* (Chapel Hill: University of North Carolina Press, 1939); E. Franklin Frazier, *The Negro Family in the United States* (Chicago: University of Chicago Press, 1939, 1957); and Federal Writers' Project, *These Are Our Lives* (Chapel Hill: University of North Carolina Press, 1939). Depression life in other parts of the nation may be seen in articles collected in Bernard Sternsher, ed., *Hitting Home: The Great Depression in Town and Country* (Chicago: Quadrangle Books, 1970) and in what Americans remembered of its effects upon their own lives, as in Studs Terkel's *Hard Times: An Oral History of the Great Depression* (New York: Pantheon, 1970) and Tom E. Terrill and Jerrold Hirsch's *Such As Us: Southern Voices of the Thirties* (New York: Norton, 1979).

The plight of the city dweller and industrial worker is the subject of *Citizens without Work* and *The Unemployed Worker* by E. Wright Bakke (New Haven, Connecticut: Yale University Press, both 1940) and the definitive overview may be had from Irving Bernstein's *The Lean Years: A History of the Industrial Worker, 1920–1933* (Boston: Houghton Mifflin, 1960) and *The Turbulent Years: A History of the American Worker, 1933–1941* (Boston: Houghton Mifflin, 1970). An incisive account with emphasis upon workers' attempts to organize apart from government control, is James R. Green's *The World of the Worker: Labor in Twentieth Century America* (New York: Hill & Wang, 1980).

Explicit, coordinated, national planning by the federal government is a fairly modern concept for any number of good reasons. For a survey, see Otis L. Graham, Jr.'s *Toward a Planned Society: From Roosevelt to Nixon* (New York: Oxford University Press, 1976) and *An Encore for Reform: The Old Progressives and the New Deal* (New York: Oxford University Press, 1967), and, more specifically, "The Planning Ideal and American Reality: The 1930s," in *The Hofstadter Aegis*, Stanley Elkins and Eric McKitrick, eds. (New York: Alfred A. Knopf, 1974), pp. 257–299. Given the time involved in planning, enacting what they planned, and then defending what they had enacted, it seems hard to believe that those surrounding FDR had any time left in which to write, much less, to write privately. But write privately they did, in addition to a torrent of public hearings and public reports—though the serious reader will be disappointed in their numerous autobiographies, memoirs, diaries, and assemblages of anecdotes because these are, in the main, rehearsals of political machinations rather than substantive discussions of any kind of social policy. Thus, one can scan Rexford G. Tugwell's *The Striken Land* (1947), *The Democratic Roosevelt* (1957), or *The Brain Trust* (1968), learning less than what Tugwell set down in seventeen pages in "The Principle of Planning and the Institution of Laissez-Faire," in the *American Economic Re-*

view, XXII, Supplement (March 1932), pp. 75–92—and this from the most prominent planner of them all. Better to turn to Tugwell's superior and the man who hired him, Henry A. Wallace, whose *New Frontiers* (1934) contains the ideas FDR's first secretary of agriculture brought with him to Washington, whose *Technology, Corporations, and the General Welfare* (Chapel Hill: University of North Carolina Press, 1937) shows him wrestling with the contradictions of a planned economy on the eve of the second depression, the recessions of 1937–38, and whose *Pathways to Plenty* (Washington, D.C.: GPO, 1938) defends the New Deal's farm program and the various institutional reorganizations from 1933.

Turning to secondary assessments, Ellis W. Hawley, *The New Deal and the Problem of Monopoly* (Princeton, New Jersey: Princeton University Press, 1966) is the most penetrating analysis of the New Deal's inability (or unwillingness) to deal with increasing concentrations of economic power, given that consolidation and centralization were increasingly explicit goals of Roosevelt's administrations. Focusing upon the Department of Agriculture, Richard S. Kirkendall's *Social Scientists and Farm Politics in the Age of Roosevelt* (Columbia, Missouri: University of Missouri Press, 1966) demonstrates what planners and reformers achieved and, rather than learning from Tugwell what he was about in those years, we must turn to Bernard Sternsher's *Rexford Tugwell and the New Deal* (New Brunswick, New Jersey: Rutgers University Press, 1964). Unfortunately, Kirkendall and Sternsher share not only a distaste for comprehensive indexes (neither the Historical Section nor its director, Roy Stryker, merit an entry), but seem to have consulted with each other on how best to cleanse Agriculture of any progressive, socialist, or left-wing taint. As a consequence, the anticommunist and anticollectivist attacks by Congress, the press, and various sectors of the public seem inexplicable and crucial issues affecting planning are lost. More helpful are David E. Conrad's *The Forgotten Farmers*

(Urbana: University of Illinois Press, 1965), Paul E. Mertz's *New Deal Policy and Southern Rural Poverty* (Baton Rouge: Louisiana State University Press, 1978), and most to the point, Sidney Baldwin's *Poverty and Politics: The Rise and Decline of the Farm Security Administration* (Chapel Hill: University of North Carolina Press, 1968), whose detailed story of relations, internal and external, is congruent with the charged content of the celebrated FSA photographs. A model study is Norman D. Markowitz, *The Rise and Fall of the People's Century: Henry A. Wallace and American Liberalism, 1941–1948* (Glencoe, Illinois: The Free Press, 1973), whose wide-ranging attention to social structure and institutional change, to shifts in ideology and the nature of political and economic power during this period in American history, embodies an attempt to raise questions outside the conventional framework of electoral politics, whether liberal or conservative, and outside traditional American economics.

2 Primary Care Medicine and Practice in the 1930s

A History of Medicine, Vols. 1 and 2, Henry E. Sigerist, M.D. (New York: Oxford University Press, 1951), provides a sound and readable survey. The American scene, with divergent thematic attention, is treated in two chronologically overlapping studies: *Medicine and Society in America, 1660–1860*, Richard H. Shrylock (New York: New York University Press, 1960) and *American Medicine and the Public Interest*, Rosemary Stevens (New Haven, Connecticut: Yale University Press, 1971). Shrylock's other books are relevant—*The Development of Modern Medicine* (New York: Alfred A. Knopf, 1947) and *Medicine in America: Historical Essays* (Baltimore, Maryland: Johns Hopkins University Press, 1968)—as are Joseph F. Kett's *The Formation of the American Medical Profession: The Rise of Institutions, 1780–1860* (New Haven, Connecticut: Yale University Press, 1968) and William G. Rothstein's *American Physicians in the*

Nineteenth Century (Baltimore, Maryland: Johns Hopkins University Press, 1972).

Much general data may be had from the American Medical Association (Chicago, Illinois), particularly from committees such as their Council on Medical Education's publications, "Medical Education in the United States," 1915, 1920, 1930, 1940, 1950 (see the August issue in the *Journal of the American Medical Association* for each of the years indicated). The National Library of Medicine (Bethesda) contains valuable government documents, including Public Health Service surveys and reports which bear upon disease, illness, and various interventions by national, state, and local agencies. Periodical medical literature is available through the library, and by consulting the Surgeon General's Index, an extensive topical listing of books and articles relating to medicine which begins to fill in the very great gaps between statistics. The *Committee on the Costs of Medical Care* [CCMC] (Chicago: University of Chicago Press, 1932) is, given the varied composition of the committee and its broad mandate, an essential source, though its 27 volumes may slow even the most diligent of readers. See, then, *Medical Care for the American People, The Final Report* (1933), reprinted by the U.S. Department of Health, Education, and Welfare (Washington, D.C.: GPO). Seymour Harris's *The Economics of American Medicine* (New York: McGraw-Hill, 1948) is soundly researched, clearly written, and helps to put the difficulties providing adequate health care for all Americans in perspective. More specific data, either in terms of policy or cost, may be found with state medical societies and associations, state boards of health, state bureaus of labor, announcements and publications by state (and private) medical schools and colleges, and individual hospitals and clinics within each state.

Medicine, as it reached the average American in the 1920s and 1930s, is best seen in the Lynds's two Middletown studies cited earlier. Valuable supplements are the relevant sections in Rosemary Stevens's *American Medicine and*

the Public Interest; Frederick Mott and Milton I. Roemer's *Rural Health and Medical Care* (New York: McGraw-Hill, 1948), Robert Cooley Angell's *The Family Encounters the Depression* (New York: Scribner's, 1936; reprinted 1965); and "Medical Care during the Depression," by George J. Perrott, Edgar Sydenstricker, and S. D. Collins, in the *Milibank Memorial Fund Quarterly*, Vol. 12, No. 2 (April 1934).

While medical achievements of an institutional or technological nature have a thousand articulate fathers, medical practice has remained an orphan. Few analytic or comparative studies exist; interested scholars have had to search out widely scattered pieces such as "The Country Doctor and the Hospital," Nathaniel W. Faxon, *Boston Medical and Surgical Journal*, Vol. 177 (1917), pp. 167–171, "The Other Side of Country Practice," Ralph W. Tuttle, *New England Journal of Medicine*, Vol. 199 (1928), pp. 874–877, or "General Practice in England Today: A Reconnaissance," Joseph S. Collings, *Lancet*, Vol. 1 (1950), pp. 555–585. More recently on 1930s practice, see "The Future of Health Care," John D. Stoeckle, M.D., in *Poverty and Health: A Sociological Analysis*, John Kosa, Aaron Antonousky, and Irving Zola, eds. (Cambridge, Massachusetts: Harvard University Press, 1969), pp. 292–318, and "The Neighborhood Health Center—Reform Ideas of Yesterday and Today," John D. Stoeckle, M.D., and Lucy M. Candib, *New England Journal of Medicine* Vol. 280 (June 19, 1969), pp. 1385–1391. Thanks to developments in the new social history of the past two decades, however, the situation has greatly improved—at least in terms of available models and continuous discussions concerning methodology.

Major journals that we used to provide orientation were the *Journal of Social History*, the *Journal of Interdisciplinary History*, and, most suggestively, *History Workshop* (Oxford and London). Important models included E. P. Thompson's *The Making of the English Working Class* (New York: Pantheon, 1964), Peter Laslett's *The World We have Lost* (New York: Scribner's, 1965), Eugene D. Genovese's *Roll, Jordan, Roll: The World the Slaves Made* (New York: Pantheon, 1974), and Herbert G. Gutman's *The Black Family in Slavery and Freedom, 1750–1925* (New York: Pantheon, 1976). See also, *Essays in Social History*, M. W. Flinn and T. C. Smolt, eds. (Oxford: Oxford University Press, 1974), especially, "Time, Work-Discipline, and Industrial Capitalism," E. P. Thompson, pp. 39–77 and "The Language of 'Class' in Early Nineteenth-Century England," Asa Briggs, pp. 154–177; *Anonymous Americans: Explorations in Nineteenth Century Social History*, Tamara K. Hareven, ed. (Englewood Cliffs, N.J.: Prentice-Hall, 1971); and *Work, Culture & Society in Industrializing America*, Herbert G. Gutman (New York: Alfred A. Knopf, 1976).

Essential social history discussions are the Editors' Statement, *Journal of Social History*, Vol. 1, No. 1 (Fall 1967); Harold Perkin's "Social History in Britain," *Journal of Social History*, Vol. 10, No. 2 (Winter 1976), pp. 129–143; Elizabeth Fox-Genovese and Eugene Genovese's "The Political Crisis of Social History," *Journal of Social History*, Vol. 10, No. 2 (Winter 1976), pp. 205–220; Herbert G. Gutman's *Slavery and the Numbers Game* (Urbana: University of Illinois Press, 1975); Paul G. Spagnoli's "Social History With and Without Numbers," *Journal of Interdisciplinary History*, Vol. X, No. 1 (Summer 1979), pp. 107–120; and especially "A Clown in Regal Purple: Social History and the Historians," Tony Judt, *History Workshop*, Issue 7 (Spring 1979), pp. 66–94, and "Critique: On the Methods of the History Workshop," David Selbourne and "A Reply," Raphael Samuel, *History Workshop*, Issue 9 (Spring 1980), pp. 150–161, pp. 162–176.

Interviewing is central to the doctor-patient relationship and to the construction of oral histories which are data for social history. For exemplary works, see *All God's Dangers: The Autobiography of Nate Shaw*, Theodore Rosengarten (1974), and the *Children of Crisis* series by Robert Coles, M.D. (vols. 1–5, and in progress), cited earlier. Coles's introductions are of

great value; other discussions of method are "The Peculiarities of Oral History," Alessandro Portelli, *History Workshop*, Issue 12 (Autumn 1981), pp. 96–107; "The Hem of My Garment: An Interview with Theodore Rosengarten about the Making of Nate Shaw," George Abbott White, *Massachusetts Review* (Winter 1980), pp. 787–800; and "Using Oral History: A Biographer's Point of View," Milton Meltzer, *Oral History Review* (1979), pp. 42–46. For a fruitful exchange on the nagging question of what constitutes authenticity and validity see "How Valid Are the Federal Writers' Project Life Stories: An Iconoclast among the Believers," Leonard Rapport, *Oral History Review* (1979), pp. 6–17 and "Replies to Leonard Rapport," Tom E. Terrill and Jerrold Hirsch, *Oral History Review* (1980), pp. 81–85, 85–89, 89–92.

Beyond the approach of social history and its methodology and techniques, there is a body of material, formal and popular, which we used to make our composite picture. This ranged from doctors' accounts—celebrity, plain, and then foreign physicians for contrast and perspective—and the accounts of patients—again, celebrity, plain, and foreign—to the more distanced accounts of professionals and nonprofessionals who are still a part of the health-care scene: nurses, laboratory technicians, technicians, pharmacists, and druggists, ambulance drivers, patent medicine salespeople, and the inevitable quacks of every shade and stripe. Thousands of novels have been written with doctors either as the protagonist or one of several main characters. Hundreds of films and dozens of comic strips also portray the physician or deal with the drama of accident and illness—and these reach millions of readers each day, to say nothing of the current plethora of "soaps" in which the doctor and his or her hospital are where the action is centered. Major newspapers and magazines run columns by physicians—even small-town newspapers contained these during the Depression—and if one looks closely enough, there are usually letters to the editor on almost any aspect of health care. Doctors themselves keep a variety of records, professional and personal (including account books, journals, and letters), each having a range of value from the literary to the purely documentary. We have looked at dozens of medical texts, first-aid handouts, and medical advice books—this latter a genre that expands each day, it seems, and threatens to engulf the bookstores we have visited. Finally, there are the photographs doctors themselves took (very few) and the (even fewer) taken by patients. (Who would think, for example, to photograph the hospital where they had a major operation, or the clinic they visited when a youngster?)

Each reader will have his or her favorite motion picture, novel, comic strip, newspaper advice column, or medical advice book. For our purposes, we found most interesting the following: *The Magic Mountain*, Thomas Mann (New York: Alfred A. Knopf, 1944); *The Plague*, Albert Camus (New York: The Modern Library, 1948); *Doctor Zhivago*, Boris Pasternak (New York: Pantheon Books, 1958); *Letters of Anton Chekhov*, Selected and Edited by Avrahm Yarmolinsky (New York: Viking, 1973); *The Moviegoer*, Walker Percy (New York: Alfred A. Knopf, 1960); *Arrowsmith*, Sinclair Lewis (New York: Harcourt, Brace, 1925); *The Autobiography of William Carlos Williams* (New York: New Directions, 1951); *William Carlos Williams, The Doctor Stories*, compiled by Robert Coles, M.D. (New York: New Directions, 1984). *Winston Churchill. The Struggle for Survival: 1940–1965*, Lord Moran (London: Constable, 1966); *Doctor Spock, Biography of a Conservative Radical*, Lynn Z. Bloom (Indianapolis, Indiana: Bobbs-Merrill, 1972); *Men, Medicine and Myself*, S. Vere Pearson (London: Museum Press, 1946); *'Doctor Himself,' An Unorthodox Biography of Harry Roberts, 1871–1946*, Winifred Stamp (London: Hamish Hamilton, 1949); *The Life and Work of Sigmund Freud*, 3 vols., Ernest Jones (New York: Basic Books, 1953–1957); *Freud: Living and Dying*, Max Shur, M.D. (New York: International Universities Press, 1972); *Memories, Dreams, Reflections*, C. G. Jung, Recorded and Edited by Aniela Jaffe (New York: Alfred A. Knopf, 1983); *Free Associations: Memories of a Psycho-Analyst*, Ernest Jones (London: Hogarth Press, 1959); "How the Poor Die," George Orwell, *In Front of Your Nose, 1945–1950*, Sonia Orwell and Ian Angus, eds. (New York: Harcourt, Brace, 1968), pp. 223–233; *Bellevue: A Documentary of a Large Metropolitan Hospital*, Don Gold (New York: Harper & Row, 1975); *Pioneer Doctor*, Lewis J. Moorman, M.D. (Norman: University of Oklahoma Press, 1931); *A Family Doctor's Notebook*, I. J. Wolf, M.D. (New York: Fortuny's, 1940); *Strictly Private! Being the Intimate Diary of a Medical Practitioner*, Dr. Maurice Chideckel (Boston: Stratford, 1928); *Corner Druggist*, Robert B. Nixon, Jr. (New York: Prentice-Hall, 1941), and "Medical Advice Books: The Search for the Healthy Body," John D. Stoeckle, M.D., *Social Science and Medicine*, Vol. 19, No. 9 (Oxford, 1984), pp. 707–712.

Appendix A: List of FSA Doctor-Patient Photographs

1
Siloam, Greene County, Ga. (vicinity). Nov. 1941.
Midwife going out on call.
LC-USF 34-46536-E.
JACK DELANO.

2
Kempton, W.Va. May 1939.
Company doctor leaving the home of a sick miner.
LC-USF 33-1384-M2.
JOHN VACHON.

The Doctor's Office
3
Kempton, W.Va. May 1939.
Office of a company doctor.
LC-USF 33-1370-M3.
JOHN VACHON.

4
Transylvania, La. June 1940.
The doctor's office on the U.S. Department of Agriculture, Farm Security Administration project.
LC-USF 34-54063-D.
MARION POST WOLCOTT.

5
Elkins (vicinity), W.Va. June 1939.
The Tygart valley subsistence homesteads, a project of the U.S. Resettlement Administration. Health center.
LC-USF 33-1397-M2.
JOHN VACHON.

6
Oran, Mo. Feb. 1942.
Doctor receiving call in his office.
LC-USF 34-64355-D.
JOHN VACHON.

7
Penasco, New Mexico Jan. 1943.
Clinic operated by the Taos County Cooperative Health Association.
LC-USW 3-14178-C.
JOHN COLLIER.

8
San Augustine, Tex. Apr. 1943.
Dr. Jones in his office.
LC-USW 3-25011-D.
JOHN VACHON.

9
Baltimore, Maryland Apr. 1939.
Baltimore street.
LC-USF 33-3035-M2.
ARTHUR ROTHSTEIN.

10
Chicago, Ill. Apr. 1941.
Doctor in his office in the southside.
LC-USF 34-38835-D.
RUSSELL LEE.

11
Shafter, Calif. Mar. 1940.
The Farm Security Administration camp for migratory workers. Patient leaving health clinic.
LC-USF 34-24287-D.
ARTHUR ROTHSTEIN.

12
Yakima, Wash. Sept. 1941.
FSA migratory labor camp for farm families. The clinic is a big drawing card.
LC-USF 34-70208-D.
RUSSELL LEE.

13
Faulkner County, Ark. May 1940.
A patient waiting at a doctor's office in the rear of a country store.
LC-USF 34-53764-D.
MARION POST WOLCOTT.

14
Scranton, Iowa. May 1940.
A doctor's office and a water tank.
LC-USF 34-60749-D.
JOHN VACHON.

15
Gee's Bend, Ala. May 1939.
Clay Coleman showing an interest in a food chart while waiting in the health clinic.
LC-USF 34-51582-D.
MARION POST WOLCOTT.

16
Pittsburgh, Penna. May 1938.
Quack doctor's sign.
LC-USF 33-2797-M2.
ARTHUR ROTHSTEIN.

17
Fairfield bench farms, an FSA scattered home-
stead development, Mont. May 1939.
*Doctor who is hired by the Farmers' Cooperative
Health Association.*
LC-USF 34 2731-D.
ARTHUR ROTHSTEIN.

18
Faulkner County, Ark. May 1940.
*A medicine and drug shelf in a country store
which has a doctor's office in the rear.*
LC-USF 34 53737-D.
MARION POST WOLCOTT.

19
Merigold, Miss. Oct. 1938.
Negroes in front of a doctor's office.
LC-USF 33 30664-M3.
MARION POST WOLCOTT.

20
San Augustine, Tex. Apr. 1943.
Dr. Rulfa in his office.
LC-USW 3 25207-D.
JOHN VACHON.

21
Circleville, Ohio. Summer 1938.
Doctor's office, on Main and Court streets.
LC-USF 33 6391-M5.
BEN SHAHN.

Waiting on the Doctor
22
San Augustine, Tex. Apr. 1939.
*Line of women waiting to see the doctor on Satur-
day morning.*
LC USF 33 12155-M5.
RUSSELL LEE.

23
West Aliquippa, Penna. Jan. 1941.
House.
LC USF 34 62202-D.
JOHN VACHON.

24
Greene County, Ga. June 1941.
*A young boy in bed with measles in the home of a
Farm Security Administration borrower.*
LC USF 34 44581-D.
JACK DELANO.

25
Belle Glade, Fla. June 1940.
*The waiting room at the health clinic on typhoid
inoculation day at the Osceola migratory labor
camp, a Farm Security Administration project.*
LC USF 34 54091-D.
MARION POST WOLCOTT.

26
Woodville, Calif. Mar. 1941.
*Agricultural workers waiting in the clinic at the
Farm Security Administration farm workers'
community.*
LC USF 33 13230-M3.
RUSSELL LEE.

27
Oran, Mo. Feb. 1942.
Farmer waiting to see the doctor.
LC USF 34 64283-D.
JOHN VACHON.

28
Penasco, New Mexico Jan. 1943.
*The waiting room of a clinic operated by the Taos
County Cooperative Health Association.*
LC USW 3 13655-C.
JOHN COLLIER.

29
Irwinville Farms, a U.S. Resettlement Adminis-
tration project, near Irwinville, Ga. May 1938.
*Women and children waiting to see the doctor
who visits the project once a week.*
LC USF 33 1151-M5.
JOHN VACHON.

30
Oran, Mo. Feb. 1942.
Doctor's office and waiting room.
LC USF 34 64353-D.
JOHN VACHON.

31
Questa, N.M. Jan. 1943.
The waiting room of the clinic operated by the Taos County Cooperative Health Association.
LC USW 3 17927-C.
JOHN COLLIER.

32
Chicago, Ill. Apr. 1942.
Provident Hospital. In the waiting room of the clinic.
LC USW 3 675-D.
JACK DELANO.

33
Eleven Mile Corner, Ariz. Feb. 1942.
Cairns General Hospital, Farm Security Administration farm workers' community. The waiting room at the clinic.
LC USF 34 71928-D.
RUSSELL LEE.

34
Nyssa, Ore. July 1942.
FSA mobile camp. Japanese-Americans patronize the camp clinic.
LC USF 34 73344-D.
RUSSELL LEE.

Doctor Attending: Infants, Children, Young
35
Cleveland (vicinity), Miss., in the Delta area. June 1937.
Grandmother, mother, and newborn baby of a sharecropper.
LC USF 34 17327-C.
DOROTHEA LANGE.

36
Merrill, Klamath County, Ore. Oct. 1939.
Farm Security Administration mobile camp for mi-gratory farm labor. Doctor examining children in the trailer clinic.
LC USF 34 21833-E.
DOROTHEA LANGE.

37
Dailey, W.Va. Dec. 1941. Tygart valley home-steads, and Farm Security Administration proj-ect, 11 miles southwest of Elkins, W.Va.
Dr. Tabor, examining Randolph Darkey before in-oculating him against measles, in the community health center.
LC USF 34 24416-D.
ARTHUR ROTHSTEIN.

38
Calipatria, Imperial County, Calif. Feb. 1939.
The Farm Security Administration emergency camp for workers in the pea harvest. Visiting pub-lic health doctor conducting a well-baby clinic in a local school building adjacent to the pea harvest. Many migratory mothers bring their children.
19069-E.
DOROTHEA LANGE.

39
Bridgeton, N.J. June 1942.
Farm Security Administration agricultural workers' camp. The camp clinic.
LC USF 34 83202-C.
JOHN COLLIER.

40
Penasco, N.M. Jan. 1943.
Preventive medicine is an important part of the program of the clinic operated by the Taos County Cooperative Health Association.
LC USW 3 14540-C.
JOHN COLLIER.

41
Scott County, Mo. Feb. 1942.
Doctor at bedside of sick child.
LC USF 34 64220-D.
JOHN VACHON.

42
Merrill, Klamath County, Ore. Oct. 1939.
Farm Security Administration mobile camp for mi-

gratory farm labor. The doctor examining a boy
from Texas.
LC USF 34 21832-E.
DOROTHEA LANGE.

43
Southington, Conn. May 1942.
*At the health center, the people of Southington
may receive medical advice and a certain amount
of medical care (such as physical checkups, which
this girl is receiving) without cost.*
LC USW 3 42143-D.
FENNO JACOBS.

44
St. Charles County, Mo. Nov. 1939.
*A physician cooperating with an FSA medical
health plan, visiting the home of a rehabilitation
client.*
LC USF 34 29111-D.
ARTHUR ROTHSTEIN.

45
Bridgeton, N.J. June 1942.
*Farm Security Administration agricultural workers'
camp. The camp doctor has a large practice in
Bridgeton but also gives his time to the migrant
camp, where he works to curb venereal disease,
malnutrition, and general run-down conditions of
health.*
LC USF 34 83194-C.
JOHN COLLIER.

46
Chaffee, Mo. Feb. 1942.
*Little girl who was bitten by a dog, receiving
antihydrophobia vaccine.*
LC USF 34 64304-D.
JOHN VACHON.

47
Transylvania, La. June 1940.
*A U.S. Department of Agriculture, Farm Security
Administration project. Mrs. M. E. Chappell with
her daughter, Sybil Lee, being examined by
Dr. F. A. Williams, director of East Carroll Parish
health unit, in the project school clinic.*
LC USF 34 53986-D.
MARION POST WOLCOTT.

48
Caswell County, N.C. Oct. 1940.
*Dr. S. A. Malloy examining Louis Graves and his
family on their front porch.*
LC USF 34 56376-D.
MARION POST WOLCOTT.

49
Greendale, Wis. Sept. 1939 [?].
*A community planned by the suburban division of
the U.S. Resettlement Administration. Boy being
examined by the doctor. This is the Greendale
branch of the Milwaukee Group Health
Association.*
LC USF 34 60153-D.
JOHN VACHON.

50
Coffee County, Ala. Apr. 1939.
*A doctor and a nurse (Miss Teal) examining and
advising about treatment for a child at the health
room of the Goodman Consolidated School.*
LC USF 34 51441-D.
MARION POST WOLCOTT.

51
Box Elder, Utah. Aug. 1940.
Medical cooperative of the FSA.
LC USF 34 37409-D.
RUSSELL LEE.

52
Blanch, N.C. Oct. 1940.
*Dr. S. A. Malloy examining Mrs. William H. Wil-
lis and her family. Mr. Willis is a Farm Security
Administration borrower.*
LC USF 34 56373-D.
MARION POST WOLCOTT.

53
Maricopa County, Ariz. May 1940.
*The Aqua Fria Farm Security Administration camp
for migratory workers. Doctor at the clinic exam-
ining the son of an agricultural worker.*
LC USF 34 36025-D.
RUSSELL LEE.

54
Bridgeton, N.J. July 1942.
*Farm Security Administration agricultural workers'
camp. The clinic.*
LC USF 34 83435-C.
JOHN COLLIER.

55
Scott County, Mo. Feb. 1942.
Country doctor examining child in farmhouse.
LC USF 34 64221-D.
JOHN VACHON.

56
Blanch, N.C. Oct. 1940.
*Dr. S. A. Malloy examining Mr. William H. Willis'
son Bobby in their home. Mr. Willis is a Farm Se-
curity Administration borrower.*
LC USF 34 56367-D.
MARION POST WOLCOTT.

57
Bridgeton, N.J. June 1942.
*Farm Security Administration agricultural workers'
camp. Patients at the camp clinic receiving injec-
tions for the treatment of venereal disease.*
LC USF 34 83253-C.
JOHN COLLIER.

58
Box Elder, Utah. Aug. 1940.
*Doctor with a family who are members of the FSA
medical cooperative.*
LC USF 34 37366-D.
RUSSELL LEE.

59
Reedsville, W.Va. Apr. 1935.
*The Arthurdale subsistence homestead project of
the U.S. Resettlement Administration. Doctor ex-
amining a boy's throat.*
LC USF 34 1063-C.
ARTHUR ROTHSTEIN.

60
Penasco, N.M. Jan. 1943.
*Dr. Onstine, of the clinic operated by the Taos
County Cooperative Health Association, and Ma-
jorie Muller (right), resident Red Cross nurse.*
LC USW 3 13716-C.
JOHN COLLIER.

61
Dailey, W.Va. Dec. 1941.
*Tygart valley homesteads, and Farm Security
Administration project, 11 miles southwest of Elk-
ins, W.Va. Dr. Tabor writing instructions for med-
icine for Roscoe Loupin.*
LC USF 34 24437-D.
ARTHUR ROTHSTEIN.

62
San Augustine, Tex. Apr. 1943.
*Dr. Schreiber of San Augustine giving typhoid
inoculation at rural school.*
LC USW 3 24992-D.
JOHN VACHON.

Doctor Attending: Adults and Elderly
63
Penasco, N.M. Jan. 1943.
*Dr. Onstine making an examination in the clinic
operated by the Taos County Cooperative Health
Association.*
LC USW 3 14683-E.
JOHN COLLIER.

64
Crystal City, Tex. Mar. 1939.
*Mexican with an advanced case of tuberculosis.
He was in a bed at home with other members of
the family sleeping and living in the same room.*
LC USF 34 32401-D.
RUSSELL LEE.

65
Chicago, Ill. Apr. 1941.
*Doctor examining a patient in her home. The pa-
tient is on relief.*
LC USF 34 38702-D.
RUSSELL LEE.

66
Corpus Christi, Tex. Jan. 1942.
*Privately supported tuberculosis clinic supervised
by a retired doctor. Majority of patients are Latin-
American. Doctor recording medical history of pa-
tient. Map shows number of cases in area.*
LC USF 34 24920-D.
ARTHUR ROTHSTEIN.

67
Washington, D.C. Jan. 1942.
Self-help client getting medical examination before he applies for work.
LC USF 34 82147-C.
JOHN COLLIER.

68
Kempton, W.Va. May 1939.
Company doctor in a coal town examining a patient. Miners pay $2 a month for medical care.
LC USF 34 8999-C.
JOHN VACHON.

69
Brooklyn, N.Y. Aug. 1942.
State physician checking the blood pressure of a factory worker.
LC USW 3 5376-D.
ARTHUR ROTHSTEIN.

70
Questa, N.M. Jan. 1943.
Examination in the clinic operated by the Taos County Cooperative Health Association.
LC USW 3 18083-E.
JOHN COLLIER.

71
Woodville, Ga. June 1941.
At a cooperative prenatal clinic.
LC USF 34 44174-D.
JACK DELANO.

72
Brooklyn, N.Y. Aug. 1942.
State industrial hygiene physician examining the heart of a factory worker.
LC USW 3 5377-D.
ARTHUR ROTHSTEIN.

73
Wilder, Idaho. May 1941.
Mobile unit of the Farm Security Administration camp for migratory workers. Examination in the trailer clinic.
LC USF 34 39193-D.
RUSSELL LEE.

74
New York, N.Y. Jan. 1943.
Italian surgeon bandaging a patient's arm.
LC USW 3 14475-D.
MARJORY COLLINS.

75
New York, N.Y. Oct. 1942.
Dr. Winn, a Czech-American, has his office in his apartment at 425 East 72 St.
LC USW 3 9863-D.
MARJORY COLLINS.

76
Colp, Ill. Jan. 1939.
Dr. Springs giving prescription to patient.
LC USF 34 26813-D.
ARTHUR ROTHSTEIN.

77
Maricopa County, Ariz. May 1940.
The Aqua Fria FSA camp for migratory workers. Doctor at clinic taking case history of agricultural worker.
LC USF 34 36026-D.
RUSSELL LEE.

78
Crystal City, Tex. Mar. 1939.
After much persuasion by a local physician, this small shed was constructed to house a tuberculosis patient. This was the first time in this section that a tuberculosis patient has been isolated from his family.
LC USF 34 32345-D.
RUSSELL LEE.

Closure
79
Farmersville, Tulare County, Calif. May 1939.
Farm Security Administration camp for migratory workers. Sons, migratory workers, bringing their father who is sick and old to the camp clinic.
LC USF 34 19656-D.
DOROTHEA LANGE.

80
Questa, N.M. Jan. 1943.
Doctor Onstine, of the clinic operated by the Taos
County Cooperative Health Association, and
Father Smith, the parish priest, at the bedside of a
tuberculosis patient.
LC USW 3 17918-C.
JOHN COLLIER.

Appendix B: List of FSA Illustrative Photographs

I1
"Migrant Mother."
Nipomo, California, 1936.
LC USF 34 9058C.
DOROTHEA LANGE.

I2
He was once a Missouri farmer and is now a migratory farm laborer in California. Feb. 1936
LC USF 34 2470-E.
DOROTHEA LANGE.

I3
Smithland (vicinity), Iowa. Dec. 1926.
Christmas dinner at Earl Pauley's home on sub-marginal farmland. The dinner consisted of potatoes, cabbage, and pie.
LC USF 34 10124-D.
RUSSELL LEE.

I4
Cimarron County, Okla. Apr. 1936.
Farmer and sons walking in the face of a dust storm.
LC USF 34 4052-E.
ARTHUR ROTHSTEIN.

I5
Anniston (vicinity), Ala. June 1936.
Hoe culture.
LC USF 34 9328-C.
DOROTHEA LANGE.

I6
Hale County, Ala. 1935.
The washroom in the dog run of Floyd Burroughs' cabin.
LC USF 342 8133-A.
WALKER EVANS.

I7
A Negro church in South Carolina. Mar. 1936.
LC USF 342 8056-A.
WALKER EVANS.

I8
Church interior. Alabama, July–Aug. 1936.
LC USF 342 8285A.
WALKER EVANS.

I9
Yuma, Ariz. Feb. 1942.
Motion picture show billboard.
LC USF 33 13256-M3.
RUSSELL LEE.

I10
Sign along U.S. Highway 99, between Tulare and Fresno, Calif. May 1939.
LC USF 34 19685-C.
DOROTHEA LANGE.

I11
Roadside store (vicinity Greensboro, Ala.).
Summer 1936.
LC USF 342 8282A.
WALKER EVANS.

I12
Pennington, S.D. May 1936.
A bleached skull on this parched, overgrazed land gives warning that here is a land which the desert threatens to claim.
LC USF 34 4507E.
ARTHUR ROTHSTEIN.

I13
Kaufman County, Tex. Aug. 1936.
Plantation owner's daughter checking the weight of cotton.
LC USF 34 5199-D.
ARTHUR ROTHSTEIN.

I14
New Madrid County, Mo. Jan. 1939.
State highway officials moving sharecroppers away from the roadside to an area between the levee and the Mississippi River.
LC USF 33 2932-M2.
ARTHUR ROTHSTEIN.

I15
Kaufman County, Tex. July 1936.
Cotton pickers.
LC USF 34 5204-D.
ARTHUR ROTHSTEIN.

I16
Kaufman County, Tex. Aug. 1936.
*Cotton pickers who receive fifty cents a hundred
pounds.*
LC USF 34 5215-D.
ARTHUR ROTHSTEIN.

Index